Next Stop, Tehran:
The Neoconservative Campaign For War in Iran

Rohan Davis

Next Stop, Tehran:
The Neoconservative Campaign For War in Iran

Rohan Davis

Academica Press
Washington - London

Library of Congress Cataloging-in-Publication Data
Names: Davis, Rohan, author.
Title: Next stop, Tehran : the neoconservative campaign for war in Iran /
Rohan Davis.
Description: Washington : Academica Press, 2020. | Includes
bibliographical references and index.
Identifiers: LCCN 2020933543 | ISBN 9781680532296 (hardcover) |
ISBN 9781680531329 (paperback)
Copyright 2020 Rohan Davis

Table of Contents

Introduction

When hatred of culture becomes itself
a part of culture, the life of the mind loses all meaning.

—Alain Finkielkraut, *The Undoing of Thought*

On March 19, 2014, Elliott Abrams sat with Jonathan Silver to answer questions about US foreign policy. The conversation took place at *The Tikvah Fund* headquarters in New York City, in front of a small and learned audience. *The Tikvah Fund*, which Silver is the Senior Director of, is a US-based private philanthropic foundation dedicated to advancing the interests of the Jewish state and Jewish intellectual, religious and political leaders.[1] It is also well-known for its close working relationship with many neo-conservative intellectuals, think-tanks and media organisations. Since its founding in 1992, it has provided a platform for many leading neo-conservative thinkers, such as Norman Podhoretz, Bret Stephens, John Bolton, William Kristol, and Clifford May, to promote their views about US foreign policy, to sing the praises of the US-Israel relationship, and to warn about the evil forces threatening both US and Israel.

Abrams is amongst the most prominent and influential neo-conservatives in the modern US political and intellectual contexts to have visited the organisation in recent times. He has held numerous high-level positions within the national security and foreign policy departments during both the George W. Bush and Ronald Reagan administrations. More recently, he assumed the position as Special Envoy within a Trump administration that was initially hesitant to welcome the neo-conservatives back into the fold, in light of their previous disastrous efforts vis-à-vis the US-led invasion of Iraq. Despite his impressive CV, Abrams is perhaps best known for having withheld information from the US Congress about his dealings during the Iran Contra affair (1985-1987). Unfortunately for Abrams, but perhaps fortunately for the US and many political actors around the world, the extent and precise nature of his past impropriety has not been forgotten by all; Minnesota Democrat Representative Ilhan Omar raised his transgressions during a much publicised 2019 *House Foreign Affairs Committee* hearing, which gained global attention.

Far away from the killing fields in El Salvador, which Abrams had endorsed on the account of US efforts to 'combat communism,' on this particular day in New York City in 2014, Abrams spoke to a small crowd at *Tikvah* about the importance of the US remaining steadfast in its commitment to promoting democracy throughout the world. To remind himself to stay on message, Abrams had brought with him a piece of paper on which he had scribbled a quote he would refer to throughout the hour-long highbrow discussion - "By the end of this I would [sic] have read it four or five times". Abrams told his audience the quote was taken from Soviet physicist cum-dissident Andrei Sakharov, and went on to read another prescient line of the activist's work, "a country that does not respect that rights of its own people will not respect the rights of its neighbours".[2] These quotes appeared in Sakharov's manifesto written half a decade earlier, which, along with his political activities, saw him imprisoned by Soviet authorities for nine years on account of committing 'thought crimes' against the state. Sakharov's crimes included championing the important idea that remains at grave risk today: that it is incumbent on those lucky enough to be born into, or living in, a free and open society to struggle for the freedoms of the oppressed.

Sakharov's willingness to put his own life at risk by speaking out against the Soviet regime was applauded by many who saw him as providing the world with a moral compass that it so desperately needed at that moment in time. It is in considering Sakharov's manifesto in the context of his wider activism against the Communist Soviet regime, which included his vocal supporting of the *Refuseniks*, that we begin to appreciate precisely why Abrams was now treating him with great reverence. Taken at face value, Abrams' citing of Sakharov's idea about the contingent nature of a nation's internal behaviour seems reasonable enough. This is more likely to be accepted by those not intimately familiar with the political and religious ideas inspiring the broader neo-conservative movement to which Abrams belongs, and the duplicitous nature of rhetoric neo-conservatives routinely deploy when seeking public and government support for their foreign policy prescriptions.

It may also be reasonable to assume that many of those who had gathered at the *Tikvah Fund* to hear Abrams speak, and who had perhaps previously attended talks by other leading neo-conservatives like Bret Stephens, Charles Krauthammer and Norman Podhoretz, understood his claims as making perfect sense. It is possible that many in the audience, in addition to the thousands of people around the world who have since viewed this highbrow discussion online through popular social media platforms, understood Abrams to be part of an important historical intellectual tradition seeking to do 'good' in the world by shining a light on injustice and speaking truth to power. However, for critics and many other close observers of the neo-conservative movement who possess extensive knowledge about the kinds of ideas inspiring Abrams and his colleagues, as well as the well-crafted nature of their Sophistic rhetoric, Abram's altruism would rightly be interpreted as smoke and mirrors.

Whereas it has often been taken for granted that intellectuals in general, and neo-conservatives in particular, mean precisely what they say, many observers are cottoning on to the reality that neo-conservatives like Abrams are perhaps not as fundamentally committed to the democratic ideals that they so loudly and proudly proclaim themselves to be champions of. Keen observers of neo-conservatism are becoming increasingly aware of just how popular deceptive practices amongst its intellectuals actually are. A certain degree of duplicity has almost come to be expected by many living in the West, including many Americans, whom appear to be suffering from the kind of motivational deficit Simon Critchley describes as intimately connected to the functioning of the modern neo-liberal system.[3] However, the extent and ease with which the neo-conservatives have proven to be knavish in their speech and actions in recent times has been widely interpreted as beyond the pale.

The decisive role a small band of neo-conservatives played in manufacturing evidence in their championing of the US' most recent invasion of Iraq serves as an obvious case in point. The devastating effect of these ideas and actions, and the ease with which these neo-conservatives went about wilfully deceiving the American public, was for many a line in the sand moment when it came to determining what kind of political behaviour would now be deemed acceptable. Revelations about the nature of the roles played by this group of neo-conservatives within the Bush administration encouraged an increased focus on the movement by many scholars and commentators belonging to variety of intellectual traditions and operating from within many different fields of inquiry.[4] It is also telling that so many emerging scholars from around the world have dedicated their dissertations to studying different aspects of this phenomenon.[5]

External observers have been especially captivated about the internal dynamics of a US political system that allowed for this large-scale deception to occur. Onlookers have been equally amazed by the callous behaviour of these political actors. Some scholars have also dedicated special attention to deconstructing the inflammatory and duplicitous rhetoric deployed by neo-conservatives working in the US mass media immediately prior to the invasion.[6] It has been revealed that many neo-conservatives operating within US mainstream news media, as well as the vast network of neo-conservative organisations primarily located in and around the New York City and Washington D.C. areas, provided valuable rhetorical assistance to the core group of neo-conservatives within the Bush administration with regards to legitimising, and gaining support for, the US-led invasion.[7]

It is within this context that Shadia Drury's revelations about the relations between Leo Strauss' ideas regarding the usefulness of despotic political tactics and strategic political manoeuvring, and the neo-conservative approach to the political, gained widespread scholarly attention.[8] Scholars and political commentators became particularly interested in Strauss' notion of the noble lie and the integral role this idea played in inspiring neo-conservative duplicity 'for the greater good', whilst also recognising that many neo-conservatives were either students of Strauss at the University of Chicago or were students of his students. A plethora of self-confessed Straussians choosing not to identify as neo-conservatives pushed back against these claims, taking umbrage at both scathing critiques of their teacher and their being associated with a group of intellectuals who not only appeared to be completely devoid of a moral and ethical compass but who have also revealed themselves as perpetually eager for war.[9] This work firmly situates itself within the ongoing scholarly debates about how we can best interpret Strauss' body of work, and how we can go about determining whether or not neo-conservatives have sought and found inspiration in his teachings.

That Elliot Abrams was able to keep a straight face when drawing on Sakharov's ideas for his crowd is remarkable for so many reasons and provides the perfect entry point for this study. Chief among these is Abrams' positioning himself, and representing the neo-conservative movement as, advancing an intellectual project to which Sakharov so clearly belongs but neo-conservatives do not, despite their claims to the contrary. Sakharov was a renowned physicist when he risked his professional career and personal safety to write and distribute his manifesto in post Stalinist-Russia. In writing and disseminating his *pronunciamento*, which has become renowned for pithy quotes such as: "Freedom of thought is the only guarantee against an infection of mankind by mass myths, which, in the hands of treacherous hypocrites and demagogues, can be transformed into bloody dictatorships", Sakharov joined an illustrious tradition of intellectuals that includes the likes of George Orwell, Julien Benda, Edward Said and Vaclav Havel.[10] These authors are united in their understanding that the chief responsibility of the intellectual is to be both courageous and humble in the service of truth.[11]

This 'truth' that we speak of refers to how things appear on the ground, and is devoid of the kind of fantastical thinking that details how things *should* be according to biblical prophecy. This 'truth' to which Sakharov, Benda, Orwell, Said and others have been so committed to, involves calling out injustices in full knowledge that this unmasking may lead to persecution by a powerful elite who have a clear stake in maintaining the status quo. This 'truth' involves focusing on the relationship between the dominator and dominated, and remains free of partisan interests, especially those that are religious in nature. The late Edward Said spoke about the role and responsibility of the intellectual in seeking this 'truth' in his famous Reith Lectures:

> [Religious] Revelation and inspiration, while perfectly feasible as modes for understanding in private life, are disasters and even barbaric when put to use by theocratically minded men

and women. Indeed I would go so far as saying that the intellectual must be involved in a lifelong dispute with all the guardians of sacred vision or text whose depredations are legion and whose heavy hand brooks no disagreement and certainly no diversity. Uncompromising freedom of opinion and expression is the secular intellectual's main bastion. To abandon its defence or to tolerate tamperings with any of its foundations are in effect to betray the intellectual's calling.[12]

Said like Sakharov endeared himself to many truth-seekers around the world because he practised what he preached; Said dedicated so much of his intellectual career to shining a light on the injustices in Apartheid-South Africa and Occupied-Palestine. In casting our eyes over the historical record, and closely studying what Abrams continues to say in both his official capacity with the US Government and as an employee of neo-conservative and pro-Israeli think tanks and policy organisations, it becomes apparent that he has assumed a very different role as an intellectual to those adopted by Said and Sakharov. In fact, Abrams is in many ways the antithesis of Said and Sakharov. It is hard to imagine Said and Sakharov ever describing the El Mozote massacre in El Salvador as a "fabulous achievement", which is precisely how Abrams categorised the incident in which US-trained El-Salvadorian Government soldiers raped and killed innocent women and children as part of 'defeating the communist threat'.[13]

Particularly relevant to this book is the fact that Abrams was a key player in the Iran-Contra Affair, which he later lied about to US Congress when questioned about his involvement whilst under oath. Abrams' untruthfulness was later deemed to be inconsequential by Republican President George Bush, who exercised his presidential power to pardon Abrams on the grounds his crimes were motivated by a love for, and duty to, America.[14] Not only was Abrams spared a lengthy prison sentence, but his absolution paved the way for his more recent appointment as Special Envoy with the Trump administration. It is because of these kinds of actions, and many others that we will explore throughout this book, that Abrams has proven himself to be precisely the kind of intellectual Orwell and those of similar ilk have rallied against: he who is willing to sacrifice a commitment to truth and justice in the service of nationalism and patriotism. "Nationalism", Orwell reminds us, "is inseparable from the desire for power. The abiding purpose of every nationalist is to secure more power and more prestige, not for himself but for the nation or other unit in which he has chosen to sink his own individuality".[15] For Abrams, the neo-conservative movement is one of those other units.

We now find ourselves some four decades after the infamous Iran-Contra Affair, and both the US Government's and the neo-conservatives' thoughts about working closely with Iran have completely changed. Rather than assisting Iran to acquire weaponry, Abrams, his fellow-neoconservatives and the Trump Republican administration have been determined to ensure the Shi'a Islamic Republic does not acquire or develop the kind of nuclear technology that could disrupt the balance of power in the Middle Eastern region. Neo-conservatives have worked overtime to convince others that Iran's pursuit of nuclear capability is fundamentally driven by their long-held genocidal desire to wipe Israel from the map.

It is revealing that neo-conservatives have been unwilling to seriously entertain, or at the very least acknowledge, the possibility that Iranian antipathy for Israel and its chief supporters (namely the US) is in any way related to Israel's occupying of the Palestinian Territories. Israel's routine brutalising of Palestinians of all religious and non-religious persuasions (not just Muslims but Palestinian-Christians as well, which is an important aspect of the Occupation often ignored by Western mainstream news media) is conveniently overlooked by neo-conservatives who remain convinced the Palestinian struggle for self-determination is *solely* motivated by a deep desire to eliminate Jewish-Israel. Neo-conservatives also refuse to give any credence to the idea Iranian animosity is associated with a desire to even-out the power balance in the region, so that Israel is not the only state in possession of an impressive nuclear arsenal. These are not the kinds of arguments neo-conservative want to engage with, as it would require them to clearly lay out why Israel and the US, but not Iran, should be allowed to possess WMDs. Such a process would likely mean explicitly describing their own moral and ethical viewpoints, and the major theological and political ideas shaping their worldview. It is far easier and effective, and far less controversial, for neo-conservatives to use reductionist arguments claiming the root of the hostility between Iran, and Israel and the US, is religion.

As it stands, the neo-conservatives do not enjoy the kind of influence in the foreign policy and national security spheres they possessed under the previous George W. Bush administration. Trump has proven himself to be lukewarm to the neo-conservative persuasion, although this appeared to change slightly in light of high-profile appointments of John Bolton and Elliott Abrams to important security and foreign policy positions. The neo-conservative task of convincing Trump and his inner circle to sanction military action against Iran remains challenging, far more so than when they were able to capitalise on the 9/11 terrorist attacks to help convince Bush and the public about the necessity for a quick and decisive attack against Saddam. In the absence of such another cataclysmic event, neo-conservatives find themselves dedicating significant time, effort and resources to a rhetorical campaign aimed at convincing US policy- and decision-makers, and the US public, that Iran must be attacked for the sake of Israel and US foreign interests. Never ones to shy away from such a challenge, the neo-conservatives have engaged in a sustained and inflammatory war of ideas aimed at legitimising US and Israeli state violence against Iran, and it is the nature of this rhetorical campaign that is of great interest to this study.

Ideas & Connections Matter

That ideas matter is widely recognised by scholars working within the sociology, religious, political and international relations traditions. The art of rhetoric has been the focus of scholarly inquiry at least since Classical Antiquity when Aristotle created the touchstone of political rhetoric manoeuvring. However, it is with great trepidation that we view the current neo-conservative anti-Iranian rhetorical campaign as an extension of Aristotle's seminal work. Aristotle intended for rhetoric to be used in conjunction with a dialectical philosophical approach aimed at creating a system of persuasion grounded in knowledge. Neo-conservatives have instead made deception a cornerstone of their rhetorical approach. Neo-conservatives have proven themselves comfortable and adept in using a range of duplicitous practices, including re-writing the historical record. These actions resonate with an authoritarian conceptualisation of the political, meaning they are incompatible with the kind of commitment to democracy that Abrams and his colleagues portray themselves as champions of.

What intellectuals in particular have to say matters given they occupy privileged positions in the modern public sphere. Gilles Deleuze and Thomas Osborne are among the scholars to describe the important roles intellectuals play as mediators of ideas in today's knowledge society.[16] Both authors emphasise the responsibilities intellectuals have when it comes to communicating ideas about what is happening 'out there' in the social world to the public, many of whom have little to no experience with the kinds of people, issues and events these intellectuals are talking about. In this way, the modern intellectual is often acting as a creative catalyst of ideas exerting significant influence on the public opinion-making process. What neo-conservatives *in particular* have to say matters given their privileged access within the crowded news media landscape, and the demonstrated ability of their ideas to influence the upper echelons of the US political apparatus.

Declarations of neo-conservativism's inevitable decline, and political and intellectual irrelevance, have so far proven to be wildly inaccurate. Observations of this nature were made with surprising regularity at the beginning of the Trump Presidency in 2017. It seems as though these miscalculations were either the result of a failure to properly appreciate the fierce determination of its intellectuals, many of whom had momentarily retreated to the vast network of neo-conservative think tanks and policy organisations in the Washington D.C. and New York City areas following the end of the Bush administration, or wishful thinking.[17] The extensive and well-resourced network of neo-conservative outfits, with its seemingly unlimited financial resources and extensive political and media connections both in the US and Israel, has ensured neo-conservatism's survival.[18] There appears to be no good reasons as to why the movement will lose its status as a formidable force in the US political and intellectual spheres in the near future.

The positioning of its key intellectuals at mainstream US news media publications, their online presence, and connections with the US political elite, have all contributed to the movement's continual strong presence in the political and public opinion-making games. The neo-conservative web stretches across *The New York Times, Washington Times, Washington Post, The Wall Street Journal* and *New York Post*, where the likes of Bret Stephens, Frank Gaffney, John Podhoretz, Charles Krauthammer, Michael Ledeen, Daniel Pipes and Max Boot have all been regular Op-Ed contributors. Beyond these two major metropolises, which are best characterised as the hearts and lungs of the modern neo-conservative movement, its intellectuals have also had their works consistently published in the *Lost Angeles Times, Oakland Tribune, Boston Globe, Orlando Sentinel, Spokesman Review* (in Spokane, Washington) and *Deseret News* (Salt Lake City, Utah), just to name a few.

Having found a home in the US Republican Party where they enjoy a fruitful relationship of political convenience with the Christian Evangelical movement, the neo-conservatives continue to work tirelessly to stamp their imprimatur on the world. In recent times their efforts have been focused on Iran, with the Islamic Republic now occupying a central position in the neo-conservative mindset once reserved for Saddam's regime and, prior to that, Soviet-led Communism.

Imagining Iran

Iran has not enjoyed anything close to a positive public image in the US for quite some time. Polling of the American public reveals Iran rates as the *least trusted* nation in the Middle East.[19] These findings perplex many observers given the Islamic Republic does not appear to be substantially different to the other nations in the Middle Eastern region. This is not to deny each nation's unique traditions. Rather it has to do with understanding precisely why Iran is thought of in a far more negative way than for example Saudi Arabia, whose seemingly harsher authoritarian policies have attracted far more criticism from free-floating and unattached intellectuals and liberal interventionists. Understanding this general perception only becomes more baffling when considering Iran's dealings with the US in recent times have not been entirely negative.

Iran was one of the few Middle Eastern and Islamic regimes to stand alongside US in condemning the Islamic State from the outset – a policy stance US-ally Saudi Arabia was initially unwilling to adopt. Iran also remained firmly opposed to al-Qaeda during the period of time the US had labelled the terrorist organisation as the greatest threat to the security of the Free World. Stephen Kinzer from *Politico Magazine* perfectly sums up the situation when he claims that Iran occupies a unique position in America's pantheon of enemies, and its ongoing demonization is one of the most bizarre and most self-defeating aspects of US foreign policy.[20]

Various opinions have been offered as to why many Americans have come to think about Iran in such negative ways. A common view refers to the series of issues and events that have profoundly and uniquely affected American thinking. Chief among these are the 1979 Revolution and the Iran Hostage Crisis, where fifty-two American diplomats and citizens were held in the US embassy in Tehran for a whopping 444 days. While many similar events associated with other nations in the Middle Eastern region have largely disappeared from the public memory, the Revolution and Hostage Crisis appear to have remained firmly ensconced in the American consciousness.

There also exists a popular school of thought that Iran's ability to remain a prominent fixture in the minds of many Americans has a lot to do with how the Islamic nation has been consistently re-imagined through creative media. Hollywood's 2012 release of the film *Argo*; an adaption of a book by former CIA operative Tony Mendez, provides an ideal example of how creative reconstructions littered with historical inaccuracies help audiences to relive these traumatic events involving Iran, thereby continuing to encourage negative associations.[21] It is noteworthy that this film was released during a particularly sensitive time in US-Iranian relations – negotiations between Western Powers (France, Britain and the US) and Iran about its nuclear program were retarded from 2009-2012 as Iran continued to baulk at Western interference. The framework for the *Joint Comprehensive Plan of Action* (also known as the *Iran Nuclear Deal* or the *Iran Deal*) was developed in 2013 and ratified in 2015.

It may be surprising to some just how big an affect popular films can play in shaping public perception. Film has long assumed a pivotal role in propaganda campaigns, and successive US administrations have sought to use this to their advantage throughout both World Wars, the Vietnam War, and the Cold War, just to name a few.[22] Edward Said has revealed the great extent to which creative accounts produced by Westerners played in shaping their historical imaginings about the Orient. "Every [Western] writer on the Orient", writes Said "assumes some Oriental precedent, some previous knowledge of the Orient, to which he refers and on which he relies. Additionally, each work on the Orient affiliates itself with other works, with audiences, with institutions, with the Orient itself". Said claims these "ensemble of relationships between works, audiences, and some particular aspects of the Orient therefore constitutes an analyzable formation...whose presence in time, in discourse, in institutions...gives it strength and authority".[23]

Neo-conservatives certainly recognise how this process works, which is a major reason why they were so critical of Mel Gibson's *The Passion of the Christ* (released in 2004). Despite the historical accuracy of the blockbuster film as per the Christian biblical account, which is relatively uncommon for a big Hollywood production, neo-conservatives were concerned that the recounting of the events leading to Jesus' crucifixion, specifically the key role played by a group of Jews in organising his capture, would harm Jewish-Christian relations in America. This is an aspect of the Christian biblical narrative neo-conservatives prefer the US public ignore, given its potential to inspire anti-Jewish sentiment amongst the sizeable Christian population in the US. The neo-conservative response to the releasing of this film is best exemplified by the late Charles Krauthammer. In his article 'A compassion-free Passion,' in which he decried Gibson's making of the film, Krauthammer claimed:

> The Crucifixion is not just a story, but it is a story with its own story – a history of centuries of relentless – at times savage – persecution of Jews in Christian lands. This history is what moved Vatican II, in a noble act of theological reflection, to decree in 1965 that *The Passion of the Christ* should henceforth be understood with great care so as to unteach the lesson that had been taught for almost two millenniums: that the Jews were Christ-killers...[24]

We have also seen American children, young adults and older gamers purchase *en masse* realistic shoot-em'-up video games depicting

Iranians as the bad guys.[25] *Battlefield 3*, a first-person shooter video game produced by *Electronic Arts*, sold five million copies alone during its first week of release. This game allows players to take on the role of US Marines as they fight enemies in Paris, New York and ultimately Tehran, under the looming threat of a nuclear war. Gunfights are depicted in various military, industrial and urban locations in Tehran including in its historic Grand Bazaar. The game was understandably banned in Iran by authorities. *ARMA 3* and *1979 Revolution: Black Friday* are other popular video games that have been met with the same response by the Iranian Government because of their similar graphic depicting of Iranian landscapes and representing Iranians as an enemies of the 'Free World'.

It is also worth mentioning that the US military uses shoot-em'-up video games that are set in Middle East locations to both inspire and familiarise military recruits. Important research undertaken by Scott Romaniuk and Tobias Burgers, which involved interviewing current and former members of the U.S. military with the aim of understanding the role violent first-person shooter games played in their recruitment and training, found that the majority of participants believed these especially violent games were important "to staying in the mindset of a soldier even when not on duty".[26] The impact of films, video games and other fictional and interactive media should not be overstated; however, it is important to recognise some of the different elements that have the ability to shape public perception about a particular nation, culture and religion.

Discerning the Neo-Conservative Voice

Neo-conservatives have played significant roles in the sustained anti-Iranian campaign that has also attracted great support from US-based pro-Israeli movement intellectuals as well as many Israeli political, intellectual and religious actors. This campaign intensified in the US during the official withdrawing of US troops from Iraq (2007 – 2011) and following the ratifying of the *Iran Nuclear Deal* (2015). The neo-conservative voice is easily discernible from the chorus of anti-Iranian rhetoric emanating from the US due in part to its especially inflammatory nature and penchant for racial stereotyping. Neo-conservatives have proven themselves far more willing than many others when it comes to criticising the Iranian regime and the Iranian people on account of their religious beliefs, and their 'failure to evolve' and 'adapt' to modern living. These claims are problematic not only because of their ethnocentric assumptions, but also given the US' long history of interference in Iranian politics, which neo-conservatives appeared to have forgotten.

The US was heavily involved in propping up the brutal dictatorial regime led by Mohammad Reza Pahlavi in Iran that lasted from the 1950s to the end of the 1970s. This impeded the kinds of democratic advances neo-conservatives claim Iran should have achieved by now. Declassified documents reveal that it was the Central Intelligence Agency (CIA) that orchestrated the coup against Iran's *democratically elected* prime minister Mohammad Mosaddeq in 1953: "The military coup that overthrew Mosaddeq and his National Front cabinet was carried out under CIA direction as an act of US foreign policy, conceived and approved at the highest levels of government".[27] Archived CIA documents, which include an internal history of the coup titled *Campaign to install a pro-Western government in Iran*, clearly outline the aim of the US-led campaign: "through legal, or quasi-legal, methods to effect the fall of the Mosaddeq government; and to replace it with a pro-western government under the Shah's leadership with Zahedi as its prime minister".[28]

Iranian-Armenian historian Ervand Abrahamian is among those to have argued that Prime Minister Mohammad Mosaddeq, unlike many other nationalist leaders in the North Africa and Middle East regions at this time, epitomised a unique anti-colonial figure who had proven himself dedicated to democratic values and human rights.[29] This is not however the kind of information or context one is able to glean from the many neo-conservative accounts about Iran. In spite of consistent and significant US meddling, neo-conservatives remain steadfast in their beliefs that it is the radical Islamist Iranian leaders who are entirely to blame for the 'backwards' situation they now find themselves in – a state of being that they claim results in its leaders acting in increasingly 'irrational' and 'brutal' ways.

In surveying the plethora of anti-Iranian texts produced by neo-conservatives in recent times, it also becomes apparent that many of their criticisms originate from places of nationalistic and moral clarity. Neo-conservative rhetoric routinely asserts the universal values exhibited by the US and Israel; both of whom are considered to be global leaders of the Judeo-Christian civilising project. Put another way, neo-conservatives view the US and Israel to be the originators and purveyors of all that is good in the world. Neo-conservatives locate demonic Iran as existing beyond the bounds of the modern civilised world. The 'timeless' nature of its Islamic society and its continual refusal to acquiesce to US demands, have inspired neo-conservatives to represent Iran as the quintessential modern expression of evil, with a lineage that can be traced all the way back to the Fall of Man.

As it stands, the neo-conservative movement is comprised of a significant, but by no means exclusive, Jewish-American element. Whereas it once may have been accurate to describe the movement as an uniquely Jewish phenomenon - as Jacob Heilbrunn has done, it has experienced significant change in recent times. We are now seeing a marked increase in the number of Christian-American intellectuals associating with the movement, particularly when it comes to collaborating on policy briefs, articles and research projects with well-known Jewish neo-conservatives, and working for established neo-conservative think tanks and media organisations.[30] There exists a range of possible reasons for this significant increase in Christian participation: financial rewards, professional opportunities within a well-funded and resourced network, seeking of political appointments within Republican administrations, and a shared interest in supporting Israel in the face of ongoing criticism from many intellectuals, groups and political leaders.

There however appears to be great hesitation on the part of many emerging scholars when it comes to characterising some of the younger, and sometimes female, American intellectuals as neo-conservatives. This is somewhat understandable when considering many researchers beginning their careers in the academe take their cues from the existing sizeable body of work on neo-conservatism, which for the most part is dedicated to studying the ideas and actions of household names like Irving Kristol, Charles Krauthammer and Norman Podhoretz. This work seeks to chart new waters in its characterising of who is a neo-conservative, whilst remaining mindful that all categories in the social world are inherently fuzzy in nature. Determinations in this study about 'who is in and who is out' are informed by Max Weber's notion of the ideal type, and are buttressed with a scrutinising of each intellectual's known political, religious and professional associations.[31]

Neo-conservatism like any category in the social world is fuzzy in nature. This means there will always exist conjecture about 'who is in and who is out'. There is an academic way of dealing with this unique challenge; making use of Max Weber's notion of the ideal type. "An ideal type", writes Weber "is formed by the one-sided accentuation of one or more points of view", according to which we are able to arrange individual phenomena into a unified analytical construct. It is best imagined as a "thought-picture" whose "conceptual purity" is unable to be located elsewhere in reality.[32] Its purpose, as Susan Hekman points out, is to synthesise meaningful and characteristic aspects of a phenomena in order to describe the occurrence of social events.[33]

The defining elements of the Weberian ideal type informing this study are as follows: an unwavering support for Israel, a binary view of the world clearly distinguishing between good and evil, which are considered natural parts of the God-created-world, and a religious and/or political commitment to the ideas of US, Israeli and Jewish Exceptionalism. Added to these are: a favouring of unilateralism over multilateralism, a rejection of US isolationism in favour of a muscular foreign policy that is accompanied by a strong commitment to a powerful military, viewing US and Israeli national interests as inextricably linked, a Machiavellian conceptualisation of the political organised around the idea of enmity, and the *appearance* of a commitment to the promotion of democracy. These elements reflect the fundamental religious and political concerns of this study. Neo-conservatism has interests beyond the aforementioned areas, including in the areas of social welfare, the family unit and sexuality, however these are beyond the scope of this work. Marx's dialectical imagination teaches us that studies like this can only ever expect to provide a snapshot of a much larger and more complicated whole.

When considering the political and religious affiliations of neo-conservative intellectuals producing texts about the perceived threat posed by Iran, special attention is paid to the fact they have found a home in the Republican Party since the late 1970s. Rather than fleeing or dissociating themselves from the Grand Old Party following the electing of Trump, who was not their first, second nor third choice amongst the Republican Presidential candidates, neo-conservatives understand they have no other viable political options at this moment in time given the duopolous nature of the US political system. Returning to their previous home in the Democratic Party is not an option for neo-conservatives who have burned their bridges with its leaders, whom they have long considered to be hostile to the best interests of Israel. Their hatred for the Democratic Party reached a crescendo during the Presidency of Barack Obama, who they viewed as the most anti-Israel US President in living memory.

When it comes to distinguishing a neo-conservative it also worth noting that they tend to work for the same media organisations and think tanks, are typically believers in Judaism or Christianity, and will often lend their services to Jewish and Christian organisations advocating for a strong US-Israel relationship on theological grounds. Some neo-conservatives such as Norman Podhoretz, Charles Krauthammer and John Bolton have been far more public than others like Frank Gaffney, Michael Ledeen and Reuel Marc Gerecht, when it comes to publicly advertising their religious beliefs. However, as we will see throughout this study, even the less theologically boisterous neo-conservatives have produced texts peppered with religious language and which are clearly informed by religious ideas.

Objectives

The religious aspects of neo-conservatism, especially with regards to how these beliefs have helped to shape the movement and influence their perception of Iran, is of great interest to this study for a number of reasons. First there appears to be a widespread cautiousness amongst scholars to hone in on this aspect for fear they will be the focus of *ad hominem* attacks by (neo-conservative) critics. It is sometimes the case that professional appointments in the academe prevent the exploring of sensitive and controversial areas like many of those touched on in this study, due in part to the inevitable backlash that follows from neo-conservatives and the wider pro-Israel lobby. Speaking truth to power is not always easy to do, which is why this process has often been left to free-floating and unattached intellectuals, as is the case in this study.[34]

It is hypocritical that so many neo-conservative intellectuals have employed the kinds of *ad hominem* attacks, particularly racial slurs, they claim others are guilty of committing, when it comes to responding to critiques of the religious elements of their movement. One need only peruse the growing body of literature aimed at understanding how neo-conservatives have gone about Othering Middle Easterners and Muslims to find clear evidence of this.[35] Attempts at silencing and intimidating critics in these ways must not prevent future researchers from speaking truth to power, shining a light on injustice and, more specifically, questioning the wisdom associated with developing foreign and security policy based on the idea that a supernatural figure will one day emerge from the sky and arrive in Jerusalem with the explicit purpose of saving all believers. It is hoped this work is viewed as part of a scholarly tradition characterised by its refusal to cower to intimidation and unfounded aspersions that it will more than likely attract from neo-conservatives and their supporters.

A second reason for focusing on the key religious elements of the movement is related to the neo-conservatives' demonstrated willingness to extensively draw on biblical ideas and language, which appears to have reached a high point in recent times. This has coincided with the electing of President Trump, raising the possibility his routine use of inflammatory rhetoric has helped set a new standard for what is deemed acceptable political speech. Irrespective of where one sits on the political spectrum, it is hard to refute claims Trump has spoken in provocative and offensive ways completely foreign to his predecessor. There is a marked difference in how these two US Presidents have spoken publicly about Muslims, Islam and the Middle East. It remains a point of contention whether uncivil language comes naturally to Trump, is shrewdly deployed to appeal to his political base, or is a combination of both of these and other factors.[36]

There now seems to be an increased level of comfort amongst US political and intellectual actors to publicly reveal their commitment to particular ideas irrespective of how fantastical in nature they are. That so many of these ideas are primarily informed by biblical narratives outlining specific criteria needing to be met in order for the Saviour to emerge and save those demonstrating their commitment to Him, is extremely worrying for many observers. It is especially concerning for those who value the more secular aspects of modern liberal democracies. It must be acknowledged that neo-conservatives are not the only ones to have adapted to the shifting in arbitrary standards governing public discourse. The alt-right also seems to have embraced this change, with many of its intellectuals appearing to have interpreted Trump's initial condoning for their ideas as a green light for spouting hateful and racist ideas. It may also be the case these changes are somehow connected to what many people of faith interpret as the fast approaching of the End Times - one need not worry about offending the sensibilities of others when The Rapture is on the horizon.

Alongside this exploration into the key roles religious ideas are playing in neo-conservative thinking, this study aims to understand the nature and role played by popular political ideas when it comes to shaping the movement and influencing its intellectuals' interpretations of Iran in recent times. Undertaking this task involves engaging with the ongoing scholarly debate about the 'true' nature of Leo Strauss' writings, and the extent to which his ideas have influenced neo-conservatives, many of whom were either his students or students of his students at the University of Chicago. Informed by John Caputo's notion of truth - that we are no longer living in an age where there exists all-encompassing narrative able explain all the happenings in the social world, this study makes no objectivist claims to truth, including when it comes to the dealing with Strauss' ideas.[37] Instead it engages in the act of interpretation, which like all sense-making exercises in the social world is profoundly influenced by what Hans-Georg Gadamer's hermeneutic conception of knowledge calls one's *Vorurteile*.[38]

Another factor driving the focus of this work on key political aspects of the neo-conservative movement has to do with the widespread misunderstanding about their stated commitment to promoting democracy abroad. Very few critics have rightly identified this as rhetorical foil for the pursuit of specific geopolitical aims and goals. It has proven to be the case that these aims and goals are often intimately connected to helping secure Israel's interests. It is deeply worrisome that so many scholars and commentators are still taking neo-conservatives at their word when they claim to be fundamentally committed to democratic ideals and to spreading the 'rule of reason' throughout the world. As we will soon see, this rhetorical approach exists in an intimate relationship with the concept of the noble lie as is reprised in great length by Strauss.

It is with all of these considerations in mind that this study has been carefully crafted to answer the following questions: What are the key religious and political ideas motivating the neo-conservative movement? From what sources do neo-conservative intellectuals draw their inspiration for these ideas? How are these ideas influencing their making sense of the perceived threat posed by Iran? What are some of the key rhetorical techniques neo-conservatives have relied on when seeking to influence US public opinion and the policy- and decision-making processes with regards to this perceived Iranian threat? And why have they *chosen* to employ these specific techniques?

Sitting behind these are deeper philosophical issues concerning the roles and responsibilities of the modern intellectual as is outlined in the sociology of intellectuals tradition. Ground-breaking twentieth century works by Karl Mannheim, Julien Benda and Edward Said sought to describe how the intellectual *should* act when confronted with extremely challenging political situations.[39] Each author's work was profoundly shaped by, and was in direct response to, the pressing issues confronting them at a particular moment in time and within a specific context. Mannheim, in *Ideology and Utopia,* dealt with the role intellectuals were playing in legitimising the atrocities associated with World War One. Benda, in *The Treason of the Intellectuals,* was concerned with European intellectuals' gradual immersion into the practical and material world of nationalistic and patriotic passions. And Said's ideas were informed by his activism on behalf of those oppressed by colonial regimes in South Africa and Palestine. All of their thoughts continue to have great merit; however, we are now operating in very different political, religious and social contexts – less so in the case of Said's more recent observations.

The sociology of intellectuals is not a fixed body of knowledge whose illuminating insights about the roles and responsibilities of modern intellectuals are to be treated as unchanging and providing eternal truths. It is a scholarly tradition that needs to be continuously engaged with in order for its benefits to be fully realised. The task becomes all the more important in light of the dynamic changes the social world has undergone in recent times. Since the 9/11 terrorist attacks in New York and Washington, we have witnessed a series of events and issues that have had far-reaching and deep-seated implications. We have witnessed the rise and fall of ISIS, the Syrian Civil War, which has morphed into a proxy battle between international powers and regional actors, the US' formal recognising of Jerusalem as the (eternal) capital of Israel, and the creating of what are essentially massive open-air prisons in Gaza and the West Bank, which are enclosing a profoundly traumatised Palestinian population.[40] These events have contributed to the fragmenting of an already fractured global politic, where the trend has been for states and actors to pull away from multilateral and international bodies in favour of increased political autonomy.

In light of these changing dynamics, it pays to reflect on the roles modern intellectuals are currently playing in these processes. Are they helping to identify injustices, and challenging traditional and oppressive political structures, with the aim of creating a just world for all inhabitants? Or, are we witnessing an increased commitment to the promoting of partisan interests by intellectuals fully aware of the negative implications their approach has for those people not deemed worthy enough to belong to the in-group? Neo-conservatives portray themselves as playing integral roles in the former process, however a detailed analysis of their actions suggests the latter description is far more accurate. This is especially the case when it comes to how they speak, write, blog and tweet about Iran.

An inclusive definition of the term 'intellectual' is used in this study. Any actor engaging themselves in tasks of translating information to an audience within the public sphere, and who makes use of some kind of media apparatus when doing so, is treated as an intellectual. There exists a tendency in social science research to adopt more exclusive definitions; many scholars including neo-conservatives themselves have relied on determinations about intellectual capacity and specific locations within a society. These elitist conceptualisations have proven to be out-dated in light of rapid advancements in social media, which has resulted in many new actors receiving the kind of attention once reserved for those holding privileged positions in the old media. It can no longer be taken for granted that mainstream media figures are the first port of call for an inquisitive public. Traditional media sources are far from redundant; however, they provide only one option in an increasingly fragmented public sphere. This research appreciates this new reality, which is a why a variety of texts appearing in the old and new media are drawn on when deconstructing the neo-conservatives' anti-Iranian rhetorical campaign. This helps to provide a more complete picture of what is taking place within the public sphere than would otherwise be case should we limit our attention to just one of these mediums.

It was Joseph Dietzgen who famously asked, "Where do I begin and where do I stop"? Impressing upon scholars the importance of clearly outlining a study's beginning and end points, and the kind of journey readers can expect to be taken on.[41] This study has been orchestrated with this advice in mind. Chapter One is dedicated to making sense of the nature of human be-ing, and to describing the dialectical imagination through which we are able to fully appreciate the dynamic, intricate and interconnected nature of the social world. A snapshot of the well-resourced and inter-connected neo-conservative network is also provided, with special attention dedicated to the outfits established with the clear goals of persuading the public and policy- and decision-makers about the specific threat Iran poses to US and Israeli interests.

In Chapter Two we begin exploring some key religious and political ideas profoundly shaping the movement, as well as locating the sources for these ideas. This journey takes us to back to the events and issues associated with the Holocaust. There has been a tendency amongst scholars studying neo-conservativism to use the 1970s as the starting point, however these studies have tended to overlook the profound and lasting influence certain political and religious responses to the Holocaust provided by prominent (and mainly Jewish-American intellectuals) have had on the development of the neo-conservative movement. The key ideas of Leo Strauss are also introduced, namely his notion about the natural order of things. This signals the beginning of our exploration into the relation between his works and actions, and the neo-conservative approach to the political.

In Chapter Three we continue our journey of understanding and locating the origins of some key political and religious ideas influencing neo-conservatives, with a clear view of appreciating the extent to which they have influenced their representations of Iran. We take a close look at the façade that is the neo-conservative global promotion of democracy, and at the three interconnected ideas of US, Israeli and Jewish Exceptionalism. Special attention is dedicated to the David and Goliath myth, which has its roots in sacred religious texts and has proven integral to neo-conservatives' recent attempts at legitimising US and Israeli-led military strikes against Iran. We also look at how claims of anti-Semitism have been used rhetorically; a sensitive topic but one needing to be dealt with given its frequent use and corrupting by many neo-conservatives.

In Chapter Four we outline the sense-making process with an eye firmly fixed on deconstructing a wide range of texts that have featured in the neo-conservative campaign against Iran. The analytical model used is adapted from two interrelated linguistic fields; Systemic Functional Linguistics and Cognitive Linguistics. This original approach consists of elements abstracted from ground-breaking and recent work undertaken by those part of the Sydney School, and from more well-known advances made in the fields of cognitive metaphors and the cognitive structuring of violent accounts by George Lakoff and Karen Cerulo respectively.

In Chapter Five we begin reaping the fruits of our deconstructive labour. We see how neo-conservatives have structured their anti-Iranian campaign around the key idea that an Iranian regime with nuclear capability will allow it to realise its 'long-held genocidal fantasy' of 'wiping Israel off the map'. We take a close look at three interconnected elements acting as key pillars in this approach: using the metaphorical expression 'the spirit of Munich', the deploying of the neologism 'Holocaust 2.0' and the utilising of the haunting phrase 'never again'. All of these invoke horrific imagery associated with the mass killings on the European continent by Hitler's twentieth century Nazi regime.

In the Conclusion we reflect on the journey taken, which involves considering the neo-conservative movement's next moves, and reflecting on what it means and how it feels to experience be-ing in a world in which the threat of nuclear-war is a very real possibility, and where 'truth' is increasingly understood as a malleable idea to be used in the pursuing of partisan interests and fulfilling fantastical and violent desires.

Chapter One
On Being &The Neo-Conservative Network

Everything flows onward; all things
are brought into being with a changing nature;
the ages themselves glide by in constant movement.

— Ovid

Our understanding of the world exists in relation to what we have become, are becoming and the instruments we choose to use when making sense of these processes. Martin Heidegger is among the most famous philosophers belonging to the Western tradition who has impressed upon us the importance of getting to know the world in which are living. In his seminal work *Being and Time,* Heidegger describes both the great personal and societal value associated with committing oneself to undertaking reflective analytical exercises geared at further understanding ourselves, those around us, and the communities we are intimately bound to. Heidegger's concept *Dasein*, whose literal translation is 'being-there', draws attention to the idea human be-ing is best understood as existing within a world comprised of interrelated elements. *Dasein* is 'to be there' and 'there' is the interconnected and often complex world we are sharing with others. The human being is, as Heidegger describes, a 'relational being' whose experience in being human is characterised by a deep immersion in the happenings of the everyday world.[1]

Heidegger's philosophical ideas resonate with Karl Marx's notion of dialectics. Marx intended dialectics to offer researchers a way of thinking about the social world that brings into sharp focus its full complement of changes and interactions. Bertell Ollman, who has demonstrated himself to be a virtuoso in dialectics, makes the important point in his work *Dance of the Dialectic* that this kind of philosophical approach to social world inspires in its users a language of 'processes', 'elements', 'moments', 'expressions', 'manifestations', 'forms', and 'aspects', as these are the things comprising the dynamic world in which we are living.[2] These elements, moments and so on, are constantly experiencing processes of becoming, and exist in mutually affecting relations with each other. As observers of these processes seeking a comprehensive and accurate understanding of what is taking place, we are only ever able to take a snapshot of these elements at a particular moment in time. After stilling this picture for but a brief moment in time, we must then dedicate ourselves to making these "frozen circumstances dance by singing to them their own melody".[3]

Before describing the particular aspects of Marx's dialectic utilised in this study, it is worth drawing attention to the reality that this approach stands in stark contrast to how neo-conservatives view the world. Neo-conservative intellectuals are demonstrated adherents to an objectivist approach, where elements within the world exist in a causal relationship. This approach emphasises what we call a philosophy of external relations. This thinking maintains that there is a 'truth' to be found in the social world, and it is our roles as humans to discover it and then act accordingly, in order to produce specific and measurable outcomes. These beliefs were on display when neo-conservative trailblazer Norman Podhoretz famously declared he had discovered "the secret of life and existence and knowledge", and, following this revelation, thought it was his responsibility to communicate this profound truth others. Podhoretz claims this truth was revealed to him during a supernatural experience in which he saw appearing before him "a kind of diagram that resembled a family tree".[4] Podhoretz's ideas would not be so concerning if he existed on the lunatic fringe of the neo-conservative movement, similar to the position Rachel Abrams once occupied. However, the opposite is true: Podhoretz has done more than most to help establish and shape the movement, including infusing it with its more controversial religious ideas that have been inspired by the work of Emile Fackenheim.

The problem with an objectivist approach to the social world, which is adhered to by neo-conservatives and indeed many other thinkers, is it often lends itself towards authoritarian conceptualisations of the political. This is because it treats the social world as a battleground for the imposing of one's truth and, at the same time, the discrediting of conflicting truths. There are many Podhoretzs out there who also claim to have had similar supernatural experiences, and also believe it is their duty to communicate these revelations to others. Hannah Arendt spoke about this increasingly worrying trend at great length in *The Origins of Totalitarianism*, which she wrote in response to the widespread spreading of totalitarian ideologies throughout mid twentieth century Europe. Arendt makes the important point that objectivist thinking became so tempting to Europeans after the War and the Depression because it offered them a 'key to history' they believe they so desperately needed in order to secure themselves and their communities a safe and predictable future.[5]

No such objectivist claims to truth are informing this study; rather, the focus is to treat issues and events as they reveal themselves on the ground. It is here that Marx's ideas about the philosophy of internal relations, abstraction and vantage point become extremely useful. Marx's dialectical imagination is both dense and expansive, and it is beyond the remit of this study to fully incorporate all of his ideas, no matter how brilliant or illuminating. What we are able to do, with a clear view in answering the research questions previously set out, is abstract the pertinent elements from his dialectical framework for use. Abstraction, philosophy of internal relations and vantage point are the three pillars on which the dialectic stands, and it is incumbent on us, as good philosophers, to have a solid understanding of what precisely each of these are and how they work. This understanding is especially important given they form the philosophical foundation on which this study is built.

A dialectical analysis focuses on questions about why and how we go about drawing boundaries and establishing observable and deconstructable units that guide our thinking about the social world – this is a process that we call abstraction. It is here we can refer to Marx's *A Contribution to the Critique of Political Economy*, where he makes his most explicit remarks on this subject.[6] Marx describes this approach as beginning from the "real concrete" i.e. the world as it presents itself to us, proceeding through "abstraction" i.e. the intellectual activity of breaking this whole down into manageable mental units, and arriving at the "thought concrete" i.e. the reconstituted and now understood whole present in the mind.[7] Bertell Ollman highlights the important point that the term 'abstract' comes from the Latin *abstrahere* meaning 'to pull from', and that it can be used as both a verb and noun; an important insight worth remembering as we progress throughout this study.[8] Ultimately the great power in the abstraction process comes from its ability to encourage social scientists to focus on a specific element or small number of elements within a large, complex and dynamic whole, as opposed to biting off more than one can chew and reaching mundane and surface level conclusions.

The philosophy of internal relations encourages researchers to see the social world as an interconnected whole rather than as a conglomeration of loosely connected things. Nothing exists in isolation and everything is experiencing constant change. Like a body of water incapable of remaining still, changes in elements are mutually effecting, setting in motion ripples throughout the entire body. Implications for this study become apparent when considering operational definitions for fuzzy categories like 'neo-conservatism' and 'intellectual', which are existing in a constant state of flux.[9] These fuzzy categories exist in a dynamic space where contexts, ideas and experiences are always undergoing change. T.S. Eliot recognised this when he presciently wrote in *Four Quartets* "For last year's words belong to last year's language, And next year's words await another voice".[10] In understanding the social world in this way, one soon comes to the realisation that it is only possible to provide a snapshot of relations at a particular moment in time. Any kinds of definitive claims to truth, political, religious or otherwise, i.e. claims about the way things always have been, and will always be, in the social world, are nonsensical and serve only to betray the promises of the dialectical imagination.

The notion of vantage point encourages us to consider the happenings in the social world from different standpoints. An abstraction itself, vantage point can be understood as a sense-making process undertaken from different positions at different moments in time. Ollman draws our attention to Marx's using of this idea in *Theories of Surplus Value*, where he refers to capital and labour as "expressions of the same Relation, only seen from the opposite pole".[11] In more recent times, social scientists are more likely to associate this idea with Karl Mannheim, who emphasised the mutually affecting relations between the distinctive conditions in which people live and work.[12]

One particular vantage point needing to be recognised is that adopted by the researcher driving this study; free-floating and unattached to a specific interest group, and inspired by desire to speak truth to power. An important and relevant point made by Hans-Georg Gadamer in his hermeneutic conception of knowledge, is that all sense-makers, no matter their connections or lack thereof, are significantly influenced by their pre-understandings.[13] Gadamer describes how anticipatory structures within our minds affect the ways in which we come to know and understand the world. Every act of understanding presupposes a pre-understanding, the elements of which are one's *Vorurteile*, prejudgments or prejudices. These "absolutely fundamental anticipations, that is, anticipations common to us all", are what Gadamer terms "tradition".[14]

The place and time in which we are thrown into the world, as Heidegger describes in his notion of *Dasein,* affects the kinds of traditions we develop. This point becomes important as we seek to understand how and why neo-conservatives have come to understand the world in particular ways, and how these experiences have affected their interpretations and representations of Iran. Arriving at a thoughtful and nuanced understanding about the different vantage points adopted by different neo-conservative intellectuals within their intellectual tradition, requires a multi-layered exigent analysis. This is especially salient when we it comes to recognising and considering the subtle differences in viewpoints between the first, second and third / current generation of neo-conservative intellectuals; each of whom have been profoundly shaped by their immediate experiences in a dynamic world.

Sources of Guidance & Inspiration

In setting about this sense-making exercise, and in thinking about how we can best communicate this scholarly endeavour, we are able to look for guidance and seek inspiration in the work of serious thinkers whom have previously engaged in similar activities. Russian theorist Mikhail Bakhtin, who played an integral role in laying the groundwork for what we now call the Systemic Functional Linguistics tradition, reminds us that to speak and write about the sense-making and communicative processes is to refer, or take up in some way, that which has been previously spoken and written about.[15] "[A]ny speaker is himself a respondent to a greater or lesser degree", writes Bakhtin. "He is not, after all, the first speaker, the one who disturbs the eternal silence of the universe…Any utterance is a link in a very complexly organized chain of other utterances".[16] It is with this advice in mind that we cast our eyes over the great body of knowledge that we call the Western philosophical tradition. We do this with clear intentions in mind: locating and understanding philosophical insights that enhance our ability to make use of intelligible words and concepts that both recognise and encourage others to appreciate the interconnected nature of the human condition.

In addition to drawing on Marx's ideas about dialectics, for the purposes of this study there is great utility in the idea of the movement intellectual. The notion of the movement intellectual has been reprised at great length by many writers in the sociology of intellectuals tradition.[17] Twentieth century Italian writer Antonio Gramsci did more than most in terms of conceptualising the unique role played by an intellectual with explicit ties to an interest group. Gramsci's idea of the organic intellectual, which he describes in his seminal work *Prison Notebooks*, claims these kinds of political actors are inspired by a desire to use whatever ideological tools are available to them in order to advance the interests of a particular class or group. "Every social group, coming into existence on the original terrain of an essential function in the world of economic production, creates together with itself, organically, one or more strata of intellectuals", writes Gramsci, "which give it homogeneity and an awareness of its own function not only in the economic but also in the social and political fields".[18]

Whilst Gramsci's ideas shed light on understanding the important relation between intellectuals and interest groups, his conception can be categorised as Marxist in nature in that it encourages determinations about being and function according to class origin and affiliation. There is great merit in understanding the current structure of Western society as comprised of elite and subordinate classes, however this study is not guided by, nor is it built on, this assumption. Moving away from a strictly

Marxist lens, movement intellectuals are understood in this work as those with explicit links to an interest group. The notion of the intellectual used here has a slightly broader and more inclusive meaning; encompassing those who many other scholars would perhaps otherwise describe as political commentators and media personalities. The increasingly fragmented nature of the public sphere, which is perhaps best exhibited by the great ability of social media in influencing public opinion about important political processes, has rendered elitist conceptions of the intellectual unviable.

Many intellectuals who enjoy prominent and privileged positions in the old media have a stake in promoting elitist and exclusive notions of intellectual, however one need only look at the huge impact Facebook, YouTube and Twitter played in influencing public opinion in the 2016 US election in order appreciate the reality that the politic is increasingly relying on social media when seeking information about current political issues and events.[19] Elisa Shearer and Jeffrey Gottfried at the *Pew Research Center* found that, as of August 2017, just over two-thirds of Americans reported that they get at least some of their news on social media, and rather interestingly, about three-quarters of non-white Americans now report getting their news from social media sites.[20]

This study is informed by revelatory ideas provided by authors widely categorised as Marxists (Karl Marx and Antonio Gramsci), however this study is not Marxist *per se* as it does not make determinations about the functions of intellectuals *solely* according to their roles within the current capitalist structure and as primarily expressions of a particular class. It is certainly accurate to describe neo-conservatives as largely belonging to the wealthier sections of US society, and they certainly have a vested interest in maintaining the status quo; these points will be expanded upon at pertinent times throughout this work, especially as we begin to explore Leo Strauss' ideas about the natural order of things, however it is the neo-conservatives' religious and political beliefs rather than their economic allegiances that are acting as the glue holding the movement together. It is also their religious and political beliefs, more than their vested interests in acquiring as much capital as possible, that are acting as the major sources of friction when it comes to their ongoing struggles with other intellectuals and movements.

It is also worth here making explicit the operational definition of 'text' used in this study. This clarity is important as some more general understandings of the term tend to exclude things like speech, and also fail to properly appreciate the profound influence of recent developments in social media. In this study 'text' includes all forms of written and verbal communication; from highbrow intellectual discussions at *The Tikvah Fund* that are recorded on YouTube, speeches made at public rallies like the *Stop Iran Rally* in New York City, to tweets and other kinds of social media posts provided by neo-conservatives belonging to a movement that has its finger on the pulse when it comes to tapping into the power of the new media. The dynamic and relational understanding of 'text' informing this study is perfectly described by prominent linguistic theorist M.A.K Halliday:

> A text is the product of its environment, and it functions in that environment...[it is] a continuous process of semantic choice. Text is meaning and meaning is choice, an ongoing current of selections each in its paradigmatic environment of what might have been meant (but was not)...text is interpreted as the process of continuous movement through the system, a process which both expresses the higher orders of meaning that constitute the "social semiotic", the meaning systems of the culture, and at the same changes and modifies the system itself."[21]

Since Halliday's formative work in linguistics, which helped in laying the foundation for the emerging Systemic Functional Linguistics tradition, we have witnessed the creating and increasingly prominent role played by the Twittersphere. Whilst some traditional public sphere theorists are loathed to treat this medium as a serious and important part of the modern public sphere, due in part to its inability to meet the conditions of the popular and normative account provided by Jürgen Habermas, this study has no qualms in recognising the power the 240-character tweet has in influencing the public opinion and policy-making processes.[22] President Trump has played a key role in the emergence of the Twittersphere, as Twitter has proven to be one of his preferred methods of public diplomacy when communicating with foreign leaders and when engaging with the public.[23]

Neo-conservatives have appeared to follow Trump's lead in recent times, using Twitter to take pot-shots at supporters of the *Joint Comprehensive Plan of Action* (*Iran Nuclear Deal*) and Iranian leaders, and to advocate for military action against the Shi'a Islamic Republic. Some of the more incendiary tweets by neo-conservatives in recent times include Michael Ledeen's re-tweeting an image of Iran displaying the military options available to the US should it decide to launch an attack, Bret Stephens' sharing of a video demonstrating why "you're not allowed to be a human in Iran", Nikki Haley's calls for "maximum pressure" to be put on Iran in light of their intentions to "violate the disastrous nuclear deal" and Frank Gaffney's promoting of claims "The National Iranian American Council (#NIAC)" is acting as a "faithful transmission belt of the mullahs' line in Tehran".[24] Stephens' dehumanising of the Islamic enemy, which we catch a glimpse of here, has proven to be a popular technique of neo-conservatives wanting audiences to understand any future attack against the Iranians as 'not that bad' given 'they' will not feel the kind of pain 'we humans' otherwise would.[25]

In spite of their yearning for a period in history where traditional values are favoured to neo-liberalism's excesses, neo-conservatives have proven themselves adept in utilising the newest developments and trends in social media when seeking to connect with the public. The role of the Twittersphere, whilst hugely important, should not however be overstated; this study is also informed by texts representing the perceived Iranian threat appearing in the neo-conservative echo-chamber i.e. the Op-Ed sections of the *The Wall Street Journal, Washington Times, Washington Post* and now the *New York Times* (in light of Bret Stephens relocation), as well as neo-conservative flagship publications *The Weekly Standard* and *FrontPageMag*, and the vast array of neo-conservative think tanks and policy organisations – all of which produce a constant stream of information aimed at US policy and decision-makers on Capitol Hill. Popular books that appeal to the public such as Joshua Muravchik's *Making David into Goliath: How the World Turned Against Israel* have also been harvested for information about how neo-conservatives have gone about constructing their anti-Iranian rhetorical campaign.

Well-Resourced, Interconnected & With An Ideological Axe To Grind

Serious research has been dedicated to detailing the existence and operating of the well-resourced and interconnected network of neo-conservative outfits primarily concentrated in the Washington D.C. and New York City areas.[26] These locations make perfect sense for a movement with its finger on the pulse, given they are; hubs of the US government and international bodies like the UN, key sites of production for leading national newspapers, and places of residence for many of the US political and intellectual elite. The neo-conservative network shares many similarities with the wider and much more influential and well-funded pro-Israeli movement, and is often understood by scholars and mainstream intellectuals alike as subset of the pro-Israel Lobby. 'Pro-Israel Lobby' is a phrase many neo-conservatives bristle at, despite demonstrating they have no qualms in identifying the existence of, and heavily criticising, what they call the 'Muslim Lobby' and the different elements that comprise it like the Saudi-aligned 'Wahhabi Lobby'.[27] As we will come to learn, the timeless proverb 'what is good for the goose is good for the gander' holds no currency with a neo-conservative movement who views itself as beyond reproach.

The neo-conservative movement and the pro-Israel movement are united in their strong and unwavering support for Israel, however the former is typically distinguishable by its identifying with domestic conservative politics expressed in the form of the Republican Party. In contrast, the pro-Israel movement is bipartisan, and enjoys comparable political influence and support from members belonging to, and identifying with, both the Democratic and Republican Parties. Revelations about the extent of the pro-Israel Lobby's influence, particularly with regards to US foreign policy-making process, has not been well-received by neo-conservatives and likeminded individuals and groups. These political actors prefer the Lobby's operations, particularly their political lobbying, remain largely concealed from public view, and the nature of the current US-Israeli relationship *not* be a focus of ongoing debate. They seek to maintain the status quo – to say that Israel currently enjoys a sweet deal, given it continues to receive billions of dollars in US 'aid' and is the beneficiary of a US foreign policy that helps to safeguard its interests in the Middle East, is an understatement.

Existing within this web of networks is a range of religious and political organisations presenting as Christian-Jewish alliances. Their interests overlap with neo-conservatives and the pro-Israel movement to the extent they seek to ensure the Holy Land remains firmly in control of the Israeli state. That Jerusalem must remain under the control of the Jewish nation is a prescription they understand as having Biblical authority, and as key to the returning (for Christians) or welcoming (for Jews) of the Saviour. The interconnectedness of these networks also reveals itself in the often explicit and extensive links in terms of co-hosting and sponsoring initiatives in the forms of websites, excursions to the Holy Land, events, rallies, education programmes, research funding and sharing of board members. These organisations often distribute the same publications produced by members of affiliated organisations, are typically financed by the same wealthy individuals and groups, and routinely call on each other to provide 'expert opinions' when discussing pressing issues and events. In this sense, this network bares a strong resemblance to Herman and Chomsky's describing of the processes involved in the US mass media's manufacturing of consent.[28] In the midst of all these joint initiatives, it is these groups' involvement (typically financial) in the supporting of settler initiatives in the Palestinian Territories that remains a major concern for those intellectuals and human rights activists who oppose the Occupation.[29]

Pertinent to this study are the aspects of this interrelated network of religious and political outfits that are aligned with the neo-conservative movement, and whose primary functioning is to 'educate' the public and policy- and decision-makers about the 'inherently evil nature' of Iran and the existential threat it would pose to Israel should it acquire nuclear weapons. These organisations typically promote the adopting of an ultra-aggressive US foreign policy, and rally against multilateral diplomatic negotiations like the *Iran Nuclear Deal*. These groups are not in the business of discussing how US foreign policy might have helped contribute to the current frosty relationships between the US and much of the Islamic world, nor do they encourage serious debate about why some nation-states should be allowed to possess nuclear weapons and others should be forbidden.

Proficiency in Sophist rhetoric is only one element needed when winning the war of ideas; the other is having an apparatus that allows for these ideas to be continually reinforced. Antonio Gramsci understood this, which is part of the reason why he dedicated so much time and effort to understanding the ideological structures available for use by intellectuals seeking to impose their views.[30] Providing a finely detailed account about the functioning of *all* the organisations and individuals comprising the neo-conservative and associated networks is beyond the remit of this study, nonetheless it is important that some kind of suitable abstraction is provided so readers are not expected to accept claims of influence and intent on face value alone. It is with this in mind that we turn our attention to an organisation called *United Against Nuclear Iran* (UANI), which is among the most prominent neo-conservative associated outfits engaged in the modern anti-Iranian campaign in the US political context.

Founded in 2008, the UANI has dedicated itself to championing a bellicose US foreign policy when dealing with Iran. The UANI is an initiative of the *American Coalition Against Nuclear Iran* (ACANI) - a New York based outfit promoting itself as a non-partisan and broad-based coalition committed to preventing Iran from becoming a regional super-power and from possessing nuclear weapons.[31] UANI's stated aims include informing the US politic about the *true* nature of the Iranian regime, and to raise awareness about the threat posed to US interests by a nuclear-armed Iran.[32] UANI claims to represent a group of similarly minded advocacy organisations that include *Christian Leaders for a Nuclear-Free Iran, American Iranian Democracy Initiative, Democratic Party of Iranian Kurdistan, Iran Task Force, Iran Watch, The Free Muslims Coalition, Progressive American-Iranian Committee, Wisconsin Project on Nuclear Arms Control, Arcadia Foundation* and the *Non-Proliferation Policy Education Center*.[33]

UANI operates under the chairmanship of long-time neo-conservative ally and former US Senator Joseph Lieberman. Lieberman has previously worked for the *Committee for the Liberation of Iraq* (CLI) and, like all neo-conservatives, was a strong advocate for the US invasion of Iraq. The CLI was a short-lived yet hugely influential body organised in direct response to the George W. Bush administration's stated goal to seek regime change in Iraq in the immediate aftermath of the 9/11 terrorist attacks. Lieberman replaced Gary Samore, who following his resignation, expressed his public support for the *Iran Nuclear Deal* – a cardinal sin for anyone associated with the neo-conservative network who are in principle opposed to multilateral negotiations with leaders they consider authoritarian.[34]

A brief look at Lieberman's known professional associations helps to highlight the interconnected nature of the neo-conservative and pro-Israeli networks. His appointments have included working for the *Jewish Institute for National Security Affairs*, *American Enterprise Institute*, *Washington Institute for Near East Policy*, *Committee on the Present Danger* and the *Foundation for the Defense of Democracies*. All of these outfits played prominent roles in advocating for the US' invasion of Iraq, and all are currently playing equally significant roles in the campaign to strike Iran. Liberman, a recipient of the *Christians United for Israel* (CUFI)'s *Defender of Israel* Award, gained widespread attention for his speech at the 2008 CUFI annual conference, in which he expressed his explicit support for CUFI Founder and Chairman Paster John Hagee. Hagee previously made global headlines for calling the Catholic Church "the great whore" and claiming Adolf Hitler was sent by God in order to necessitate the returning of Jews to Israel.[35] This is the kind of individual now responsible for helping lead the campaign for the US' bombing of Iran.

A review of UANI's current and former advisory board members also reveals numerous positions have been held by the likes Jeb Bush and John Bolton. Bush's association with the neo-conservative movement is well-known; he was a founding signatory of the prominent neo-conservative outfit *Project for the New American Century*, he enlisted the support of leading neo-conservative intellectuals as advisors for his 2016

Republican Presidential Candidate campaign, and he has made regular appearances at neo-conservative-aligned think-tanks like the *Council on Foreign Relations*, where he has called for the moving of the US embassy from Tel Aviv to Jerusalem. Bolton is a member of the neo-conservative movement's Christian faction. He served as the National Security Advisor in the Trump administration and his appointment alongside Elliott Abrams as Special Envoy to Venezuela, helped put paid to the idea Trump is 'pushing neoconservatives into the wilderness' as has been claimed by prominent mainstream US and international media commentators like Nicole Hemmer.[36]

Beyond the functioning of the UANI, it is also worth abstracting the case of leading neo-conservative Bret Stephens. Stephens' recent move from the *The Wall Street Journal* to the *New York Times* helps highlight the increasingly prominent role neo-conservatives are playing in mainstream US news-media. A former Pulitzer Prize winner, Bret Stephens has been a regular Op-Ed contributor at the *Times* since April 2017. His move from the neo-conservative echo chamber at *The Wall Street Journal* (prior to which he was at *The Jerusalem Post*, which should give readers some initial indication about the nature of his beliefs) has been a major coup for the neo-conservative movement, as it has granted them access to a market of readers they previously had great trouble reaching. The *Times* still has the kind of *je ne sais quoi* that attracts a very particular segment of US public and which is also very appealing to international readers. There also exists a general feeling amongst international readers that the *Times* alongside *Le Monde* in France and *Die Spiegel* in Germany, is one of the most renowned newspapers in the world. Leading neo-conservative Richard Perle wrote for the publication in the early 1990s and occasionally in the 2000s, however the movement has not previously enjoyed the kind of consistent contributions that Stephens has been able to provide in recent times.

In spite of its allure, it is worth recalling that the *Times* echoed neo-conservative calls for the US' most recent invasion of Iraq, and later admitted it 'got it wrong' when it was revealed its writers relied on 'manufactured evidence' to support their warmongering.[37] Whilst somewhat admirable given the general lack-of quality and objectionable behaviour of many Western newspapers today, these admissions offer little solace to the millions of Iraqis who became 'collateral damage' as well as the generations of surviving Iraqis who are now living with war-related trauma. If there is something that many neo-conservatives learnt from their families' experiences in the Holocaust, it is that war-related trauma has a tendency to exist for many generations.

Stephens, who expresses a quintessential neo-conservative foreign policy view, wasted no time in using his influential position at the *Times* to take up the two interrelated causes dominating neo-conservative thinking in modern times: framing the Palestinian resistance as part of the wider Global War on Terror with the aim of justifying and supporting Israel's ongoing Occupation of the Palestinian Territories, and convincing the US public about the existential threat a nuclear Iran would pose to Israel. The neo-conservative presence in mainstream US media does however extend far beyond Stephens' influential position at the *Times*.

Frank Gaffney has been a regular Op-Ed contributor for the *Washington Times*, and David Pryce-Jones, Irving Kristol and Michael Ledeen have occupied similar positions at *The Wall Street Journal*. John Podhoretz has written regularly for the *New York Post*, Robert Kagan, Marc Reuel Gerecht and Charles Krauthammer for the *Washington Post* and Max Boot for the *Los Angeles Times*. Many of their articles, as well as those written by the plethora of neo-conservatives not mentioned here, have been re-published by newspapers all over the US: a long list that includes Minnesota and Wisconsin's most widely circulated newspapers *The Star Tribune* and *Milwaukee Journal Sentinel, The Orlando Sentinel* in Florida, *Deseret News* in Salt Lake City, Utah, and *The Chicago Tribune* in Chicago. This speaks to the reach of the neo-conservative movement. Whilst its heart and lungs are located in the New York City and Washington D.C. areas, the movement has been able to connect with many of the so-called 'deplorables' living in the 'fly over states', as well as large swathes of the US population not living in its major (and mostly liberal leaning) metropolises.

When it comes to understanding the influential and interconnected nature of the movement, including its close links with the US-based pro-Israel movement, it is also worth abstracting the particular case of leading neo-conservative Frank Gaffney. Gaffney serves as an ideal choice also because he has spearheaded the neo-conservative anti-Iranian campaign. Gaffney has at one time or another been associated with the *Centre for Security Policy*, *Committee on the Present Danger*, *Foundation for the Defense of Democracies*, *Americans for Victory Over Terrorism*, *Set America Free Coalition*, *Project for the New American Century*, *Middle East Forum*, *Coalition for Liberty, Security, and the Law*, *Defense News*, *Benador Associates* (a media company that books its conservative clients media spots, especially within the Murdoch-operated press), *Ariel Center for Policy Research* and *National Review Online*. He has gained attention in recent times for the particularly inflammatory nature of his rhetoric, which is extreme even according to neo-conservative standards. Gaffney has long-displayed a penchant for using neologisms like 'Islamofascist' and 'Islamofascism' when describing any number of 'radical Islamist' enemies he believes poses some kind of threat to Israel and US interests; a list that includes any group or individual supporting Palestinian self-determination, the 'Wahhabi's' in Saudi Arabia, and the modern Iranian Shi'a regime.[38]

George Lakoff was spot on when he pointed out in *Moral Politics: How Liberals and Conservatives Think*, that a significant part of the conservative media's success in influencing political processes has to do with its investing massive amounts of financial resources into its movement intellectuals, and its constructing the kind of ideological infrastructure required to help achieve cultural hegemony.[39] Lakoff, a cognitive linguist by trade, emphasises the important point that successful political campaigns require carefully constructed rhetoric and a framework through which these messages can be consistently promoted. Neo-conservatives certainly came to this realisation some time ago, and the kind of ideological apparatus they have available to them is unparalleled in the US context relative to the numerical size of the movement. Neo-conservatives are without doubt among those US political actors to have heeded Hannah Arendt's important advice about the pitfalls associated with possessing great wealth but not enjoying commensurate ability to influence political processes, which becomes especially important when it comes to pushing back against targeted hatred: "wealth without visible function is much more intolerable because nobody can understand why it should be tolerated. Antisemitism reached its climax [in Europe] when Jews had similarly lost their public functions and their influence, and were left with nothing but their wealth".[40]

The primary focus of this study is the war of ideas neo-conservatives are engaging in the US political and intellectual contexts, however in addition to having an understanding of the national apparatus available to neo-conservatives, it also helps to have an appreciation of the global reach of the movement, especially when it comes to their interference in the internal happenings of foreign sovereign nations. Here it is worth drawing attention to the movement's behaviour vis-à-vis the domestic political situation in Iran. Many intellectuals belonging to the neo-conservative movement, which has long history of supporting international actors and groups who share similar interests and end goals to themselves, have been supporters of a group called *Mojahedin-e Khalq-e Iran* (MEK) (commonly translated as the People's Mujahedin of Iran). Established in Iran in 1963, the MEK was conceived with clear Islamic- and Marxist-inspired ideas in mind. It aimed to overthrow the Islamic Republic of Iran, however it famously lost out in its quest for power to Ayatollah Khomeini and his supporters in the 1978-79 revolution. The MEK responded by engaging in a prolonged paramilitary style campaign against Iranian leaders, launching co-ordinated and violent attacks from neighbouring Iraq.

Saddam Hussein was receptive to the plight of MEK, providing its members refuge throughout the 1980 Iran-Iraq war. The MEK was allowed to live in the Camp Ashraf settlement in Iraq, which was located near the Iranian border in Diyala Province, until moving to Camp Liberty nearby to Baghdad's international airport in 2013. In 2003 the MEK decided not to involve itself in the US-led invasion of Iraq in response to assurances from the US government they would not be targets of the US military, so as long as they remained neutral throughout the conflict. The MEK were betrayed by US forces, who soon bombed MEK sites as part of a deal it struck with Iranian leaders.[41] That a US administration was willing to double cross the MEK was not particularly surprising, particularly to those familiar with the history of US foreign policy in the region. What was bemusing was the MEK decided to take the Bush administration at its word. Admittedly, the extent to which this administration had proven itself willing to employ duplicitous practices, remembering it was heavily influenced by a core group of neo-conservatives in foreign policy and national security positions, was not fully revealed at this moment in time.

Both official US Government and neo-conservative opinion about the MEK however experienced a qualitative change in 2012. Following lobbying by neo-conservatives and other conservative figures and groups, the MEK was officially removed from the designated terror list. A lot of this bidding was done through the *Iran Policy Committee* (IPC), which at the time was spearheaded by Raymond Tanter.[42] Tanter was a former National Security Agency staffer, who was also a member of the neoconservative outfit *Committee on the Present Danger* and an adjunct scholar at another neo-conservative and well-known pro-Israeli outfit *Washington Institute for Near East Policy*. The neo-conservative connection with the IPC is also revealed through the involvement of key figures like Paul E. Vallely and Bruce McColm. Both members of the IPC have long been heavily involved with neo-conservative outfits; Vallely as a military committee chairman for Frank Gaffney's *Centre for Security Policy*, advisor to *Family Security Matters* and writer for *FrontPageMag*, and McColm primarily through his involvement with *Freedom House* and *Coalition for Democracy in Iran*.

It also pertinent that Vallely was among the speakers at the *Stop Iran Rally* in Times Square, New York, in 2015, where he shared the stage with the likes of James Woolsey, Caroline Glick, Monica Crowley and Frank Gaffney – this is an important revelation to keep in mind as we progress throughout this study. A close review of Vallely's past political and religious commentary, and general warmongering, reveals precisely why he has endeared himself to leading neo-conservatives like Gaffney. For e.g. in an interview for PJTV, Vallely declared that the Bush administration's Global War on Terror was a war between the Judeo-Christian project and Islam: "That's what's going on. If you don't understand that, then you don't get it".[43] Vallely was also a promoter of the Obama Birther conspiracy, and has been involved with Jewish and

Christian organisations like the *Jerusalem Summit*, that support the occupation of Palestinian lands on the grounds Israel has a theological right to the land as clearly promised by God, and have sought the relocating of the Palestinian population to prevent their interference with 'Israel's divinely inspired rebirth'.[44]

Neo-conservatives and those with similar aims and goals in Iran, arrived at the realisation that the MEK could now be useful in their quest to at least destabilise, and at the most overthrow, the current Iranian regime. The Islamist and Marxist inspired MEK did not experience any substantive internal change warranting such a re-categorising in 2012; what changed was external perception of the group in light of changing US administrations and shifting US geo-political interests. With the Iraqi threat to Israel's balance of power in the region now neutralised, neo-conservatives and many others shifted their attention to Iran. This entire process helps to demonstrate just how fickle the categorising of terrorist organisations actually is. It is a process that has very little to do with a history of violence and ideology, and more to do with compatibility in terms of furthering US interests.

It is revealing that so many neo-conservatives, and those with strong links to the movement, who have proven themselves to be supporters of the MEK, have made conscious decisions to overlook defining aspects of the group they are otherwise happy to both point out and/or create, in other enemy groups. In addition to its clear Islamic and Marxist-inspired ideas, the MEK is well-known for its totalitarian and cultish aspects, which are reported to include requiring all recruits swear a Koranic oath of devotion to the MEK's leader and that they abstain from sexual relations as a sign of commitment to the MEK's cause.[45] These kinds of characteristics would undoubtedly be highlighted and criticised by neo-conservatives should they relate to pro-Palestinian or pro-Iranian groups.

The key point is that for neo-conservatives there exists no definitive metric for determining who is classified as good or bad, violent or peaceful, despite their claims to the contrary. Neo-conservatives are in the habit of making arbitrary assessments about leaders, groups and movements, which are informed by their own shifting aims and goals, and changes in the national and international political environments. These determinations are heavily influenced by their unwavering support for Israel, as well as their deep desire for the US to maintain its global superpower status. These are important considerations to keep in mind as we go about deconstructing the ongoing neo-conservative anti-Iranian rhetorical campaign.

As it currently stands, the MEK has become a permanent fixture in Washington through its ongoing involvement with the *National Council of Resistance of Iran* (NCRI). The NCRI has provided financial support to influential US political actors like John Bolton, Rudy Giuliani, James Woolsey and Newt Gingrich, who have responded in kind by acting as vocal supporters of the group.[46] "Appeasement of dictators leads to war, destruction and the loss of human lives", proclaimed Giuliani at a pro-MEK rally in Paris in 2010, "For your organization to be described as a terrorist organization is just really a disgrace".[47] That many Iranians consider the MEK to be pariahs appears to be of little to no concern to Bolton, Giuliani, Woolsey and many others associated with the neo-conservative movement, whose public position is that the group provides a viable democratic alternative to the current Iranian regime.[48]

This is by no means an exhaustive account of all activities of a neo-conservative network, which Eli Clifton has accurately described as well-oiled machine that has evolved in ways its early progenitors could never have imagined.[49] As yet, we have not even begun probing the inner-workings and studying the influence of arguably the most powerful neo-conservative outfits like the *American Enterprise Institute*, *Washington Institute for Near East Policy*, *Committee on the Present Danger*, *Foundation for the Defense of Democracies* and the closely associated *American Israel Public Affairs Committee*. The workings and profound influence of these outfits, and many others, will be explored throughout this study as we begin to deconstruct texts produced by neo-conservatives representing the perceived Iranian threat. It is now time to turn our attention to understanding the nature and origins of the key ideas influencing the neo-conservative perception of Iran. This journey takes us back to the horrific events associated with the Holocaust, and the political and intellectual responses it inspired in prominent Jewish-American intellectuals.

Chapter Two
Trauma & Inspiration

I think commitment can carry to the point where you no longer think.

—Hannah Arendt, *The Recovery of the Public World*

Frank Gaffney warns listeners of his local Washington radio show and podcast, *Secure Freedom Radio*, that an Iranian perpetrated Holocaust 2.0 targeting Jewish-Israel is a foregone conclusion should Iranian leaders acquire nuclear weapons. In New York, Monica Crowley delivers a similar message to crowds gathered in Times Square for the *Stop Iran Rally*. She tells Americans 'never again' means dealing swiftly and violently with an Iranian regime intent on fulfilling its long-held genocidal desires to wipe Israel off the map. Also in Washington D.C., Clifford May from the neo-conservative think tank *Foundation for Defense of Democracies*, joins Jeff Jacoby at the *Boston Globe*, Bruce Thornton at *FrontPageMag* and a plethora of other neo-conservative intellectuals writing online, in mainstream newspapers, books and magazines, in telling readers the 'sprit of Munich' is alive and well, and clear for all to see, in the US Government's dealings with an Iranian regime hellbent on acquiring nuclear weapons for the sole purpose of destroying Israel. These abstractions highlight the different expressions of a common rhetorical technique neo-conservatives have made a cornerstone of their current and ongoing anti-Iranian campaign; that is, Holocaust rhetoric.

Before exploring each of these techniques in greater detail, with a view of understanding precisely how they aim to influence the politic and policy - and decision-makers, it is important to understand what has encouraged neo-conservatives to arrive at the point where they believe it both acceptable and effective to write about Iran in these ways. This sense-making journey takes as back to twentieth century America, specifically to the aftermath of the Holocaust. The Holocaust inspired a host of political and religious responses by Jewish, including Jewish-American, thinkers, which would profoundly shape the ideas and actions of many Jews. Amongst the most affected were those Jewish-Americans who would soon become the first generation of neo-conservative intellectuals. The profound influence of these ideas did not however stop there; in fact, the social, political and religious responses provided by a host of Jewish thinkers would also resonate with second and third generation neo-conservatives. Whilst these intellectuals did not directly experience the horrors associated with Hitler's systematic killing programme, they still appeared to suffer from a similar kind of trauma as their elders.

Despite these horrific events occurring some seventy years ago and counting, the events and issues associated with the Holocaust, as well as the mass killing itself, continues to act as a major source of inspiration and motivation for a modern US neo-conservative movement known for looking back as much as looking forward and for its tendency to ascribe a fixed-nature to happenings in the social world. Of specific interest here is how different prescriptions for be-ing provided by influential figures operating in the Jewish-American intellectual scene have influenced how many neo-conservatives have set about ensuring that such a catastrophe perpetrated against the Jewish people would never be repeated.

Many of the more popular academic studies focused on the neo-conservative movement have tended to focus on two key moments in its history. One is when a core group of influential neo-conservatives used their influential positions within the George W. Bush administration to advocate for the US' invading on Iraq based on manufactured evidence.[1] Two is the movement's generally agreed upon point of conception in the 1970s, which was signalled by Irving Kristol's self-identifying as a neo-conservative and Michael Harrington's using the term neo-conservative to describe a group of Jewish-American intellectuals who had transitioned from the anti-Stalinist left to the US political right.[2] However, as our up until-now brief foray into the nature of the current anti-Iranian rhetorical campaign suggests, and for other important reasons that will soon become clear, there is a strong case for journeying decades earlier in order to *fully* appreciate some of the key ideas, issues and events inspiring many neo-conservatives.

In undertaking such a task, this work is following the lead of a handful of scholars such as Jacob Heilbrunn, who has helped demonstrate how the memory of the Holocaust has profoundly impacted neoconservatives' general perceptions of threats to the Jewish people. It was Heilbrunn who made the important and somewhat controversial point that "neoconservatives have invested the Holocaust with a contemporary political significance that warrants caution".[3] Also relevant are David Biale's insightful observations: "Clearly, no one would advocate that the Holocaust not be remembered, for it is unquestionably the most important event in recent Jewish history. But there is a difference between remembrance and constructing a collective identity around an event and an experience alien to the realities of American Jewish life".[4] Biale's prescient comments are worth keeping in mind as we closely study how neo-conservatives have made the Holocaust a central part of their anti-Iranian campaign.

It is unsurprising that the Holocaust, given both its enormity and harrowing nature, would profoundly shape successive global intellectual, theological and political climates. It is understandable that its effects would be most profound in parts of the world like the US where Jews migrated *en masse* following the mass killings on the European continent. Mid twentieth century Jewish-America certainly experienced a qualitative transformation as many of its (newer) members engaged in political and theological debates about how to best make sense of this tragedy and ensure a similar targeted-killing campaign would never again happen. Many of these discussions were, understandably, characterised by a profound sense of loss and deep feelings of consternation about a future in a modern world that had revealed itself capable of producing such evil.

Of specific concern here is how these discussions profoundly impacted Jewish-American thinkers who would soon emerge as the first generation of neo-conservatives. It was their ideas that would help lay the ideological foundation for the movement's sequential generations. The original neo-conservatives produced a large body of work that has provided valuable reference points for how Jewish-Americans in particular should engage with a post-Holocaust world. As we will soon see, their advice has also appealed to Christian elements of the neo-conservative movement, who are similarly motivated by the ideas that Jews are God's Chosen People, and the Holy Land must remain under control of the Israeli state, as per Biblical specifications.

The Existentialist Attraction & God's Chosen Ones

The Holocaust inspired a variety of Jewish thinkers to reconsider their religious and political beliefs. Some decided to turn their backs on Judaism, finding solace in the increasingly popular existentialist ideas that had begun to gain serious traction throughout the Western world. The works of French philosopher Albert Camus in particular attracted a lot of this attention following the translation of his works into English. Holocaust survivor, American *immigré* and popular Jewish-American personality Elie Wiesel was among those who seemed especially receptive Camus' ideas. Wiesel's writings and discussions at this time exhibited the kind of existential crises he and many other Jews found themselves struggling with post-Holocaust. Wiesel's ideas were famously expressed in his seminal and widely-acclaimed literary work *Night*, in which he hauntingly wrote of the Holocaust: "Never shall I forget those flames that consumed my faith forever... Never shall I forget those moments that murdered my God and my soul and turned my dreams to ashes. Never shall I forget those things... Never".[5]

Alongside Wiesel's reflections and flirtations with the Western existentialist tradition, designed to help fill the void where a strong faith in God once existed, were popular meditations on God's (in)existence provided by thinkers like Martin Buber. The Jewish philosopher encouraged his fellow Jews to seriously consider the idea that God may no longer be receptive to hearing the cries of His people. Buber sought to understand God's reasons for severing the once direct line of communication Jews enjoyed as His Chosen Ones. Buber famously asked:

> How is a life with God still possible in a time in which there is an Oswiecim? The estrangement has become too cruel, the hiddenness too deep. One can still 'believe in the God who allowed these things to happen,' but can one still speak to Him? Can one still hear His word? . . . Dare we recommend to . . . the

Job of the gas chambers: 'Call to Him; for He is kind, for His mercy endureth forever'?[6]

Writing in *Commentary Magazine* in 1966, whose target audience was the local Jewish-American population, Chaim Potok notes that whilst Buber was "often the object of mass adulation" amongst the Jewish people, "the most influential Jewish philosopher of our time" was largely rejected by his own people due to his promoting of an interpretation of a Western Existentialist-infused Judaism. Buber's explicit embracing and admiration for the important role played by Jesus Christ in the history and future of mankind, was also not looked upon favourably by many Jewish people who had only a handful of years earlier experienced the Nazi German regime's exploiting of Christianity for their anti-Jewish programme.[7] The Nazi's co-opting of Christianity left a bad taste in the mouths of many Jewish neo-conservatives, particularly Irving Kristol and Norman Podhoretz, who as a result, and in combination with their strict adherence to a more orthodox interpretation of Judaism, remained resentful of the Christian faith. In more recent times, many Jewish neo-conservatives have had to downplay this general concern given they heavily rely on their political alliance with the Evangelical Christians under the banner of the Republican Party.

Richard Rubenstein was another prominent intellectual in the Jewish-American community who joined the Austrian-born Israeli Buber, and equally famous Wiesel, in this sense-making exercise. In *After Auschwitz*, Rubenstein recommended Jews adopt an understanding of the human experience that rightly acknowledged the absurdity and ultimately tragic nature of the universe. "[W]e live in a time of the Death of God", wrote Rubenstein in 1966, "I am however a religious existentialist after Nietzsche and after Auschwitz…the thread uniting God and man, heaven and earth, has been broken. We stand in a cold, silent, unfeeling cosmos, unaided by any purposeful power beyond our own resources. After Auschwitz, what else can a Jew say about God"?[8]

Rubenstein wanted Jews to re-imagine Judaism as a system of ritual and myth that offered its followers coping mechanisms when navigating life's traumas, as opposed to understanding the faith as offering a set of rules that must be interpreted literally and closely followed in order to receive God's favour. "For many who live after Auschwitz, however, it is God, not genocide, that is inconceivable", wrote Rubenstein,

> "[t]he Holocaust simply reveals the obvious fact that the Jews were targeted for annihilation. The fate of Europe's Jews demonstrates…that in times of acute stress Jews are in danger of becoming the target *par excellence* of the nations of the world. This is hardly identical with being chosen by God".[9]

Rubenstein advocated for a re-establishing of the special relationship Jews viewed themselves as enjoying with Israel; however, this new understanding was couched in secular rather than theological terms.

In a post-Holocaust world Rubenstein wanted Jews to think of Israel as a sanctuary for Jewish people where they could be in total control of their destiny. Having their own land would mean not having to rely on the kindness of Gentiles when living in *their* lands according to *their* laws. According to Rubenstein, the European Jewish experience was evidence that this way of living was fraught with danger. This specific idea, which is also integral to the global Zionist project, is shared by many modern neo-conservatives and has perhaps best been expressed in recent times by the late Charles Krauthammer: "We defend ourselves. We don't depend on others, we aren't the court Jews, we don't have to go ask favors of the Gentiles to protect us".[10]

According to Rubenstein, God's Covenant with the Jews – the special status extended to them as His Chosen People conditional on their strict obedience to the Holy Law, had become implausible. It was now the responsibility of Jews around the world to acknowledge this new reality and adapt accordingly: "The Covenant as something that actually happened may no longer be credible, but the Jewish people must live, and there are times in our lives that remain sacred, that is, of decisive importance, to us, even if objectively we are not a Chosen People".[11] Whilst Rubenstein's ideas about the importance of a Jewish-Israel deciding its own fate have strongly resonated with neo-conservatives, his claims that Jews are no longer objectively God's Chosen People have been uniformly rejected by Jewish elements within the movement. "I never thought of not being Jewish" remarked neo-conservative godfather Irving Kristol, "I was always very pleased to be Jewish. After all, not everyone is a member of the Chosen People".[12] Norman Podhoretz has expressed similar sentiments: "I believe in God and I believe that the Jews are the Chosen People", he proudly declared to his New York audience at *The Tikvah Fund*, "Israel is the key issue as far as I'm concerned".[13]

Neo-conservatives have been receptive to some of the advice offered by the likes of Rubenstein, Buber and Wiesel, however, the idea that Jews no longer enjoy a special privilege granted exclusively to them by God has been strongly pushed back against. In addition to explicit claims to this exceptional status made by leading neo-conservative thinkers like Kristol and Krauthammer, a popular way in which neo-conservatives have promoted this idea has involved giving voice to and publishing 'scientific works' attributing Jewish brilliance to God's grace. There are many prominent outfits within the neo-conservative network, including *Commentary Magazine* and the American Enterprise Institute (AEI), that have published works by Christian-leaning American writer Charles Murray, in which he makes these kinds of claims.[14]

A darling of the neo-conservative movement who has also been a recipient of the AEI's highest honour, the *Irving Kristol Award,* Murray claims the success Jews have enjoyed in the arts and sciences is directly attributable to their relatively high IQ.[15] Murray makes the point that no other ethnic or religious group of people have enjoyed comparable success in these fields. The reason for this Jewish brilliance, according to Murray, is God's covenant with them as His Chosen People:

> Why should one particular tribe at the time of Moses, living in the same environment as other nomadic and agricultural peoples of the Middle East, have already evolved elevated intelligence when the others did not? At this point, I take sanctuary in my remaining hypothesis, uniquely parsimonious and happily irrefutable. The Jews are God's chosen people.[16]

That there exists a long list of outstanding thinkers with Jewish heritage who have profoundly shaped the world and the human condition for (what many would consider) the better is undeniable. Hannah Arendt, Noam Chomsky and Albert Einstein all provide examples. However, there are major problems in using reductionist and causal arguments identifying their Jewishness as the distinguishing reason for their brilliance. Similarly, there are major problems when referring to any individual's or group's racial or cultural identity as the determining reason for their behaving in negative ways. This is precisely what neo-conservative critic and American academic Kevin MacDonald has done when claiming Jewish evolutionary psychology is primarily responsible for how Jewish intellectuals, including those part of neo-conservative movement, think and act. [17] MacDonald's reasoning is as equally disturbing as Murray's for precisely the same reasons, despite him arriving at very different conclusions.

In spite of disagreements between influential twentieth century writers like Rubenstein and neo-conservatives about the status of Jewish people living in a post-Holocaust world, Rubenstein's ideas have been important in helping promote an idea very popular amongst neo-conservatives today; the Jewish people must fully accept responsibility for their own fate. This idea inspires many neo- conservatives in their rejecting and criticising the advice and directives offered by others, both national and international actors, including UN figures and leading apolitical humanitarian organisations, about the courses of action Israel and the US should be adopting in order to help right their wrongs. Many understand policy prescriptions offered by international non-government organisations to be non-partisan given their *raison d'être* is helping end injustice. Neo-conservatives however typically view this (often expert) advice, particularly when it concerns Israeli and US interference in the internal happenings of other nations in the Middle Eastern region, as unwanted and accusatory.

To help illustrate this, it is worth here abstracting remarks made by President Trump's former National Security Advisor and leading neo-conservative John Bolton. Bolton's case is telling because it also helps in illuminating the strong links between right-wing Israeli political actors and the neo-conservative movement. Bolton has been extremely critical about the existence and functioning of the UN and bodies like the International Criminal Court, which was established as the result of a lengthy consultation process within the UN (referred to as the Rome Statute). "It is a big mistake for us to grant any validity to international law even when it may seem in our short-term interest to do so", Bolton famously claimed, "if I were redoing the Security Council, I'd have one permanent member: the United States". [18]

It is telling that Bolton's appointment to the influential position in the Trump administration was celebrated by many on the right, including the far-right, in Israel, in addition to US political actors with clear links to these groups. Bolton had already endeared himself to these Israeli elements following his recent efforts at rescinding the 1975 *Zionism is Racism* UN resolution. Joseph Frager, the Vice President of the National Council of Young Israel, offered a response typical amongst the Israeli right when he congratulated his "old friend" on his "well-deserved appointment". Interestingly, Frager claimed Bolton was the ideal candidate for the position given his demonstrated level of skill and sensitivity: "I have no doubt that the sensitivity and skill that permeates everything he does will be evident to the entire nation in his new role as President Trump's national security adviser".[19]

Frager has proven to be a middling player in the US political scene. He has played an active role in helping cement the relationship between conservative Jews and Christians under the Republican Party banner. In recent times he has hosted Republican Party leaders in Israel to tour key religious sites in Jerusalem with the aim of strengthening the relationship between the GOP and Jewish Israelis, and uniting them in their common desire to push back against the Democratic Party's 'anti-Isreali and anti-Jewish' views.[20] He is however perhaps best-known internationally for his organising of a Trump-style rally in Efrat, Israel in August 2018, which provided well-known conservative Israeli and American figures, like leading Christian Evangelical and Republican US politician Mike Huckabee, a platform for supporting the expanding of Israeli settlements in the Palestinian Territories.[21] Huckabee is a key figure in the US Christian Evangelical and Republican Party scenes, whose ideas and influence we will explore in greater detail later.

Frager's political activities and associations help us to understand how he has arrived at the perplexing viewpoint that Bolton is 'sensitive', which is a *very* interesting choice of words given the plethora of confrontational remarks Bolton has made. Amongst the most notable are his advocating for a pre-emptive strike against Iran to prevent the remotest of possibility it may one day develop nuclear capability, and his stated support for a "three-state solution which would merge Gaza with Egypt, and parts of the West Bank with Jordan".[22] Bolton's ideas about the Palestinians strongly resonate with Rachel Abrams' early claims about their supposed in-existence. Abrams, the wife of Elliott Abrams before her death, was well-known for her tendency to put the term Palestinian in single inverted commas; a linguistic technique often used in academic and intellectual circles when the phrase in question is highly contested.

For what it is worth, Abrams previously held the position as the *Meir Kahane Writing Fellow* at the neo-conservative flagship publication *The Weekly Standard*. This is interesting and pertinent to this study given Kahane is widely credited with creating and popularising the post-Holocaust slogan 'never again'. As we will soon see, this phrase has become key to the neo-conservative anti-Iranian rhetorical campaign.[23] Frager's inclusion here is purposeful; his associations and ideas helps to reveal the strong links between neo-conservatives and right-wing political individuals and groups in Israel - an important point previously made by Mearsheimer and Walt, and which many neo-conservatives and US-based pro-Israeli movement intellectuals bristle at suggestions of.[24] The precise nature of these political and religious alliances will become clearer as we dig deeper into the intimate workings of the neo-conservative movement throughout this study.

Bolton's professional appointment in the Trump administration seems to have inspired in him a more aggressive posture when publicly dealing with Iranian leaders. This led to some observers suggesting that the best way for the US to avoid an unnecessary war with Iran is to replace Bolton with someone who is far more sensitive.[25] Bolton's long list of inflammatory rhetoric directed at Iranian leaders in recent times includes his infamous tweet on February 11, 2019, (marking the 40th anniversary of Iran's Islamic Revolution) sent from the White House's official Twitter account, in which he informs Ayatollah Khamenei, "I don't think you'll have many more anniversaries to enjoy".[26]

Entrusting external actors with *any* kind of political authority when it comes to the functioning of Israel is interpreted by neo-conservatives as outsourcing the fate of the Jewish people to Others. According to them, this has happened before and it did not end well; a point well-made by Rubenstein and which prompted Elliott Abrams to make assessments like: "At the United Nations, a lynch mob for Israel is always just a moment away".[27] The cultural appropriation involved here in Abrams' using the phrase 'lynch mob' when representing the UN in this way should not be lost on American readers in particular. This becomes especially important in light of criticisms levelled by neo-conservatives, and those closely associated with the movement, against other intellectuals and various social justice warrior groups who they claim have inappropriately appropriated the slogan 'never again' for causes entirely unrelated to the Holocaust.[28]

Fackenheim & the 614th Commandment

Existing alongside the ideas espoused by Israeli philosopher Rubenstein and Jewish-American thinkers like Buber and Wiesel in the mid twentieth century, was a popular school of thought whose proponents advocated for Jews to re-embrace the Jewish faith in its original, literalist form. Whilst Rubenstein, Buber and Wiesel were united in their calls for Jews to react to post-Holocaust living in more secular rather than religious ways, this second group of Jewish thinkers distinguished themselves with their claims that the best way to avoid a similar catastrophic event from happening again was to embrace the Jewish faith with even greater *rigueur*.

This second group of thinkers wanted their fellow Jews to pay serious attention to how the sacred Jewish texts described the existence evil; that it pervades this God-created world and therefore must be constantly rallied against. According to these thinkers, the adopting of a more literalist interpretation of the sacred Jewish texts was now more important than ever for Jews when it came to surviving in a post-Holocaust world. Put another way, they claimed there existed a truthful way of living clearly laid out by God, and it was the Jewish people's role and responsibility to continue in following these prescriptions despite what had happened in Europe. These ideas strongly resonated with many first-generation neo-conservatives, and the extent of this lasting influence consistently reveals itself in modern neo-conservative discourse.

Jewish philosopher and Reform Rabbi Emil Fackenheim is arguably the most notable and relevant thinker belonging to this school of thought. His ideas are worth abstracting here given their clear relation to the thinking and actions of neo-conservative trailblazer Norman Podhoretz. Podhoretz played a critically role in laying the foundations of the neo-conservative movement, in addition to helping shape it from the mid-to-late 1970s until today. Podhoretz is still an active member, however given his older age he has understandably taken on a much lighter workload, which appears largely limited to appearances at the *The Tikvah Fund* and similar outfits, and writing the occasional text for various neo-conservative groups.

Fackenheim sought to understand the nature of evil manifested in its extreme form in the Holocaust, and was intent on providing the Jewish people with a framework for dealing with trauma and making sense of this new world. Similar to Rubenstein, Wiesel and other prominent Jewish voices at this time, Fackenheim considered the Holocaust to be revelatory for His people. His understanding distinguished itself from Rubenstein, Buber and Wiesel's ideas because of its strong theological flavour and rejection of secularism and existentialism. Of particular importance was his inventive idea he termed the 614th Commandment.

This theological addition to the pre-existing 613 Commandments appearing in the *Torah*, considered the widespread Jewish proclivity for giving up on the idea of God and turning away from Judaism as tantamount to granting Hitler a posthumous victory. Fackenheim has maintained that a firm belief in God viewed strictly through the lens of Judaism is still essential to ensuring the survival of the Jewish people.[29] Norman Podhoretz was among those to heed Fackenheim's advice, and he has since described Fackenheim's idea as *the* motivating force inspiring his engaging in the war of ideas as a neo-conservative on behalf of His people: "I believed and still believe in the 614th commandment and I think it takes precedence over many of the 613", Podhoretz recently told his audience at *The Tikvah Fund*. In the same interview in which he made these remarks, Podhoretz also claimed that history had revealed it as 'fact' that Jews *must* follow a rabbinic path in order to guarantee their existence here on earth where they are constantly surrounded by evil forces.[30]

Podhoretz so strongly believed in Fackenheim's ideas and prescriptions for Jewish living in a post-Holocaust world, that he used his position as managing editor at *Commentary Magazine* to 'sneak in' (as he describes it) the Rabbi's work for the magazine's predominantly Jewish-American readership in the immediate aftermath of the 1967 Six Day War.[31] Podhoretz's unilateral decision, as has since recounted it, signalled a substantive qualitative transformation in the content and direction of the neo-conservative flagship magazine, which up until this moment in time paid little if any attention to the intersections between Jewish culture, religion and history, and contemporary US politics. *Commentary Magazine* was now on its way to becoming a publication with a keen interest in ideas related to the survival of the Jewish people and the Jewish state, and these ideas were, and continue to be, frequently expressed in religious terms.[32]

Like many observant Jews throughout the world, Podhoretz remains firm in his belief that closely following God's prescriptions as detailed in the sacred texts is integral to ensuring the survival of a Jewish people who have consistently been the focus of violent attacks and slandering by enemies. According to many believers, including those part of the neo-conservative movement, Iran is the latest manifestation of this long tradition of evil that has existed since the beginning of time and is intimately associated with *ha-satan*.[33] It is noteworthy that 'Satan', as detailed in the Jewish sacred texts, is commonly interpreted by the faithful as 'adversary', and is often understood as representing sinful impulse (*yetzer hara*) or, more generally, the evil forces preventing humans from submitting to God's divine will. With this in mind, we begin to view explicit claims made by authors like Caroline Glick and David Horowitz, and promoted by neo-conservative-aligned outfits like *Middle East Forum* and *The Washington Institute for Near East Policy*, that Iran is an 'adversary' of the Judeo-Christian world led by Israel and the US, in a new and theological light.[34]

Many neo-conservatives have repeatedly expressed concerns that turning away from more literal interpretations of Judaism in favour of adopting more liberal variations, is tantamount to straying from the path clearly out by God for His people. This deviation leads many Jews to making 'deeply regrettable' decisions such as the adopting of liberal political ideas and supporting of liberal political parties like the US

Democratic Party. Neo-conservatives consider these political actions and beliefs to be hostile to the interests of the Israeli state and Jewish people everywhere. They maintain that in the US political system, it is only the US Republican Party that is firmly committed to the Jewish people and has proven itself unwavering in its support for the state of Israel. "I think there is no question that on Israel the Democrats can no longer be trusted", said Norman Podhoretz in an interview with *The Times of Israel* in 2016. "The liberal community, generally, and the Democratic Party, particularly, have grown increasingly unfriendly to Israel over 50 years, and it's reached a point now where there are elements within the party who are positively hostile to Israel, and many who are simply cold and unfriendly".[35]

This 'liberal crisis' remains a focus of leading neo-conservative intellectuals, as well as for writers working for the movement's outfits operating in and around the New York and Washington D.C. areas. The "crisis" writes Ronn Torossian for *FrontPageMag* "is that these liberal Jews are no longer interested in remaining Jewish – and of course if they aren't concerned about Judaism, they are less likely to care about the Jewish state". The reason for this crisis, claims Torossian, "has to do with the fact…that 71 percent of non-Orthodox Jews intermarry, 66% of American Jews don't belong to a synagogue, 25% don't believe in God". Torossian proceeds to offer a typical neo-conservative understanding about this crisis of faith:

> This crisis is that so many Jews are not concerned about Judaism, and the natural conclusion of abandoning Judaism is abandoning Israel. Traditional Jews who are concerned about the Jewish people of course do outreach to the liberal Jews because we hope they will recognize the greatness of Judaism and our people. Norman Podhoretz was a prophet when he wrote some years ago that "liberalism has become much more than a set of political opinions for political Jews: It has become a religion in its own right, with its own Torah of liberalism and its own set of commandments." For them, "The new Torah will always trump the old." These people are subscribers to a religion called liberalism. [36]

Torossian has proven himself to be a darling of the movement, both in terms of his controversial actions and in speech. In addition to supporting the Republican Party and having strong links with the Likud Party in Israel, he has joined neo-conservatives in criticising the Boycott, Divestment and Sanctions campaign and in supporting the construction of new Israeli settlements in the Occupied Territories. Torossian's political activism was also clear for all the world to see when he was arrested for protesting Yassar Arafat's winning of the Nobel Peace Prize at the award ceremony in Oslo.

In the interests of further understanding the clear relation between Fackenheim's ideas and those of the neo-conservative movement, it is also worth drawing attention to Fackenheim's advising Jews that whilst it is important to always remember the Holocaust's victims, they must never succumb to overwhelming feelings of despair about God's (in)existence. Such despair, argues Fackenheim, is tantamount to delivering this God-created world to the forces of evil. Like many Jewish intellectuals, irrespective of their political and religious persuasion and writing from the mid-to-late twentieth century to now, Fackenheim understood the state of Israel as an integral component to preventing a Final Solution, or a 'Holocaust 2.0' as has been described by modern neo-conservatives like Frank Gaffney. This is a crucial point worth reiterating: irregardless of whether Jewish intellectuals operating in a post-Holocaust world were more attracted to the theological responses offered by Fackenheim or the existentialist responses offered by authors like Wiesel and Buber, the common thread running through both schools of thought is understanding the survival of the modern Israeli state as inseparable from the survival of the Jewish people. This idea continues to inspire all neo-conservatives today.

Roberta Strauss Feuerlicht makes the important point in *The Fate of the Jews* that the Holocaust inspired in many Jewish-Americans a renaissance of Jewish existence, with the Israeli state becoming in effect their new religion.[37] Feuerlicht's insights are supported by recent polling conducted by *Pew Research Centre*, which revealed Jewish-American respondents considered 'remembering the Holocaust' to be the most important factor to their identity as Jews, trumping other aspects like 'observing Jewish law' and 'leading an ethical/moral life'.[38] Amongst the Jewish elements of the neo-conservative movement, this idea has manifested itself both in their persistent using of Holocaust rhetoric and their unconditional support for Israel - a belief held so strongly by many neo-conservatives that they often find themselves defending what many others consider the morally and ethically indefensible. This is precisely what happened with the US' invasion of Iraq. Neo-conservatives championed Saddam's removal on the basis his regime was becoming increasingly hostile to Israel, in addition to his general unwillingness to acquiesce to US demands. This is also continuing to occur with regards to the Israel-Palestinian conflict. For many it is a deeply regrettable situation, particularly given the global success of the anti-colonial movement in recent times, that Israel remains one of the few settler colonial societies still in existence today.

Beyond these noteworthy examples, we need not look too far to find other attempts by neo-conservatives at promoting and defending ideas many others deem morally and ethically reprehensible. Bret Stephens, the late Rachel Abrams, and neo-conservative darling Jeff Jacoby provide obvious examples. Stephens' long list of controversial claims include; describing most problems in the Middle East as a product of the "disease of the Arab mind", condoning waterboarding as a legitimate method for extracting information from suspects, and accusing Palestinians as suffering from a "communal psychosis" thereby debunking "comforting fictions about all people being basically good, or wanting the same things for their children, or being capable of empathy".[39] This commentary, which he provided during his time as an Op-Ed contributor at *The Wall Street Journal*, makes his appointment at the *New York Times* all the more puzzling given the paper's public declaring that "[t]here's no place for bigotry or dishonesty in intelligent discussion".[40] Many outside of the neo-conservative movement and the four walls of the *New York Times* would consider dehumanising groups of people in these ways as bigoted and dishonest.

Neo-conservatives defending the seemingly indefensible in the name of advancing the Israeli cause extends beyond one of its leading figures at the *New York Times*. Rachel Abrams infamously called Palestinian children "devil's spawn", and neo-conservative sympathiser Jeffrey Goldberg sardonically claimed Arab-Palestinian women should "compete in 'Miss Gaza Refugee Camp'" and " 'Miss Mother Who Sends Her Children into the Street to Catch Israeli Bullets with Their Heads' contests".[41] It is also significant that many neo-conservatives, as well as many closely associated with movement including the likes of Andrew McCarthy and Frank Gaffney, promoted the Birther conspiracy when it became apparent when African-American Barack Obama would assume and maintain the US Presidency.[42] These intellectuals were not promoting this conspiracy in the dark corners of the internet where *Stormfront* and similar organisations also described Obama as a traitor beholden to the Muslim God; rather, they were using their prominent positions in the mainstream US media to promote these crazy and sometimes racist ideas. Gaffney's article 'The Jihadist Vote' for the *Washington Times* serves as a case in point:

> Another question yet to be resolved is whether Mr. Obama is a natural born citizen of the United States, a prerequisite pursuant to the U.S. Constitution. There is evidence Mr. Obama was born in Kenya rather than, as he claims, Hawaii. There is also a registration document for a school in Indonesia where the would-be president studied for four years, on which he was identified not only as a Muslim but as an Indonesian. If correct, the latter could give rise to another potential problem with respect to his eligibility to be president.
>
> Curiously, Mr. Obama has, to date, failed to provide an authentic birth certificate which could clear up the matter.[43]

Gaffney's slandering was at the time part of a wider neo-conservative effort aimed at discrediting the Obama Democratic administration's attempts at resolving the Israeli-Palestinian conflict. Neo-conservatives uniformly rejected Obama's efforts on account of Israel enjoying the upper hand in the conflict over a land God promised to His People.

This section provides a snapshot of a particular period in US history where the ideas of prominent thinkers about be-ing in a post-Holocaust world influenced how many Jewish-Americans made sense of, and engaged with, their surroundings. As we have seen, and will continue to see as we closely study the nature of the anti-Iranian campaign, many of the ideas promoted by these twentieth century writers have clearly resonated with neo-conservatives. That is to say, they have provided guidance and inspiration for a movement seeking to making sense of, and deal with, the perceived threat a nuclear-Iran would pose to Jewish-Israel. Existing alongside these more theological prescriptions for be-ing are conceptualisations of the political provided by Leo Strauss, which have similarly acted as key sources of motivation for many neo-conservatives. The nature of Strauss' ideas, and their clear associations with the movement, is the focus of the next section.

The Natural Order of Things

Leo Strauss fled from Nazi Germany to the US when it became apparent his options were accepting 'the Ghetto or the Cross.' As the son of Jewish parents, Strauss decided against living at the mercy of an anti-Semitic Nazi regime, turning his back on the totalitarian regime whose political manoeuvring he had once greatly admired. Strauss' relocating to the US, and subsequent academic appointment at the University of Chicago, provided him with an abundance of eager students with whom he could discuss and translate his ideas about theology and politics. Inspired by the ideas of great philosophers ranging from Plato through to Socrates, Spinoza, Machiavelli, Hobbes and Heidegger, Strauss' huge body of work reveals a pervading concern with the foundational idea that is still core to the current war of ideas taking place within the US, and much of the world, today; namely, 'what is right'?

Understandably, Strauss had a seminal influence on the worldviews of many of his students, some of whom like Allan Bloom, Walter Berns, Abram Shulsky, Harry Jaffa, Carnes Lord and Irving Kristol, would go on to play formative roles in the neo-conservative movement. Kristol, whom is widely considered to be the godfather of neo-conservatism, describes in great detail the profound influence Strauss had on him in his pioneering work *Neo Conservatism: The Autobiography of an Idea*.[44] Many students of Strauss' students, particularly those taught by Bloom, which included John Podhoretz, William Kristol, Francis Fukiyama, Paul Wolfowitz and Tod Linberg, would adopt similar conceptualisations of the political and go on to play leading roles in the neo-conservative movement.[45] Irving Kristol is among those to have written about this intergenerational effect:

His students – those happy few who sat at his feet – became "Straussians", though they preferred to be known as "political theorists"…These students of Leo Strauss, in turn, have produced another generation of political theorists, many of whom have relocated to Washington D.C., since the academic world of positivist "political science" has become ever more hostile to Strauss and "Straussians" – even while his mode of thought has filtered down to an ever more numerous "happy few."[46]

Self-confessed Straussians have also observed the general tendency amongst Strauss' immediate students to pursue academic positions within the US higher education system, whilst also noting that many students of his students went on to seek positions of influence within the US political apparatus.[47] Despite having different career goals, the two generations of students were united by a desire to (re)shape the social world in ways that aligned with Strauss' very detailed prescriptions.

Strauss' great body of work provides readers an interpretation of the social world in which there exists a natural order of things. Two of his works in particular; *The City and Man* and *Natural Right and History*, paint a picture of an ideal society where an elite class assumes a dominant position, subordinating the common man whom Strauss refers to as belonging to the 'vulgar masses'. Whereas the pre-Socratic notion of natural right considered all men to be free and equal, Strauss' ideas demonstrate a desire to prioritise what is 'good' before what is 'right' when it comes to organising a society. Strauss' close associate, popular supporter of the Nazi Party and popular political philosopher Carl Schmitt held similar beliefs.

According to Strauss' thinking, the 'good' is the most desirable state of affairs and operates in a causal relationship with what is 'right'. In this consequential equation, what is 'right' is typically interpreted as that which is moral and ethical. For Strauss, the moral and ethical do not have standard operating definitions, nor do they suggest the existence of some kind of eternal truth; rather, they are malleable concepts designed to help achieve pre-determined aims and goals.[48] This approach is similar to how neo-conservatives went about understanding and categorising the MEK, which we described in detail earlier. Strauss' interpreting of a 'good' society is one in which an elite group assume their positions as rightful rulers, presiding over a vulgar citizenry distinguished by a general lack of intellectual ability in addition to a lack in desire to look beyond hedonistic pleasures. Strauss diagnosed this condition of the masses as a result of the disease that is modernity (or liberalism, as we have since come to describe this period in Western civilisation). This is a view that continues to resonate with many political actors and theorists today, especially neo-conservatives.

"In realising this natural order of things" writes Strauss, it is "necessary for the philosopher" as a function of the elite class to "descend again into the cave, i.e. to take care of the affairs of the city, whether in a direct or more remote manner". In ordering society in a way that it is in the 'best interests' of the politic i.e. around idea of political enmity, Strauss sees the philosopher as admitting the intrinsic truth that he is to act as an "in-between being – between the brutes and the gods". Whether these philosophers are of "good natures" is irrelevant; what is important is that the elite are able to reconcile their wisdom with the consent of the masses. The elite however must refrain from publicly acknowledging that the consent of the "unwise" is needed, as this according to Strauss is tantamount to "admitting a right of unwisdom, i.e., an irrational, if inevitable, right". [49]

We have seen how neo-conservatives dealt with issues pertaining to consent and the masses during their appointments in the foreign policy and national security divisions within the most recent Bush administration. We learnt how this group went about concocting incriminating evidence, and we also saw how the wider neo-conservative network went about providing the illusion of public agreement about the dire need to invade Iraq. This Straussian political manoeuvring had mixed results. The neo-conservatives achieved their long-held desire to remove Saddam from power, however mass demonstrations by the US public revealed they were not as successful as they had hoped when it came to convincing the vulgar masses about the necessity of this invasion. Ultimately public opinion mattered little as the Bush regime went about invading yet another foreign sovereign nation. We are now witnessing many similarities between this campaign and the current neo-conservative campaign for war in Iran.

Strauss's great body of work also reveals that he understood it was the responsibility of the elite class to ensure the great unwashed learn to prioritise the 'good' of the collective over their mindless hedonistic pursuits. This endless pursuing of pleasures has been made easier given the nature of the modern liberal state. Strauss considered Western civilisation's transition to modernity as marked by a widespread rejecting of moral absolutism, which resulted in the masses associating the 'good' with the greatest of sensory pleasures. In contrast, the elite still possessed the ability to transcend their basic human instincts in pursuit of higher ideals. Belonging to the elite involved recognising that the most pleasurable 'good' is to be found in serious philosophical pursuits, educating eager and able students, and in enjoying close relations with those of a similar ilk i.e. other members of the elite.[50] Not only did Strauss live this reality, neo-conservatives have also revealed themselves as desiring to live and work in similar ways.

A close study of the neo-conservative movement reveals that its intellectuals largely confine themselves to living and working in the most affluent parts of New York City and Washington D.C. They work and socialise amongst themselves in what Bret Stephens has described as the (neo) 'conservative echo chamber', and offer assessments and policy prescriptions about the 'catastrophic' situations in foreign nations from their plush offices, where they enjoy all of the creature comforts not afforded to most of the world's population.[51] Their situation is strikingly different to researchers who have committed themselves to undertaking the kinds of ethnographic research many believe to be necessary before labelling an Islamic nation, its people, culture and religion as timeless, evil and dangerous – a point well made by Edward Said in his seminal work *Orientalism*. Thomas Hegghammer they are not.

Political Enmity

When dealing with the more practical concerns associated with the functioning of the ideal society, Strauss found inspiration in the operating of Julius Caesar's Roman Empire. Strauss' earlier writings in particular revealed a great reverence for Caesar's authoritarian regime, which had used the idea of political enmity to great effect. Strauss understood it is not always the natural condition of the masses to kowtow to directives issued by the elite, nor to acknowledge their own inherently lesser value as human beings. Like his contemporary Carl Schmitt, Strauss realised the great utility the idea of political enmity had in channelling the energies of an otherwise lazy and occasionally disgruntled public away from the nature of the political system, and towards a group of people or nation (Others) who were envious of them and seeking their destruction. In the absence of a real existential threat posed by these jealous Others, both Strauss and Schmitt claimed it was the role of the elite to manufacture this peril for the 'good' of the society.

Ensuring the masses remain acutely aware of an existential threat posed to them by an Other helps to keep them in a constant state of arousal and preparedness for war. The thinking is that this helps in maintaining a strong and unified politic by helping divert attention away from internal squabbling, which possesses the ability to destabilise or destroy the imagined community the elite have worked so hard to create. This helps us to understand why neo-conservatives have been so scathing in their critiques of the US political Left for their waging of identity wars. The neo-conservative reaction to the Black Lives Matter (BLM) movement serves as a perfect case in point. Bret Stephens claims BLM "has metastasized into the big lie of America", and is fighting "an imaginary enemy" as "[i]nstitutionalized racism" does not exist.[52] Stephens' commentary and similar sentiments expressed by many of his neo-conservative colleagues have come at a time when new research has shown young black American men are nine times more likely to be killed by police than non-black men.[53]

Germany philosopher Carl Schmitt famously wrote that "[t]he specific political distinction to which political actions and motives can be reduced is that between friend and enemy".[54] Norman Podhoretz has more recently described this friend-enemy distinction in a slightly different way: "every animal is supposed to know who its enemies are and who are its friends: that one is going to try and devour me, and this one is only eating grass".[55] In an ideal society, Strauss claims "the just man is he who does not harm, but loves his friends and neighbors, i.e., his fellow citizens, but who does harm or who hates his enemies, i.e., the foreigners who as such are at least potential enemies of his city".[56] According to this logic, it is imperative that an out-group is always represented as posing an existential threat to the lives of the in-group, who by contrast enjoy a superior way of living that arouses envy in the Other. In constructing this enemy, Strauss recommends the elite make use of the range of tools of deception that are available to them. Strauss describes this process in detail in his work *Natural Right and History*:

> The city cannot leave it at saying, for instance that deception, and especially deception to the detriment of others, is bad in peace but praiseworthy in war. It cannot help viewing with suspicion the man who is good at deceiving, or it cannot help regarding the devious or disingenuous ways in which are required for any successful deception as simply mean or distasteful. Yet the city must command, and even praise, such ways if they are used against the enemy.[57]

Strauss identifies Sophist rhetoric as one of these tools available for use, paying particular attention to the concept of the noble lie. Deception is considered noble because it is in the service of the greater 'good' of the nation. It is a specific approach to the political that has led many observers to draw parallels between Strauss and modern neo-conservatives who have shown deception to be a cornerstone of their political approach.[58] Amongst the plethora of examples highlighting this clear relation is Elliott Abrams' actions during the Iran Contra Affair.

Abrams deliberately engaged in unlawful activities during his professional appointment with the Reagan Republican administration, and later lied about his dealings to US Congress when under oath. Despite his illegal activities, Abrams was later pardoned by Republican President Bush who deemed his intentions be 'morally sound' and for the 'good' of the nation.[59] Abrams appeared to be operating under the impression his position as part of the US political elite meant he was beyond the reproach of US law; acting honestly / truth-telling were not applicable to him in his position. Ultimately he was proven correct. However, this time around, instead of assisting the Iranian regime in its acquiring of weaponry as was the case during Iran Contra Affair, Abrams is now part of efforts aimed at hindering the Islamic Republic's ability to acquire (nuclear) arms.

When reading the works of Leo Strauss and his contemporary Carl Schmitt, and when considering the relations between their ideas and those of the modern neo-conservative movement, it is important to heed the elementary yet crucial point each is making when it comes to organising a society. The political ideas of both twentieth century political theorists and modern neo-conservatives all assume that the masses will succumb to vulgar ways of being when left entirely to their own devices. Providing the masses with structure by organising them against an existential threat, real or imagined, helps in distracting them from indulging these innate human desires. It is precisely these kinds of ideas about order, man's essential being and what neo-conservatives consider to be an increasingly debaucherous American and Western society, that helped inspire the neo-conservative movement's conception in the twentieth century. It is here worth recalling Irving Kristol's remarks in *The Neoconservative Persuasion: Selected Essays, 1942-2009*: "Neocons and religious traditionalists ... are united on issues concerning the quality of education, the relations of church and state, the regulation of pornography, and the like, all of which they regard as proper candidates for the government's attention".[60]

In spite of the claims to truth offered by Strauss, Schmitt and neo-conservatives, it is worth noting their shared conceptualisation of the political is not the only way of going about things. Around the same time as Schmitt and Strauss were developing their ideas, Sigmund Freud was also dedicating serious thought to the nature of human condition and the constructing of an ideal society. Freud believed society should provide the ideal conditions for its people to realise their full potential. Like Strauss and Schmitt, Freud understood the importance of harnessing man's libidinal energies for use in productive ways, and which would also secure the survival of the human race.

Rather than organising a society based on feelings of antipathy directed at a real or imagined threat, and therefore channelling man's lifeforce in hateful ways, Freud wanted man to focus his attention inward and embark on a journey of self-enlightenment.[61] With this goal in mind, a society could be constructed in such a way that the necessary tools and support would be available to those dedicated to this lifelong process of self-examination; this is precisely the kind of life Plato and Socrates wanted man to live. It is in comparing and contrasting these two approaches that we are able to fully appreciate just how sinister some of the ideas held by neo-conservatives really are.

Strauss as Role Model? Other Considerations

When determining the kind of role Strauss has played in terms of acting as a source of inspiration for neo-conservatives, it is also worth drawing attention to some other relevant similarities in terms of actions and beliefs. In light of Irving Kristol's famous remarks about students feeling lucky enough to have sat at Professor Strauss' feet during his lectures at the University of Chicago, it makes sense to seriously consider the idea that some neo-conservatives have also sought to emulate other aspects of their teacher's approach to the political / political behaviour.[62] Those who have been part of the academe would understand that the cult of academic personality, whilst often disturbing, is a very real phenomenon. Pertinent here are similarities associated with ideas about the UN, and identifying and engaging with internal enemies, particularly when it comes to issues associated with nuclear weaponry.

Strauss opposed the existence of the UN and its functioning as a quasi-global regime. His early thoughts on the hazards of a world state, which is what he saw the UN as representing, are made clear in his work *On Tyranny*. Strauss challenges Russian-French philosopher Alexandre Kojève's claim that a universal and homogenous world state would constitute a high point in the human story. For Strauss, the opposite was true. He pointed to the totalitarian regimes in twentieth century Communist China and the Soviet Union as providing valuable insight about what a "perpetual and universal" global regime would eventually end up looking like.[63] Strauss was decidedly enraged by the platform the UN provided to the US' enemies, whom he claimed were constantly plotting the destruction of the world's most morally superior nation. He was equally coruscating of liberals, or rather the internal enemies, supporting the US' participation in this world government.

Those who have closely followed the UN will be aware of its valuable work in terms of distributing aid, nation-building, global health initiatives, campaigning against colonial and imperial initiatives, in addition to providing a global platform through which injustices and other wrongs can be brought to light. This is not however how neo-conservatives have interpreted its function. Like Strauss, they see the UN as fundamentally anti-American, seeking to minimise US influence in the world and failing to appreciate the US' exceptional nature. Neo-conservatives were especially critical of UN members' attempts at preventing the invasion of Iraq, which the US ultimately ignored anyway. We saw how that worked out. Charles Krauthammer perfectly summed up the widespread disdain neo-conservatives feel towards the institution when he recommended on *Fox News* that President Trump draw on his expert knowledge in property development (and presumably not his experience in reality television) to transform the UN into something more useful: "I think it's good real estate in downtown New York City, and Trump ought to find a way to put his name on it and turn it into condos".[64]

John Bolton has expressed similar sentiments,

> 'I'm pro-American. It is a big mistake for us [Americans] to grant any validity to international law even when it may seem in our short-term interest to do so - because, over the long term, the goal of those who think international law really means anything are those who want to constrict the United States".[65]

That Bolton, in light of his very public disdain for multilateralism and the rule of international law, went on to serve as the US Ambassador to the UN in the George W. Bush administration, is as comical as it is disturbing. His appointment does however make some sense given it came at a time when Straussian neo-conservatives wielded significant if not hegemonic influence over US foreign policy.

Throughout his long tenure at the University of Chicago, Professor Strauss also developed a reputation for his scathing attacks directed at the Democratic Party, whom he perceived as internal enemies and traitors to the American cause. Strauss targeted Democratic President John F. Kennedy's (1961-1963) efforts to establish a nuclear test ban that sought to ease tensions between Washington and Moscow. Whilst many saw Kennedy's efforts as an important step in helping avert a nuclear war, Strauss viewed his diplomatic approach as a sign of weakness. According to Strauss, Kennedy's inclusive approach was symptomatic of his administration's inability to properly project itself as a powerful empire that intimidated the Soviets. It is both telling and horrifying that Strauss preferred the risk of a nuclear war between US and Communist-Soviet forces as opposed to retreating to the ways of what he termed the "last men".[66]

According to Strauss, liberals like Kennedy who were prepared to exhaust diplomatic efforts in search of peace rather than readying themselves for a devastating war, were weak and misguided. Strauss made his thoughts clear in his 1963 letter to soon-to-be Republican Illinois Senator Charles Percy:

> ...there must be no concessions on our part...There cannot be genuine peace with Communism.
>
> The opponents continue to argue as follows: if we do not seek genuine peace, then we heighten the danger of thermonuclear war, which confronts us with the alternative of annihilation or surrender. Without genuine peace, we must face this alternative.
>
> There is a profound cleavage of opinion in this country as to which of the two alternatives is preferable...If this issue is brought before the American people, I believe the large majority will be opposed to surrender—if for no other reason than for this: because the speakers against surrender will be more trusted by the American people than the speakers for surrender...
>
> We must start from the premise that the American people, as a strong, virile, and free people will prefer to perish rather than to surrender.[67]

A similar harum-scarum approach has been advocated by modern neo-conservatives when dealing with the perceived threat posed by a nuclear-Iran. It certainly appears as though John Bolton had been reading the Straussian playbook providing the following commentary on recent US dealings with Iran: "When you have a regime that would be happier in the afterlife than in this life, this is not a regime that is subject to classic theories of deterrence".[68]

Neo-conservatives have similarly attacked Democratic President Obama, specifically for the role he played in helping set up and committing the US to the *Joint Comprehensive Plan of Action*. Like Strauss, neo-conservatives do not appreciate these kinds of multilateral diplomatic efforts when it comes to averting a nuclear or any other kind of war. They similarly view these as the actions of 'last men' who are willing to stake the US' reputation as the global superpower and its future in an increasingly chaotic world, on what they understand to be fantastical and doltish notions of peace, dialogue and freedom. It is ironic that neo-conservatives understand these ideas as fanciful yet have no qualms in expressing how US foreign policy should be dictated by their religious beliefs in a supernatural being emerging to save all believers. To say neo-conservatives were overjoyed when the reality television star-cum-US President decided to withdraw the US from the *Joint Comprehensive Plan of Action* is an understatement. "We are pulling out of the Iran Deal" tweeted John Podhoretz upon hearing the news, "Truly this is a historic day".[69]

The Strauss Debate

The aim so far has been to help reveal some of the relations between Strauss' political ideas and actions, and those of the neo-conservatives. We have gained some understanding about the key sources that have offered inspiration and motivation to neo-conservative intellectuals, however it should be acknowledged that previous scholarly attempts aimed at revealing similar relations have been pushed back against by many self-confessed Straussians. Many Straussian academics have bristled at claims their political ideas are in anyway similar to those held by neo-conservatives, and more specifically, that Strauss' teachings and texts could have inspired in any of his students, and students of his students, an approach to the political that encourages deception, elitism and authoritarianism. These denials have at times become so fervent that they have crossed from the realm of robust and respectful debate (the kind prized by democratic public sphere theorists) into the domain of threats of violence and *ad hominem* attacks, and have been informed by questionable (objectivist) claims to truth.

Shadia Drury, in *The Political Ideas of Leo Strauss*, provides a serious attempt at revealing the authoritarian nature of Strauss' works, and helps to reveal the links between his ideas and those of modern neo-conservatives. This text, like a lot of her work since, has infuriated

Straussians to the point we have seen Peter Minowitz dedicate his book, *Straussophobia: Defending Leo Strauss and Straussians against Shadia Drury and Other Accusers*, to refuting her claims. Some of Drury's critics have threatened her in ways reminiscent of Edward Said's experiences during his time at Columbia University in New York, where his support for the Palestinian cause resulted in (pro-Israeli) individuals and groups following through on their threats and ransacking his workplace and residence.[70] Much of the baleful responses directed at Drury are similar in their aims, content and style to the duplicitous claims of anti-Semitism deployed by neo-conservatives against critics of the *Iran Nuclear Deal*, a U.S. foreign policy geared towards Israel, and supporters of Palestinian self-determination. That is to say, they are deliberately inflammatory and aimed at shutting down serious academic and political debate.

It has not helped the neo-conservative and general Straussian causes that the godfather of neo-conservatism Irving Kristol acknowledged the profound impact Strauss' teaching had on his political ideas. Kristol, in his formative work *Neoconservatism: The Autobiography of an Idea,* claims "Strauss's work" produced in him "the kind of shock that is a once-in-a-lifetime experience. He turned one's intellectual universe upside down. Suddenly, one realized that one had been looking at the history of Western political thought through the wrong end of the telescope".[71] Nor has it helped that some of the world's most influential public intellectuals like the late Christopher Hitchens have drawn links between Strauss and neo-conservatives, particularly in light of the Iraq War debacle.[72] It is philosophically erroneous to think links made by free-floating intellectuals like Hitchens should be immediately accepted as veracious given both his privileged standing in the global intellectual environment and his long history of speaking truth to power. However, it is accurate to say that in the war of ideas neo-conservatives have chosen involve themselves in, such claims by prominent public intellectuals with a demonstrated history in shining a light on injustice does not do the neo-conservative reputation nor Strauss' legacy much good.

Strauss' daughter Jenny Strauss Clay has recognised this, and felt compelled to pen the article 'The Real Leo Strauss' for the *New York Times* in an attempt to refute claims her father has inspired a sinister approach to the political in his students and general readers of his work.[73] Clay refutes many of the relations that are revealed in this work. Similar valorous attempts have been provided by self-confessed Straussians Peter Minowitz, Catherine Zuckert and Michael Zuckert. Their works however have tended to have the opposite effect to what they set out to achieve. They all claim their experience as students of Strauss, in addition to their superior intellectual and academic abilities, perfectly positions them to both access and communicate the objective truth that exists within Strauss' large body of complex works. Their defences rely in part on *ad hominem* attacks against critics they deem intellectually inferior and therefore unable to properly understand the nuanced ideas of their teacher. It is here that we can draw parallels between the ontological and political ideas of Straussians and neo-conservatives – a truth exists, they believe they are among the few who can access this truth, and it is their responsibility to communicate this truth to vulgar masses whom for whatever reason (intellectual, religious, political or otherwise) have proven themselves incapable of understanding this truth.

In *The Truth About Leo Strauss,* Catherine Zuckert and Michael Zuckert claim that in providing readers with a truthful reading of his work they are putting an end, once and for all, to the ongoing debate about the nature and influence of Strauss' ideas on neo-conservatives. Their litany of attacks against Strauss' critics include the following:

> ...there is little evidence that the reporters and columnists have "done their homework," that is, that they have read much of Strauss at all, to say nothing of reading him with the kind of care that their own description of his work suggests is necessary for understanding his elusive and politically remote thinking.[74]

These kinds of arguments speak to the elitist ideas about the positions Straussians believe themselves as occupying in modern society. Zuckert and Zuckert seem to be under the impression that their ability to properly understand the 'true' nature of Strauss' works solidifies their position as part of an intellectual elite whose role is to educate the masses.

Similarly Peter Minowitz's in his work *Straussophobia* claims those associating Strauss' ideas with the neo-conservative conceptualisation of the political lack the requisite intelligence that is needed to discern the truthful nature of his work. Minowitz's takes specific aim at Shadia Drury, accusing the Canadian academic of "defiling the scholarly process," and warns others about the "dangers of intellectual haste".[75] In his eagerness and resoluteness to defend Strauss' legacy, Minowitz makes exactly the same mistakes he accuses Strauss' critics of committing. First, he glosses over some of Strauss' earlier writings, in which Strauss speaks glowingly of the fascist, imperialistic and authoritarian political techniques employed by Julius Caesar.[76] Relevant is Strauss' May 19, 1933 Löwith letter, in which he writes:

> I am reading Caesar's Commentaries with deep understanding, and I think of Virgil's Tu regere imperio... parcere subjectis et debellare superbos. There is no reason to crawl to the cross, neither to the cross of liberalism, as long as somewhere in the world there is a glimmer of the spark of the *Roman* thought. And even then: rather than any cross, I'll take the ghetto.[77]

The Roman thought Strauss is referring to is a Caesarian conceptualisation of the political, where the ideal state is comprised of a single authoritarian ruler whose claim to power is legitimised by subordinate military, political and religious authorities. This stands in stark contrast to the ideas informing the founding of the American Republic, where the functioning of the church and state must remain separate, and the military is held to account by a democratically elected civilian authority. These views were clearly expressed by Samuel Adams in 1768 when he proclaimed it a matter of necessity that a wise and prudent people always cast a watchful and jealous eye over their nation's military power. Adams' ideas have been abstracted here because they help highlight the fundamental incompatibility between Strauss' commitment to authoritarianism and the democratic principles upon which the US was founded and many Americans still cherish. This is an important point to keep in mind as we further our understanding of the neo-conservative movement, especially when it comes to the key role played by US Exceptionalism, which we will explore in some detail in the coming chapters.

This chapter has functioned as an abstraction dedicated to seriously considering the notion that Strauss' ideas and actions have in some way acted as sources of inspiration for many associated with the neo-conservative movement. In this chapter we have also considered the influence specific political and religious responses to the Holocaust provided by popular writers like Fackenheim, have played in shaping the ideas of neo-conservative intellectuals. Let us now continue our sense-making journey, shifting our focus to some of the other major ideas that have profoundly influenced the movement in general and have shaped their specific responses to the perceived Iranian threat.

Chapter Three
Duplicity & Democracy

I believe that the members of my family
must be as free from suspicion as from actual crime.

—Julius Caesar, Quoted in Suetonius, *Life of Caesar*

In 2013 John Bolton joined a growing list of illustrious but occasionally controversial speakers to address students and faculty at the hallowed Oxford Union in England. Bolton used this opportunity to warn his audience about the dangers associated with political liberalism and to justify the notion of American Exceptionalism. Bolton gave his address at a moment in time when he, and his fellow neo-conservatives, were pre-occupied with the Obama administration's alleged sabotaging of brand Americana. Bolton and his colleagues were concerned about what they perceived to be the US Government's tending towards isolationism, and its failure to properly understand and embrace American Exceptionalism.

Bolton told his English audience the Obama administration's shift was communicating the dangerous idea to the rest of the world that the US was now vulnerable to attack: "He [Obama] doesn't see the rest of the world as threatening or particularly challenging to American interests", Bolton claimed, "he may think a decade of war is ending, but the terrorists didn't get the memo and the war is still very much on. I think the President believes that American decline is natural and something he can accept, and not something that concerns him greatly".[1] Neo-conservatives wanted the Obama administration to follow the aggressive foreign approach set into motion by the preceding Bush administration – an approach that signalled to the other nations of the world that the US, the pre-eminent force in the international political and military arenas, would intervene in the affairs of foreign nations whenever it pleased.

Three years after Bolton's address at the Oxford Union, leading neo-conservative Charles Krauthammer told his audience who had gathered at the *Tikvah Fund* in New York, that his (in)famous essay 'At Last Zion' was one of his proudest intellectual and political achievements. Krauthammer rightly noted the profound influence his ideas had on many of the US and Israeli intellectual, political and religious elite. His 1998 essay provided a sweeping analysis of Jewish peoplehood from Temple times to the modern return to Zion, and also offered stern warnings about Israel's vulnerability in the face of existential threats posed by Iran, Iraq and Libya:

> ...in its vulnerability to extinction, Israel ... is the only small country...whose neighbors publicly declare its very existence an affront to law, morality, and religion and make its extinction an explicit, paramount national goal. Nor is the goal merely declarative. Iran, Libya, and Iraq conduct foreign policies designed for the killing of Israelis and the destruction of their state. They choose their allies (Hamas, Hezbollah) and develop their weapons (suicide bombs, poison gas, anthrax, nuclear missiles) accordingly.[2]

Referring to Israel as a "small country" is a common technique deployed by neo-conservatives to belie the relatively strong military and nuclear power it enjoys in contrast to its Muslim neighbours. This technique cleverly ignores the reality that Israel is the only nuclear power in the region, and that it enjoys the unconditional support of arguably the world's most lethal military force. Neo-conservatives like Krauthammer are no doubt aware that readers are naturally inclined to associate metaphorical expressions about size with strength – a process that has to do with cross-domain mappings occurring in the parts of our brains dealing specifically with cognition (the precise nature of this mapping will be described in some detail later as we take a closer look at George Lakoff's work in metaphor theory). It is counter-intuitive for our brains to associate small with strength, large with weakness, and yet this is precisely what the current geo-political situation reveals itself to be. Israel with its nuclear capabilities, its advanced military capability, and the support it receives from its security guarantor (the US), is far more capable and deadly than its Islamic and Middle Eastern neighbours who do not enjoy commensurate capabilities or support.

Despite living and working in America, Krauthammer regularly received heavy praise from the right-wing and religiously conservative Israeli political and intellectual elite throughout his career. Following his death in 2018, Israel's Prime Minister Benjamin Netanyahu lamented the loss of his 'brother in arms', whilst Eva Harrow at *Arutz Sheva* (rather peculiarly) wrote: "The passing…of this great columnist and political commentator has left a void, in our world of partisan and even fake news, of honesty, decency and brilliance. A man who valued true liberalism and democracy, loved America and was an ardent Zionist".[3] These assessments about Krauthammer's role as an intellectual stand in stark contrast to the determinations reached in this study. Remembering this was a man who, amongst other things, advocated for a Berlin Wall-type solution designed to separate Palestinians from Israelis.[4] It is worth noting that Krauthammer offered his 'solution' long before walls became popular solutions for Republican politicians seeking to keep the host population separate from Others (Donald Trump was still the star of his own reality television program *The Apprentice* at this time).

These two abstractions help illuminate the combative mindset many neo-conservatives have adopted when engaging with a world they view as inherently unstable, violent and unpredictable. Krauthammer, Bolton and their neo-conservative colleagues are not inclined to understand the world as place that offers its inhabitants valuable opportunities to realise their full potential as human beings, where the human experience is about finding ways to work together to bridge religious and cultural divides to achieve mutually beneficial outcomes. Neo-conservatives' assumptions about the world as an inherently dangerous and volatile place have instead encouraged them to place onus on the distinguishing between friends and foes; a process that has proven to have far-reaching and often deadly consequences. We saw this in the case of Iraq, we continue to see this with regards to Israel's treatment of the Palestinians, and we are now seeing this with how neo-conservatives have gone about interpreting and representing all things Iranian. All of these groups have filled, or are filling, the role of the enemy that Leo Strauss and Carl Schmitt saw as integral to the proper ordering of a modern society.

This chapter is dedicated to exploring the nature, pertinence and origins of these kinds of antagonistic ideas. This exploration also helps in laying the groundwork for the later deconstructing of neo-conservative texts detailing the perceived threat posed by Iran. The first part of the chapter deals with the global democratic project myth as promoted by neo-conservatives, which many have failed to recognise as an important rhetorical foil used for pursuing partisan interests. Amongst these interests is recalibrating the balance of power in Middle Eastern nations to ensure it is remains tipped in Israel's favour. These insights are particularly important when considering recent neo-conservative calls that the US and/or Israel must intervene in Iran on the grounds of 'helping to end the totalitarian government's oppressing of its own people'.

It should come as no great surprise that neo-conservatives do not have the wellbeing of the everyday Muslim Iranian at the forefront of their minds. The fact that many neo-conservatives support economic sanctions against Iran as a temporary measure until US leaders pluck up the courage for a military strike is testament to this claim. US-imposed economic sanctions during Trump's Presidency have shown to only have substantively affected the livelihoods of the common Iranian, and has done very little by the way of punishing the elite who are in charge of governing the Islamic Republic.[5] James Woolsey is amongst those to express his support for this interim approach:

> I think it would be superb if we got it [regime change] because Iran is a government of theocratic, totalitarian, genocidal imperialists. However, setting a policy of trying to implement regime change with all the steps and all the ancillary considerations that would come out as you would try to do that seems to me to be a very troubling approach...I don't think we're ready for that yet. Steps such as various economic restrictions that upset the Iranian regime a great deal seem to me to be perfectly fair game, however.[6]

Echoing the sentiment of his neo-conservative colleagues; that Israel and the US are partners in this struggle against Iran, and expressing the core neo-conservative belief that the interests of the two nations are intimately bound together, Woolsey went on to tell viewers of *Newsmax TV*: "I think that a far better way to move this along is to work with the Israelis on destabilizing the Iranian state and trying to help the Israelis undermine what is, as I said, a theocratic, totalitarian, genocidal empire".[7]

The second part of this chapter is dedicated to understanding the nature, origins and influence the interrelated ideas of US, Israeli and Jewish Exceptionalism have had on neo-conservatives. The neo-conservatives' often duplicitous using of anti-Semitism rhetoric will also be closely studied. There are a number of important reasons supporting an exploration into the use of this rhetorical technique, which has been deliberately employed by many neo-conservatives, as well as by many intellectuals belonging to the over-arching pro-Israeli movement. The rhetoric of anti-Semitism has often revealed itself to be a political tool aimed at intimidating and silencing critics of calls for war with Iran, as well as critics of the current Republican administration's pro-Israel foreign policy. This pro-Israel foreign policy, which is perhaps best exemplified by Trump's recognising of Jerusalem as the eternal capital of Israel and his decision to move the US embassy from Tel Aviv to Jerusalem, has come at the expense of closer and more fruitful relationships with much of the Islamic world.

The Great Façade: Promoting Democracy in the Middle East

As US forces readied themselves to invade in Iraq 2003, leading neo-conservative and US Vice President Dick Cheney told a crowd of American military veterans the intervention should aim to establish "a government that is democratic and pluralistic, a nation where the human rights of every ethnic and religious group are recognised and protected".[8] Cheney's seemingly altruistic rhetoric, which complimented the general neo-conservative message that Saddam Hussein's regime must be forcibly rid of their WMD for the 'good' of the world, struck a chord with many liberal interventionists. Responding to Cheney's claims, American liberal intellectual Maureen Dowd argued that, according to the same logic, the US should also be seeking regime change in Saudi Arabia.

Dowd, like many Western intellectuals, was deeply disturbed by reports that Saudi Arabian religious police decided against rescuing a group of schoolgirls from a school fire, on the grounds they were not appropriately covered. It was reported that the young Saudi girls had removed their religious dress during their attempted escape from the burning flames. Dowd told readers of the liberal-leaning newspaper *The Guardian*: "Once we make Saudi Arabia into our own self-serve gas pump, its neighbours will get the democracy bug".[9] Dowd's sardonic response to Cheney's claims and the wider neo-conservative chorus is revealing in that it suggests she, like many others, believes the rhetoric used by her many of her fellow American intellectual elites was foil for the pursuing of ulterior motives. In this particular instance, Dowd was repeating the common claim held by many on the US political Left: that the US' invasion of Iraq was inspired by a desire to gain control of Iraq's vast oil supplies.

What Dowd failed to consider, and what many other commentators similarly failed to seriously contemplate at the time, was the possibility that the neo-conservative chorus for war in Iraq was *primarily* motivated by a desire to recalibrate the balance of power in the region back in clear favour of Israel. These observers chose to ignore previous calls by the neo-conservatives for an invasion of Iraq, thereby 'finishing the job' Israeli Prime Minister Menachem Begin kick-started in 1981. Begin had ordered the Israeli Air Force to bomb Iraq's nuclear reactor (17km from Baghdad) as part of *Operation Opera*. This daring strike has been celebrated many times over by neo-conservatives and pro-Israeli movement intellectuals, who viewed Iraqi President Saddam Hussein's increasing belligerence when dealing with the US as a worrying sign with regards to the future security of Israel.

At that time, leading neo-conservative and US delegate to the UN Jeane J. Kirkpatrick told fellow UN representatives that Israel's bombing of the Iraqi nuclear reactor must be understood in the context of a region ravaged by instability. She claimed Israel had legitimate reasons for thinking Iraq would attack it given it had failed to formally recognise the Jewish-state's existence.[10] Whilst US President Raegan had proven himself receptive to the plight of Israel, neo-conservatives criticised him for not being unconditional in his support, which meant Israel had to take the Iraqi 'situation' into their own hands. Robert Tucker at *Commentary Magazine* was among those to lambast Reagan for failing to unequivocally support Israel's pre-emptive attack against Iraq: "The move to censure Israel for its strike against the Iraqi nuclear reactor could have been readily vetoed had Washington only desired to do so".[11] In more recent times, it is revealing that neo-conservative darling Meir Soloveichik has described Israel's pre-emptive strike against Iraq as an example of the Jewish people following God's directives as laid out in *Ecclesiastes*: 'there is a time for peace but there is also a time for war'.[12] Many not associated with the neo-conservative movement have been less inclined to interpret this devastating and illegal strike against a sovereign Islamic nation as a realising of God's will.

We now find ourselves in a similar situation. Neo-conservatives are again campaigning for a pre-emptive strike against the nuclear infrastructure in another Islamic nation, which has so far demonstrated itself unwilling to bend to Israeli demands. Again we are witnessing widespread concern among neo-conservatives that Israel's pre-eminent position in the Middle East as the only nuclear power in the region; a capability that has played a pivotal role in enabling it to continue its occupation of the Palestinian Territories largely unimpeded, is being challenged. Acutely aware that these are not ideas that will resonate with the majority of the US public, meaning they will not generally inspire the average American to risk their life in any US military operations against Iran, neo-conservatives have deployed a vast array of rhetorical techniques in an attempt sell the idea of another war. Key to this campaign is the rhetorical foil that the US must promote democracy in Iran.

We are again bearing witness to arguments made by neo-conservatives and by many of those closely associated with the movement, that another Islamic regime must be toppled because of its ongoing violating of the human rights of its own people, especially their right to live in a democratic society. Bret Stephens was amongst those to employ this human rights rhetoric during the end of Bush's Presidency in 2007 when it became clear that Obama would soon take the Presidential reins: "Is it a testament that there is no meaningful difference between free and unfree, Bushworld and Ahmadinejadland? Take that view seriously, and you wind up taking the notion of gay rights, and human rights, too lightly for anyone's good [sic]".[13] More recently at *United Against Nuclear Iran*, its intellectuals like Mark Wallace have sought to enlist the support of private American companies, calling for them to "pull out of Iran" in order "to protect human rights".[14] While neo-conservatives often maintain the neo-liberal market is, and should remain apolitical, these rules clearly do not matter when it comes to advancing their partisan interests.

In light of neo-conservative claims that a US-led attack against Iran is warranted on the grounds it will be removing a totalitarian regime denying its people their fundamental human rights, we may also ask what is so unique about the Iranian situation that it has attracted the lion's share of neo-conservative attention in recent times? As Dowd and others have pointed out, there are *many* other regimes in the region, and indeed the world, that are not currently living in the image of the US liberal democracy that neo-conservatives claim they are so proud of. If we are to accept neo-conservative claims that the US is the global champion of freedom, why then are they not advocating for interventions in nations like Jordan, Qatar, Morocco and Dagestan?

It soon becomes apparent that these nations do not appear on the neo-conservative radar because they are not viewed as posing a serious threat to the balance of power currently enjoyed by Israel. These determinations may not be revelatory for close observers of neo-conservativism, US foreign policy and Middle Eastern politics, however it is surprising that so many people continue to take neo-conservatives at their word when they proclaim themselves to be truly committed to the global promotion of democracy because it is 'for the good of all people.' This becomes increasingly perplexing when considering the neo-conservative predilection for an authoritarian approach to the political, which we will continue to become increasingly aware of throughout this study.

Like Leo Strauss and the Ancient writers he so admired, neo-conservatives understand the importance of using ideas and language associated with freedom and democracy to help conceal some of their more controversial values and beliefs. Concealing such views from the vulgar masses is considered by neo-conservatives to be a matter of necessity, as it helps in preventing the kind of robust intellectual and political debate about US foreign policy sparked by the likes of John

Mearsheimer, Stephen Walt and Ilhan Omar. Whilst these kinds of rigorous debates are crucial to a healthy democratic politic – a point emphasised by many democratic theorists and intellectuals committed to speaking truth to power, the neo-conservative prioritising of their partisan interests over a fundamental commitment to democratic principles often means they are willing to use the kinds of authoritarian tactics Strauss and Schmitt have promoted when seeking to realise their political and religious aims and goals.

Strauss wrote extensively about how it is necessary for the elite to conceal their true intentions in their dealings with the masses, and there exists an ever-growing body of scholarship studying this important aspect of his political thought.[15] Political actors using duplicitous techniques in the political arena is not an entirely new phenomenon, and Strauss is certainly not the only political theorist to endorse these kinds of actions. Nor are neo-conservatives the only intellectual movement continually choosing to act in objectionable ways. The compendium of political dishonesty also stretches far beyond Steve Tesich's relatively recent and popular coining of the term 'post-truth politics' to describe the tenuous relationship between many political actors and historical facts. The genealogy of lying and deception in politics dates back to at least the work of Plato, who endorsed such actions when they contributed to the overall psychological and moral health of the citizens i.e. when employed for the 'good' of society.[16] Strauss certainly appears to have exerted some kind of influence on neo-conservative thinking, however it is disingenuous to crucify the German-cum-American political theorist as providing the *only* source of inspiration for a group of intellectuals determined to do whatever is necessary to re-create the social world in ways reflective of their values and beliefs.

There is also merit in considering the neo-conservative propensity for engaging in duplicitous practices, in addition to this general inclination amongst political actors, in evolutionary biology terms. Scientists have long understood this kind of behaviour as fundamental to the human condition and forever woven into our biological fabric. Lying as a behavioural pattern is understood to have emerged soon after our ability to use language. The ability to manipulate others without using physical force has been critical to the human's ability to provide for themselves and their families, giving them a clear advantage when competing against others for resources and mates. This human behaviour is reflective of the deceptive strategies prevalent in the animal kingdom for e.g. the developing and using of camouflage to deceive prey and hide from predators.

In engaging in the sort of self-examination Aristotle recommends, we may be encouraged to embark on a self-reflective journey aimed at resisting this part of our human nature both for own good and for the good of the society. This is precisely the type of reflective task Sigmund Freud's project of self-enlightenment set out to achieve. According to this view, neo-conservatives choosing to act in duplicitous ways are succumbing to their basic biological inclinations. This is revealing considering neo-conservatives have long worried about, and warned others against, not giving into their vulgar desires. If we are to emulate neo-conservatives when it comes to thinking about, representing and treating Others, it could be said that we are failing to realise our full potential as human beings.

Tesich's observations at the end of the twentieth century about his fellow Americans "rapidly becoming prototypes of a people that totalitarian monsters could only drool about in their dreams", appears to have merit when closely studying the actions of neo-conservatives. Less accurate are Tesich's claims "we, as a free people, have freely decided that we want to live in some post-truth world".[17] It is a motivating idea of this work that many of us comprising the public or the 'vulgar masses' as Strauss prefers, do not want to be purposefully deceived nor do we want to forfeit control of our futures to a group of intellectuals whose ways of living, values and beliefs are for the most part *very* different to our own.

There certainly appears to exist a general lack of political and intellectual know-how on the part of the everyday citizen. This is particularly the case when it comes to possessing the acumen required to properly sift through and understand the sizeable body of information expertly crafted for mass consumption by movement intellectuals occupying privileged positions. Whether this general lack of ability amongst the public is due to temporal, monetary or educational constraints, or perhaps is as a result of sustained propaganda campaigns, is debatable. What is clear is that studies like this play a role in addressing this situation by helping provide readers with the necessary tools needed for them to make their own informed assessments.

US Exceptionalism

Exceptionalism as a general idea enjoys many different expressions including moral, ethical, intellectual, political, religious and even physical. This notion assigns superiority to an in-group at the expense of an out-group who, by definition, is unexceptional. Those who are unexceptional are often Othered, which is a process often involving dehumanising techniques. This process stands in stark contrast to those thought of and portrayed as belonging to the in-group, who are generally represented as modern and evolved in their ways of being. The exceptionalism journey is an interesting one for those wanting to understand how particular groups of people during different moments in time have gone from being viewed as equals, to then acquiring a superior or inferior status. The neo-conservatives' different political and religious conceptualisations of exceptionalism are particularly interesting and relevant here given these ideas have profoundly influenced their interpreting and representing of enemies, which now includes Iran.

American Exceptionalism is one of the major ideas pervading the neo-conservatives consciousness. It has roots in the establishing of the 1787 US Constitution, which is considered by believers to be *the* innovative political experiment. Neo-conservatives and other subscribers to this narrative understand the ingenious and enterprising spirit of the Founding Fathers as continuing to live on in the American consciousness. This wellspring of inspiration is said to be readily available and easily accessible to Americans wanting to promote the interests of the US project. According to believers, American Exceptionalism offers a promise of freedom that should be shared with the rest of the world. However, when closely observing many texts produced by neo-conservatives, one can be confused as to just how far back this idea can be traced. In reading texts written by Christian neo-conservatives, it becomes clear that its origins go as far back as 1620 when the Pilgrims fled their homes in Europe and established the New England colony. However, the narrative is slightly different when reading many of the texts produced by the Jewish elements of the neo-conservative movement.

Rather than expounding the achievements of the Pilgrims and seeking inspiration in their journey, the Jewish element of the movement tends to only think as far back as 1787. There are very good political reasons for these differences in interpretation from Christian and Jewish vantage points. The Pilgrims, fleeing religious persecution in their homeland on the European continent, understood their journey across the Atlantic in predominantly theological terms. They viewed their voyage as an exodus of biblical proportions, and their influence following their arrival as helping civilise an uncivilised land. The Pilgrims were commonly understood as acting under the guidance of God, fulfilling His desire by playing their roles in the establishing of His millenarian kingdom on earth. The Pilgrims were Christians, which is part of the reason why so many Christian Americans continue to identify with their journey.

David Horowitz, Mark Tapson and John Bolton are among those associated with the neo-conservative movement who have sought to promote this Christian interpretation of US Exceptionalism. Horowitz in *Dark Agenda: The War to Destroy Christian America*, reminds Americans of the importance of continuing to interpret their nation as "the logical, if not inevitable, development of the Protestant Reformation" that "led directly to the principle at the heart of the Declaration of Independence, that 'all men are created equal' and endowed with rights by their Creator".[18] Mark Tapson at the flagship neo-conservative publication *FrontPageMag*, has repeated Horowitz's message:

> We are engaged in "a war against this nation and its founding principles: the equality of individuals and individual freedom. For these principles are indisputably Christian in origin. They are under siege because they are insurmountable obstacles to radicals' totalitarian ambition to create a new world in their image".[19]

It was the desire for freedom that inspired the Pilgrims' transatlantic journey. Bolton has also declared he believes US Exceptionalism to be "a historical reflection of the difference of the American experience…when the Pilgrims came John Winthrop the first Governor of Plymouth colony said: "we must consider that we shall be as a city upon on a hill", and obviously he was quoting scripture. It's something that has always appealed to Americans".[20]

US Exceptionalism has gained serious attention in recent times due to the substantial, if not hegemonic, influence wielded by neo-conservatives in the George W. Bush administration (2001-09). Scholars have helped to reveal the extent to which this idea shaped US foreign policy-making during Bush's two-terms in office. [21] The conceptualising and application of this idea during Bush's time stood in stark contrast to how it was imagined by the following Obama administration. Obama and his foreign policy team sought to distance the US from the hawkish unilateralism that had inspired the previous Republican administration's invasion of Iraq, and they promoted an interpretation of US Exceptionalism that was in many ways un-exceptional.

Obama claimed to believe in the idea in a similar way to how anyone belonging to any nation tended to think about their country as the best in the world. Obama also embraced many of the more tragic elements in US history, recognising the critical role the masses, irrespective of colour and religion, played in affecting positive change. In doing so, he challenged pervading ideas about the roles played by society's elite as the sole actors in advancing the American experience.[22] This did not sit well with neo-conservatives, who have tended to view African-Americans and other non-Jewish minority groups as doing, for the most part, more harm than good to the American experience.[23] Here we can abstract the ideas of John Bolton, Marco Rubio and Rudolph Giuliani in order to both fully appreciate the neo-conservative opposition to Obama's 'liberal' interpretation of this themata, which they claim has irrevocably damaged America's standing in the world, and to gain a sense of how neo-conservatives have chosen to think about and employ this notion in recent times.

A leading Christian voice within the neo-conservative movement, John Bolton used his 2013 Oxford Union address to clearly outline his interpretation of American Exceptionalism. He detailed the major problems with the interpretation adopted by the presiding "post-American" Obama administration:

I understand that for many people American Exceptionalism is an offensive concept. That people think when we say that we believe in American Exceptionalism that it is a statement of arrogance, of superiority. I don't believe that is the case at all. I think it is a historical reflection of the difference of the American experience... when the Pilgrims came John Winthrop the first Governor of Plymouth colony said: "we must consider that we shall be as a city upon on a hill," and obviously he was quoting scripture. It's something that has always appealed to Americans. Ronald Reagan, the only politician I know who can improve on scripture, used to call us 'a shining city on the hill,' others use the phrase 'new Jerusalem.' ...the first person to comment on American Exceptionalism was a Frenchmen, Alexis De Tocqueville, who said in *Democracy of America*: 'the position of the Americans is quite exceptional' [sic].[24]

Bolton, like his neo-conservative colleagues, strongly opposed the idea the US should be thought of by Americans and non-Americans alike as existing on an equal footing with other nations. This belief is intimately connected to their general disdain for the UN, as well as other multilateral bodies, seeking to exert any kind of influence over the US policy- and decision-making process. The UN's fundamental democratic approach to problem-solving is rejected by neo-conservatives who favour authoritarian approaches to the political, and want to think of Americans, alongside God, as in firm control of their destiny.

Following John Bolton's remarks about the 'true' nature of US Exceptionalism, neo-conservative darling and Republican Senator Marco Rubio revealed his ideas when preaching to the converted at *The Council on Foreign Relations* in New York. Rubio told his audience at the neo-conservative think tank, who were exclusively comprised of members belonging to the US political and intellectual elite, that President Obama "demonstrated a disregard for our [America] moral purpose that at times flirted with disdain".[25] This reconciled with Rudolph Giuliani's comments at the *21 Club* in New York a few months earlier. Giuliani, a hugely popular Republican politician, told a small and private audience comprised of fellow Republican politicians and extremely wealthy Republican donors "I do not believe — and I know this is a horrible thing to say — but I do not believe that the president [Obama] loves America. He doesn't love you. And he doesn't love me. He wasn't brought up the way you were brought up and I was brought up through love of this country". Giuliani claimed that in spite of "all our flaws" we are still the "most exceptional country in the world". [26]

In typical neo-conservative fashion, Giuliani also reprimanded Obama for his failure to both properly understand the *true* nature of Islam and demonstrate his commitment to the ongoing global Judeo-Christian civilising project: "You've got to be able to criticize Islam for the parts of Islam that are wrong…I'm not sure how wrong the Crusades are. The Crusades were kind of an equal battle between two groups of barbarians…What's wrong with this man that he can't stand up and say there's a part of Islam that's sick"? Giuliani suggested Obama look to the example set by neo-conservative favourite and Israeli PM Benjamin Netanyahu for advice on how to think and act: "That is a patriot, that's a man who loves his people, that's a man who protects his people, that's a man who fights for his people, unlike our president."[27]

Those familiar with the Birther conspiracy will not only see clear traces of this thinking in Giuliani, Rubio, and Bolton's speeches, but will also gain valuable insight into how such fantastical ideas have been able to take root in the neo-conservative movement and the Republican Party. It is worth noting that Giuliani's offering Netanyahu as a role model came long before the extent of his, and his wife's, alleged corruption was revealed. However, these criminal actions appear to have done little to damage his reputation amongst neo-conservatives, who have preferred to downplay the crimes in favour of emphasising his national security achievements.[28]

It is revealing that the same kinds of accusations and charges levelled against leaders of Islamic nations and groups have been met with *very* different responses by neo-conservatives.[29] The standard neo-conservative trope is that corruption within Arab and Islamic regimes makes their government and the institutions they preside over like the military, incubators for radical Islamist ideas and supporters of terrorism. However, similar charges levelled by critics against Israeli leaders like Netanyahu are only indicative of them, as Vivian Bercovici at *The Weekly Standard* describes, 'losing their way'.[30] Conspicuous by its absence is any kind of serious discussion about the US continuing to fund a corrupt Israeli regime to the tune of around $US 10 million per day in 'aid.'

In addition to speaking to the ways in which neo-conservatives understand the US Exceptionalism idea, and the intimate relationship between the neo-conservative movement and the Republican Party, these abstractions highlight the neo-conservative preoccupation with the security of Israel. A lot of these criticisms were motivated by a worry that Obama's conceptualising of US Exceptionalism was leading to an increasingly isolationist US that no longer firmly believed its role and responsibility as the global superpower included a proclivity for inserting itself wherever and whenever it so desired. Neo-conservatives saw this as posing a great threat to the security of Israel given its heavy reliance on unconditional US support. This support is not only expressed through the providing of massive amounts of 'aid', but also through the US adopting of an aggressive foreign policy posture that assists in warding off enemies and perceived threats to the Jewish state.

There are other important reasons for abstracting Giuliani and Rubio's ideas. Both examples help reveal the influential political associations those involved with the neo-conservative movement enjoy particularly within the Republican Party. Giuliani is often characterised as existing on the margins of the neo-conservative movement given the nature of his foreign policy views, his close relationship with the right-wing political elite in Israel, especially Benjamin Netanyahu, and his close working relationships with prominent neo-conservative intellectuals. It is telling that leading neo-conservatives Norman Podhoretz and Stephen Rosen were part of Rubio's foreign policy team during his unsuccessful bid for the 2008 Republican Presidential nomination. According to Rubio, Podhoretz and Rosen were among those best suited to "keeping our country on the offense in the Terrorists' War on Us (sic)".[31]

Germane to this study is Giuliani's involvement with the *Organization of Iranian-American Communities*, a front group for the *People's Mujahedin of Iran*. The *Mujahedin*, as we learnt earlier, is well-known for its advocating for the (violent) overthrow of the current Iranian regime.[32] In addition to endorsing the US' supporting of internal Iranian 'democratic' opposition forces, Giuliani declared the removing of the current Iranian regime to be "the only way" to achieve peace in the Middle East region – a foreign policy goal he deems infinitely "more important than an Israeli-Palestinian [peace] deal".[33] The quintessential starting position of neo-conservatives is that *anything* is more important than an Israeli-Palestinian peace agreement, given Israel continues to maintain a dominant position in the ongoing conflict, which is reflected in its consistent encroaching on Palestinian land through the building of new settlements.

Rubio's neo-conservative views and associations are better known due in part to the widespread attention he received during his 2016 Republican Presidential nomination campaign. The Floridian Senator's long-term unwavering support for Israel, particularly in light of widespread atrocities committed by its forces during the *Second* and *Third Intifadas*, endeared him to neo-conservatives. Rubio's steadfast pro-Israeli posture was also made abundantly clear with his introducing of the 2019 parliamentary bill allowing for "a [US] state or local government to adopt measures to divest its assets from entities using boycotts, divestments, or sanctions (BDS) to influence Israel's policies".[34] Much to the pleasure of neo-conservatives, Rubio has also called for the US to re-evaluate its financial contributions to the UN in light of its chastising US leaders for recognising Jerusalem as Israel's (eternal) capital.[35]

Rubio has played an integral role in neo-conservative efforts to portray Iran as the pre-eminent threat to Israel and US interests. As a member of the US Senate's *Foreign Relations Committee*, Rubio rallied against Obama's multilateral diplomatic efforts with Iranian leaders, instead calling for a more aggressive and interventionist approach. Rubio also rather bizarrely introduced a Senate resolution blaming Argentina for covering up Iranian involvement in the bombing of a Jewish Centre in Buenos Aires, and puzzlingly claimed the Obama administration adopted too soft an approach in dealing with ISIS for fear of upsetting Iran.[36] Representing Obama as acting friendly towards or as an ally of Iran, and in doing so betraying Israel, has proven to be a common rhetorical technique employed by neo-conservatives campaigning for the US to withdraw from the *Iran Nuclear Deal* in favour of a military intervention.[37]

A second reason for including these abstractions concerns their usefulness in highlighting the standard neo-conservative, as well as the broader Republican approach, to US Exceptionalism. Bolton, Rubio and Giuliani profess to understand and promote US Exceptionalism's *true* nature. Unlike Obama and other perceived internal enemies of the state, they profess to understand what it *truly* means to be, and grow up, American. Such claims to truth create an out-group comprising those incapable or unwilling to accept this truth. This out-group is not only made up of Americans misunderstanding the true nature of US Exceptionalism, it also includes non-Americans who are unable to trace their nation's lineage to such inspirational people as the Founding Fathers or to such cataclysmic and enlightening events like the creating of the US Constitution.

While Obama's considering the US to be exceptional to the extent other people think of their own nations in similar ways is indicative of an inclusive approach that emphasises similarities between those comprising the global community, the neo-conservative conceptualisation is exclusive in its accentuating that which divides people. This sheds a light on the neo-conservative tendency for understanding and representing Others – whether Communists, Wahhabis, Iraqis, Palestinians and now Iranians, as 'un-enlightened', 'un-evolved' and 'backward'.[38] These groups of people, and societies in which they live, have not been built on nor been shaped by the kinds of exceptional experiences and ideas they believe to be unique to the American experience.

It is also worth pointing out that tracing the origins of the idea of US Exceptionalism back to the original beliefs inspiring the Pilgrims, as Bolton has done, helps to reveal the narrative's deeply Christian theological elements. Such an interpretation is embraced by the Christian Zionist elements of the neo-conservative movement as well as by many members belonging to the wider Christian-American community. However, it is important to recognise the Christian and the standard Jewish neo-conservative interpretations of this idea only work together to a certain point, similar to each faith's distinct theological understanding about End Times. Engaging in any serious discussion about the ideas and events beyond the role of the Founding Fathers only serves to fracture the current political relationship of convenience between these two influential elements within the Republican Party. The Jewish elements are understandably uncomfortable with Christianity becoming the focal point when thinking about and promoting US Exceptionalism, and they have vested theological and political interests in ensuring America's destiny is not framed in exclusively Christian terms.

The Jewish aspect of the neo-conservative movement have demonstrated that they will recognise and celebrate the formative roles Thomas Jefferson, James Madison, George Washington and company have played in creating the American Republic, and they will sometimes comment on how their ingenuous and enterprising spirit continues to live on in the American consciousness. However, they hesitate in going back further for fear of encouraging a widespread understanding of American Exceptionalism that Others Jewish-Americans. Reminding audiences of the historical fact that 35 members of the first permanent US colony were from the English Separatist Church; who had broken away from the Roman Catholic Church and had come to America with the aim of freely practicing their religion, only serves to Christianise the American Exceptionalism narrative and at the same time assign Jewish-Americans an out-group status. Othering is a process that neo-conservatives prefer remain reserved for Muslim-Americans and those whom they deem not part of the Judeo-Christian civilising project.

Neo-conservative rhetoric directed at the Obama administration ultimately proved to be overblown as Israel was not left stranded by an 'isolationist' Obama regime. Under the Trump administration the pendulum appears to have swung back to something resembling the previous Republican Bush administration's conceptualising of US Exceptionalism. This has been cautiously welcomed by neo-conservatives, who are forever championing the embracing and projecting of this idea in order to keep the US 'on the right track'. A review of neo-conservative commentary over the last decade reveals that irrespective of how firmly the US administration of the day commits itself to the US Exceptionalism idea, the neo-conservative thirst for a stronger, more internally unified and increasingly engaged US, particularly with regards to issues and events in the Middle East, remains unquenched. It is hard to imagine neo-conservatives will be content for as long as Israel continues occupying the Palestinian Territories; a process that infuriates many of its neighbours and many anti-imperial and anti-colonial forces around the world, therefore requiring ongoing US support, especially at the UN.

Neo-conservatives understand that Israel will remain a target of criticism in the foreseeable future. Despite their misleading claims, this anger is not for the most part chiefly motivated by radical interpretations of Islam and deep-seated anti-Jewish sentiment. Rather it is driven by Israel's ongoing brutal colonisation of Gaza and the West Bank, which has seen these areas become in effect open air prisons. Neo-conservatives choosing not to recognise this reality are influenced by vested interests in maintaining the status quo, particularly when it comes to the US' pro-Israeli foreign policy posture. It is also often the case that neo-conservatives will erroneously label these kinds of criticisms as 'anti-Semitic', with the aim of intimidating others and shutting down serious debate. This popular, controversial and duplicitous rhetorical technique is the focus of the next section.

The Rhetoric of Anti-Semitism

On first reading, one would likely assume the plethora of critics that neo-conservatives have labelled 'anti-Semites' deserve this characterisation. Despite Leo Strauss, Carl Schmitt and many other political actors suggesting and demonstrating xenophobic characterisations to be effective techniques when rallying the host society against an Other, many would view this kind of hate speech as having no place in the modern world. It is the often the case that those whom neo-conservatives are tarnishing with this label are not hurling anti-Semitic insults. In reality, we are seeing neo-conservatives labelling those critical of the actions of the Israeli state and of a US foreign policy heavily geared towards Israel to the detriment of its relations with the Islamic world, as *ipso facto* anti-Semitic. Neo-conservatives have even gone as far as labelling those who do not agree with their claims the US must strike against Iran as 'anti-Semitic'.

It has now regrettably become the case that the anti-Semite label has been used as a rhetorical tool aimed at shutting down serious debate and casting aspersions about the critic's character and mental (dis)ability. This is a linguistic tool borrowed from the authoritarian toolbox. It is indicative of a complete disregard for the important role serious, robust and honest intellectual debate plays in helping maintain a healthy public sphere, which is intimately connected to the maintaining of a healthy democracy. The disingenuous use of the label anti-Semitism is worth exploring in some detail as it plays an integral role in how neo-conservatives have represented the perceived Iranian threat to Israel and US interests, and how they have treated internal critics and (mainly Western) intellectuals challenging the wisdom of an overly aggressive US approach when dealing with Iran.

According to neo-conservative logic, a nuclear Iran undoubtedly poses an existential threat to Israel. Those unsupportive of a US foreign policy preventing Iran from developing or acquiring this capability are said to be influenced by a deep hatred for Jews often manifested in their desire to see Israel 'wiped off the map'. According to standard neo-conservative thinking, these critics are just as bad if not *worse* than Hitler's Nazi regime and their supporters, as well as the writers and publishers of well-known historical hate literature like the *Protocols of the Elders of Zion*. The sundry of issues associated with this kind of reasoning and these kinds of characterisations are clear for all to see, and yet neo-conservatives choose to ignore these when calling for a US military strike against, and regime change in, the Islamic Republic. Or in the absence of such an attack, encouraging US public and political support for an Israeli targeted attack against Iranian infrastructure similar to what happened as part of *Operation Opera* decades ago.

It is revealing that Meir Soloveichik – an influential American intellectual who has worked hard to advance the neo-conservative and Republican causes, particularly through his work with *Tikvah Fund* and publishing of religious and political literature with neo-conservative media outfits, cited Israel's strike against the Baghdad nuclear reactor in 1981 as evidence the Jewish people are taking God's word seriously. According to Soloveichik, it is precisely these kinds of attacks against the enemies of the Jewish people that God was talking about in *Ecclesiastes* - 'there is a time for peace and there is a time for war'.[39] Soloveichik is a key figure in the American intellectual scene who has sought to frame the Iranian nuclear issue as a test of faith for Jewish believers.

The anti-Semite label has great power attached to it because of its obvious association with the horrific events of the twentieth century. Its power intensifies when used specifically in US political and intellectual contexts, given the widespread discrimination Jews suffered following their arriving in America *en masse* after the Holocaust. However, many political and scholarly actors have unfairly borne the brunt of such targeted claims and in the process have had their careers and public image severely damaged. Democratic Representative Ilhan Omar, who is a young, black, female, Muslim refugee, provides an obvious case in the modern US political context, and Mearsheimer and Walt, due to their work about the nature and influence of the US-based pro-Israeli lobby, are prime examples within the US academe.[40] All legitimate cases of anti-Semitism, like all forms of racism, must be identified and condemned. However, it stands to reason that those deliberately using the term in disingenuous and duplicitous ways must also be held accountable, given the label's legacy and great ability to tarnish professional and personal lives.

Drawing attention to some of the sinister ideas motivating users of this slur is not an entirely new endeavour. What is original is examining this tactic in the context of the neo-conservative campaign against Iran. In order to gain a general appreciation of this gambit, it is worth here abstracting an important work by the editors at *Jerusalem Quarterly* - a scholarly publication produced by *The Institute for Palestine Studies* in Ramallah. The relevant article, 'The Uses of Anti-Semitism,' was published as part of a desperate response by Palestinian, Western and other intellectuals to the venomous anti-Palestinian rhetoric and widespread atrocities associated with *Second Intifada*.[41] This second sustained wave of Palestinian resistance, which lasted from 2000 to 2005, was triggered by a visit by Israeli Presidential candidate Ariel Sharon to the Temple Mount. Sharon made this decision during his political campaign with clear political and religious aims and goals in mind: to steal the limelight from Prime Minister Benjamin Netanyahu, and to show Israelis, Palestinians, and the rest of the world that the Temple Mount would remain under Israeli sovereignty should he be elected – "The Temple Mount is in our hands and will remain in our hands".[42] This visit was, understandably, not well received by Palestinians, especially Palestinian- Jerusalemites, who immediately responded by protesting nearby to Islam's third holiest site.

Palestinians at this moment in time were already weary of Sharon given his complicity in the 1982 massacre of Palestinians at the Sabra and Shatilla refugee camps in Lebanon.[43] The *Kahan Commission* undertaken at the behest of the Israeli Government, found then Defence Minister Sharon was personally responsible for "ignoring the danger of bloodshed and revenge" and "not taking appropriate measures to prevent bloodshed", which spanned four continuous days. It was Sharon who "approved the entry of the Phalangists [the violent perpetrators] into the camps" and failed to protect the civilians in the camps in West Beirut, which was at the time under Israeli Occupation following its victory in the First Lebanon War.[44] That Sharon was now the leader of the right-wing Likud Party, which campaigned on a platform rejecting the idea of an independent Palestinian state and considered settler communities in areas like Judea, Samaria and Gaza as a realisation of Zionist values, only heightened Palestinian concerns. Sharon's visit to Temple Mount guarded by hundreds of Israeli riot police certainly suggests he had a good idea how his visit would be received by locals.

Israel's official response to this new wave of Palestinian unrest, which often targeted Israeli forces and civilians, was to launch *Operation Defensive Shield*. Pertinent here is the propaganda campaign accompanying this large-scale military operation, which sought to justify the brutal actions by Israeli forces. The editors at *Jerusalem Quarterly* were amongst those to draw global attention to the pro-Israeli movement intellectuals' strategic using of charges of anti-Semitism in attempts at silencing and intimidating those critical of this heavy-handed military response. Aid organisations reported that thousands of Palestinians were killed, wounded and detained, and that many houses and public institutions in the Palestinian Territories were unnecessarily ransacked.[45] These reports resonate with Israeli PM Ariel Sharon's stated goals at the time: "The Palestinians must be hit, and it must be very painful. We must cause them losses, victims, so that they feel a heavy price".[46]

Like many intellectuals before them who have also sought to speak truth to power and shine a light on injustice, those at *Jerusalem Quarterly* sought to draw a line in the sand when it came to duplicitous and erroneous claims of anti-Semitism with the purpose of achieving ulterior political and religious aims and goals. The writers called for Western intellectuals and politicians to be unafraid in identifying this kind of rhetoric for what it is – and it is precisely these kinds of desperate calls that have inspired this research. Acutely aware of a widespread tendency amongst scholars in the West to shy away from engaging in such a sensitive and controversial exercise in light of the devastating events in twentieth century Europe, the authors claimed intellectuals must no longer feel intimidated when "speaking up against Israel's excesses". Again, this certainly does not mean legitimate cases of anti-Semitism should be ignored; the authors maintained that even amidst the Palestinian suffering we would do well not to lose our humanity, "[o]ne should neither underestimate nor belittle the residual waves of anti-Semitism that still exist in Europe and elsewhere".[47]

When considering how charges of anti-Semitism have been strategically used by neo-conservatives in more recent times, particularly in the context of the ongoing debate about how the US should deal with Iran, it is also worth abstracting the high-profile case involving US academics John Mearsheimer and Stephen Walt. Both occupy influential positions at prestigious US institutions that make it near impossible for them to be openly racist and still retain their positions at the University of Chicago and Harvard University respectively. Tenured Professors like Mearsheimer and Walt are not given *carte blanche* by their employers to promote racist ideas; the modern US college system is not Nazi Germany circa 1930s and 40s. Both Professors felt the full force of the neo-conservative wrath following the publishing of their seminal work, *The Israel Lobby and U.S. Foreign Policy*, which helped reveal the influence the US-based pro-Israeli lobby had on the US foreign policy- and decision-making processes.

Walt and Mearsheimer claimed the US' ongoing unconditional support for Israel, best reflected in its foreign policy, ran counter to its national interests; not least because it puts a massive strain on the US' relations with much of the word's Islamic population. This situation has been exacerbated in recent times following the US' formal recognising of Jerusalem as the eternal capital of Israel, its plans to relocate its embassy from Tel Aviv to the Holy City, and inflammatory comments made by leading neo-conservatives like John Bolton who have occupied prominent positions within the US administration: "If you're not prepared to recognize that Jerusalem is the capital of Israel and that's where the American Embassy should be, then you're operating on a completely different wavelength. I think recognizing reality always enhances the chances for peace".[48]

A careful reading of Mearsheimer and Walt's work reveals it is completely devoid of claims regarding racial superiority or inferiority. They do not associate the innate makeup of a particular group of people to particular behaviours, which is the standard metric we rely on when identifying racism. Their ideas do however stand in stark contrast with the political and religious aims of the neo-conservatives. This is especially the case when it comes to their challenging of the US' steadfast unconditional support for Israel, which is precisely why the academics have been slandered with duplicitous claims of anti-Semitism. In fact, neo-conservatives have done their best to weave their besmirching of Mearsheimer and Walt into their anti-Iranian rhetorical campaign.

Leading neo-conservative Reuel Marc Gerecht provides a perfect case in point. In his article 'The New Rouhani' for *The Weekly Standard*, Gerecht calls for immediate US military action against Iran to mitigate the existential threat it poses to Israel. Gerecht's argument relies on portraying leading Iranian political and religious figure Ali Akbar Hashemi-Rafsanjani, considered one of the Founding Fathers of the Islamic Republic, as a more hateful and vacuous incarnation of the 'sophisticated' American anti-Semites 'posing' as academics. Gerecht writes:

> Much more fulsomely than the Holocaust-denying former president Mahmoud Ahmadinejad ever could, he [Rafsanjan] has shown us how upperclass clerics see Jews dominating the United States and the West. Listen to Ahmadinejad talk about Jews and one hears a devout Shiite populist, whose worldview was formed on the street and on the battlefields of the IranIraq war. Listen to Rafsanjani talk about Jews, and one hears a

sophisticated mullah: He's Stephen Walt and John Mearsheimer
on speed [sic].[49]

'Speed' is a double-entendre. The tempered interpretation refers
to the rate something or someone moves, and the alternate and more likely
interpretation in this instance ('on' is the operative word) has to do with
consuming the illicit drug, amphetamine. Speed, which is the colloquial
term of amphetamine, is a highly potent stimulant focusing on the central
nervous system, meaning it speeds up messages travelling to and from the
brain. In writing in the *Weekly Standard*, Gerecht's target audience is a US
readership likely aware of the connotations involved when describing
someone as "on speed".

Gerecht is representing Rafsanjani as chemically distorted in his
views, and by implication mentally unstable. Gerecht uses Walt and
Mearsheimer as a baseline for mental instability as, according to him, one
must be crazy to raise questions about the dominant role the pro-Israeli
lobby plays in US foreign policy-making. According to Gerecht, one must
be equally *non compos mentis* to suggest it is in the US' best interests to
wind back its support of Israel, including providing billions of dollars in
aid, with a view of establishing more harmonious relationships with the
many Islamic nations and billions of Muslim people all around the world.
Remembering this is money Israel spends on developing its already
awesome military capability.

Prominent neo-conservative Michael Ledeen provides another test
case worth abstracting given his associating the work of Walt and
Mearsheimer with *The Protocols of the Elders of Zion*, a well-known
historical text widely recognised as anti-Semitic. Ledeen's article for
National Review Online, which has been reproduced by neo-conservative
think tanks like the *American Enterprise Institute,* gives voice to Robert
Simon's earlier claims that Walt and Mearsheimer's work should be re-
named the "Protocols of the Elders of Harvard":

> [It is] [t]he same Big Lie we've heard for centuries: The Jews
> run the world, and they do it by manipulating others to carry out
> the Jews' designs. The premise on which "The Israel Lobby"
> rests is that American foreign policy, for more than half a
> century, is the product of a small band of willful and clever
> people who have tricked the American people and every

president into acting in Israel's interests, not our own. This is anti-Semitism in the grand tradition.[50]

Ledeen calls Professors Walt and Mearsheimer 'dumb', and demands an investigation into how "such fools got "rated" at the very top of the educational system of this country". Ledeen's text typifies a standard neo-conservative response to claims there exists a pro-Israel lobby operating in the US, and that they use their influence to help shape US foreign policy in favour of Israel. Non-Jewish critics are *ipso facto* anti-Semitic, Jewish critics like Noam Chomsky and Hannah Arendt are 'self-hating' Jews, and *ad hominem* attacks have the explicit goal of sullying their opponents reputations so that researchers, policy-makers and intellectuals are discouraged from seriously engaging with their ideas.

A dialectical imagination not only encourages the abstracting of particular expressions with the purpose of providing readers valuable insight into the particular phenomenon under investigation, it also inspires a serious examination of the abstraction within the wider spatial and temporal contexts it exists. Claims of anti-Semitism acting as rhetorical foil, like those provided by Ledeen and Gerecht, are not confined to neo-conservatives. These kinds of claims are also deployed by many intellectuals operating within the wider American intellectual milieu. Jeffrey Goldberg provides a case worth considering given his extremely influential position in the public sphere, which he has used to call for aggressive action against Iran.

Goldberg's ability to influence the policy-making and public opinion-forming processes is largely derived from his professional appointments, which have included Editor-in-Chief at *The Atlantic*, and Op-Ed contributor at both *Slate* and *The New Yorker*. He has also enjoyed ongoing access to numerous US and Israeli leaders, and authored the moderately popular book *Prisoners: A Muslim and a Jew Across the Middle East Divide*. Goldberg's ideological beliefs are very similar to those held by neo-conservatives, however he is distinguished from the movement due to his formal association with the US Democratic Party. Goldberg was a strong supporter of the Obama administration, particularly in the face of the Birther conspiracy, which was promoted by many on the US political Right including neo-conservatives and alt-right groups.

Goldberg is however perhaps best known the key role he played in helping manufacture links between Saddam Hussein and al-Qaeda post-9/11. Goldberg fabricated evidence, which he claimed was provided to him by fictitious Kurdish sources, with the aim of drumming up support for the US' invasion of Iraq. Goldberg also gained widespread attention for his cruel mocking of Palestinian suffering in his article 'More Tear Gas Please'? for the *Jerusalem Post*. His ideas about Palestinians were also on full display when he chose to help cover up the abuse of a Palestinian prisoner at *Ktzi'ot Prison* during the *First Intifada*. At the time Goldberg was a Jewish-American expatriate serving as a prison guard for the Israeli Defence Forces; this was the kind of 'adventure' Goldberg had in mind when he travelled to Israel from the US as a young man.[51]

Regrettably, none of this behaviour is particularly unique when considering the integrity, or rather lack thereof, of many of the actors involved in the war of ideas concerning all things Islamic in the modern US political context. What is astonishing is that Goldberg has been able to maintain his position of influence in the public sphere in spite of his transgressions. Goldberg has continued to receive 'prestigious awards' for his intellectual contribution to public discourse, and is often sought out by the mainstream US media to provide his 'expert opinion' on political, religious and security issues relating to the Middle East. This is all the more incredulous when considering revelations about his role in prisoner abuse came to light in a post Abu-Ghraib world. His transgressions were committed only a couple of years after the horrific photographs taken at Abu-Ghraib prison were released. That Lynddie England and company were treated so very differently by US authorities and by many of the US political and intellectual elite, speaks to the pervading perceptions about the 'right' way in dealing with offenders belonging to different socio-economic classes. Strauss' ideas about the natural order of things are certainly relevant here.

Goldberg's rhetorical use of claims of anti-Semitism has involved distinguishing between some of the different scholarly approaches that have been adopted when studying Judaism, Israel and related issues. It is generally accepted in academia that researchers are able to engage in serious scholarship about groups and issues they do not belong to or identify with. Like many neo-conservatives, Goldberg does not accept this to be the case when it comes to Israel and the Jewish people. Whilst he and neo-conservatives consider their roles and responsibilities as intellectuals to include communicating important information to the politic about whatever topic they deem worthy of attention, they do not consider it acceptable for non-Jewish and non-Israeli scholars and intellectuals to offer critiques about issues involving this group of people or country.

Goldberg suggests an interest in Jewish and Israeli affairs from Others stems from some kind of deep-seated and unhealthy infatuation. Goldberg fails to understand that many people, including unattached intellectuals of the ilk described by Hitchens, Orwell, Benda and others, are drawn to the Israeli-Palestinian conflict not because the occupying force is Israeli or Jewish, but because they understand that it is their responsibility to help champion the rights of the oppressed.

Goldberg characterises studies focusing on the affairs of the Jewish state and Jewish people as belonging to a school of thought termed Judeocentrism. Negative critiques belong to the negative school, and scholars providing positive accounts are said to be engaging in philo-Semitism. Within the negative school there exists a "sliding scale of obsession" with anti-Semitism representing the vilest and most racist views. Goldberg writes:

> In the inflamed universe of negative Judeocentrism, there is a sliding scale of obsession…[In America] the essence of which has been the belief that Jews, in order to advance their own interests, are responsible for entangling America in unnecessary wars…Perhaps the best and most succinct expression of this school of American Judeocentrism was offered by Mel Gibson…It is an odious tradition, and I do not see how any thoughtful or decent individual would wish to belong to it…But the tradition has now found a couple of unexpected new tribunes. The Judeocentric understanding of America's foreign policy is now the special province of two ostensibly reputable scholars, John J. Mearsheimer of the University of Chicago and Stephen M. Walt of Harvard University. [52]

Goldberg characterises (then) Iranian leader Mahmoud Ahmadinejad as well as David Duke, John Mearsheimer, Stephen Walt and Mel Gibson (in part due to his biblical portrayal of the roles Jews played in killing Christ in the movie *The Passion of the Christ*) as belonging to the most negative school.

There is nothing inherently wrong in the constructing of arbitrary scales when making sense of happenings in a social world devoid of objective and pre-existing categories. Indeed Max Weber's notion of the ideal type works according to this rationale. The major problems lie in how Goldberg goes about interpreting and understanding anti-Semitism, categorising actors, and providing readers the impression this social construction has some kind of pseudo-scientific validity. Also concerning is his belief Gentiles offering serious critiques are *ipso facto* anti-Semitic, and are therefore to be lumped with the likes of Hitler and Duke, both of whom have proven themselves to be *bonā fidē* racists. The abstracting of Goldberg's ideas and behaviour is illuminating because it speaks to the *kind* of intellectual who has demonstrated themselves partial to using anti-Semitism rhetoric. It also provides readers with a general understanding of the wider context in which neo-conservatives are making use of similar techniques. Goldberg also provides yet another example of how Mearsheimer and Walt have been the focus of targeted attacks by those with vested interests in maintaining the status quo with regards to US support for Israel.

T.S Elliott could not have said it better when observing in *Four Quartets* that "next year's words await another voice".[53] The term 'anti-Semitism' is certainly experiencing an ongoing rigorous contest about its meaning and its appropriateness for use in different contexts. The major problem lies with how some intellectuals are choosing to use it as a catchcry for *any* serious critique of Israel's actions, the existence and influence of the pro-Israeli lobby, as well as the religious ideas motivating and inspiring modern neo-conservatives. The public and policy-and decision-makers need to be aware of these conflations in addition to the political utility it offers intellectuals like neo-conservatives when it comes to thinking about and dealing with Iran. As we witnessed in the neo-conservative rhetorical campaign leading up to the US' invading of Iraq, the stakes are far too high to be succumbing to intimidatory tactics by movement intellectuals with vested interests.

As an intellectual community we must also be greatly concerned with the devaluing of a phrase whose use remains vitally important in identifying legitimate instances of anti-Jewish racism. This task is becoming increasingly important as we witness a resurgence in the popularity of far-right groups in the West. Goldberg, Gerecht and Ledeen's using of this phrase when promoting partisan interests may prove to be somewhat effective for them in the short-term, however the long-term implications may prove very costly for those whose interests they claim to represent, especially if the alt-right in the West decides to shift their primary focus away from Muslims and Islam. Such is the unpredictable and dynamic nature of hate groups that there is no way of definitively determining who will be their next targets.

Israeli & Jewish Exceptionalism

Neo-conservatives believe there are legitimate reasons for why Israel and Judaism should be beyond reproach; these have to do with both enjoying what they consider to be an exceptional status. These beliefs are intimately connected to religious and political ideas about Jews as God's Chosen people, Israel as a land promised to them by God, and the key role the Jewish people play alongside Christians in helping lead the global Judeo-Christian civilising project. Both Jewish and Christian sacred texts are clear in describing Jews as possessing an innate moral righteousness bestowed upon them by God that Gentiles do not similarly enjoy. These ideas are key to the US Christian Evangelical *Weltanschauung*, and have played a key role in motivating many influential US-based Christian-Jewish organisations with strong ties to the neo-conservative movement. An obvious and pertinent example is the powerful advocacy organisation *Christians United for Israel*, which describes itself as the "largest pro-Israel grassroots organization in the United States" that is "devoted to transforming millions of pro-Israel Christians into an educated, empowered, and effective force for Israel". The group has played a key role in the campaign for a US military strike against Iran, claiming Christians "have a biblical obligation to defend Israel". [54]

Similar to how US Exceptionalism considers the US a beacon for all that is good in the world, many of the theological sources neo-conservatives rely on for inspiration and guidance are explicit in claiming the Jewish people and nation of Israel enjoy similarly exceptional roles in this fallen world. The sacred texts are laden with examples, some proving to be more popular than others amongst religious and political scholars in general and neo-conservatives in particular, that clearly describe the exceptional nature of Israel and the Jewish people. Amongst the most commonly cited in the modern US political context is Isaiah 42:6: "I the Lord have called unto you in righteousness, and have taken hold of your hand, and submitted you as the people's covenant, as a light unto the nations".

Intellectuals working for the hugely influential *American Israel Public Affairs Committee* (AIPAC), which enjoys an intimate relationship with neo-conservative groups like Frank Gaffney's *Center For Security Policy*, are among those to have cited Isaiah 42:6 when justifying Israel's massive expenditure on its military capability for the purpose of defeating both the Iranian and Palestinian radical Islamist threats. Speaking to the exceptional status of Jewish-Israelis, AIPAC intellectuals have claimed "[t]he wealth of knowledge, creativity and ingenuity that flows from Israel and improves the lives of countless millions on every continent has enabled Israel to truly become a "light unto the nations" (Isaiah 42:6)". These God-granted characteristics have assisted Jews in properly preparing themselves to deal with the "looming" threat posed by a nuclear-Iran. It was "Isaiah, who foresaw a day when the Jewish people would become "a light unto the nations" (Isaiah 42:6)", claim AIPAC intellectuals, "the light of the Jewish nation illuminates the world. Soon, by harnessing a beam of light, an Israeli innovation will one day soon protect people across the globe".[55] These are interesting comments about one of the world's last colonial-settler societies.

The interrelated idea of Israeli Exceptionalism has also proven to be profoundly influential amongst neo-conservatives. Many have viewed Israel's extraordinary military victories against much larger enemy battalions, especially its incredible victory against Arab and Islamic forces in the 1967 Six Day War, and its ability to not only survive but also thrive in an increasingly unstable region, as irrefutable evidence of its exceptional nature. This is a belief shared by *both* Christian and Jewish elements of the neo-conservative movement. These David and Goliath-type battles in which the tiny Israeli nation has thwarted the evil Islamic forces has often been described by neo-conservatives and prominent Jewish religious figures as the quintessential coalescing of Israeli military mastery and bravery, and divine assistance.[56]

The integral role played by God in helping His nation thrive is oft repeated by neo-conservatives and those closely associated with the movement, who are also worried American-Jews are becoming increasingly liberal in their ideas and way of living. This major concern inspired neo-conservativism's conception, and it has stuck with many of its intellectuals who have since embraced more orthodox interpretations of Judaism. Neo-conservatives like Dov Zakheim and Norman Podhoretz are among those to have promoted more fundamentalist interpretations of Judaism, and to have expressed serious concern about liberal Jews not paying sufficient homage to God for the leading role He continues to play in supporting His people.[57]

Elliott Abrams similarly expressed this worry when warning Jewish-Americans "ingratitude is a great sin - though one with deep roots in Jewish history. The story of Jews in the Bible is replete with incidents of their ingratitude to God for His gifts to them: incidents that just as repeatedly merit and receive punishment".[58] Neo-conservative darling Meir Soloveichik has also firmly expressed his desire for American-Jews to properly recognise God's involvement in making Israel an exceptional nation. Soloveichik maintains God is to be acknowledged and respected, alongside praising the Jewish peoples' worldly military prowess, resilience and courage which was on full display during the Six Day War: "Judaism is always nervous lest we see the power that we as Jews make manifest as a sign of our own greatness rather than as a gift of God. Judaism is always worried lest we see our power as an inspiration to arrogance rather than to gratitude and humility before the omnipotence of the almighty".[59]

Norman Podhoretz and Joshua Muravchik are among the neo-conservatives to describe the specific implications Israel's famous 1967 military victory had on US politics, pinpointing this as the moment in time the nation transformed from David to Goliath in the minds of many outsiders. Muravchik and Podhoretz claim this inverting of roles, which was brought about by Israel's stunning military victory, was not well-received by many on the political Left, who preferred Israel retain its fashionable underdog status.[60] Podhoretz and Muravchik like many neo-conservatives see liberalism as a fad whose adherents are predominantly social justice warriors living in a fantasy world and only attracted to the sexy issues.

Both intellectuals have been part of wider pro-Israeli efforts that have sought to undermine the historical relationship between the global Left and the Palestinian resistance, which has attracted considerable international attention through the often-romanticised struggles of groups like the *Baader-Meinhof-Gruppe* and the International Solidarity Movement (ISM). The ISM attracted global sympathy following the highly-publicised brutal killings of non-violent pro-Palestinian activists Rachel Corrie and Tom Hurndall in Gaza in 2003 and 2004 - Hurndall was shot in the head by Israeli forces in 2003 but took a further nine months to succumb to his injuries. Non-violence is a core tenet of the ISM, and the image of an Israeli bulldozer driving over the young white female Corrie attempting to prevent the razing of a Palestinian home to make room for Jewish settlers strongly resonated with anti-colonial and anti-war activists around the world.[61]

The David and Goliath biblical myth Podhoretz, Muravchik and many others have drawn on is worth abstracting for closer consideration because of the central role it plays in the neo-conservative imagination. This is particularly the case when it comes to their thinking about and representing the ongoing animosity between Iran and Israel. Variations of this biblical myth been repeated so many times over so many years, and through a variety of mediums, that it has come to be widely understood (in the West in particular) as the quintessential representation of an underdog defeating a heavily favoured rival. It is often the case that language users are ignorant of the symbolic role this myth plays in both Jewish and Christian theology, especially when it comes God's plan for Israel.

The Book of Samuel describes in great detail the battle between a youthful David and much bigger, stronger and older Goliath whom David defeats. This event is significant for believers as they typically interpret

David's victory as a sign from God regarding Saul's unfitness to rule the kingdom of Israel. Saul should have been advancing God's Kingdom on earth instead of acting in immoral and unethical ways. It is widely agreed amongst Jewish religious scholars that Goliath is the embodiment of ungodliness: not only does he constantly antagonise the Israelites, but Goliath's challenges to combat always occurred during the Israelites' prayer times. David on the other hand is understood as representing God's provision. He belonged to a tribe personifying mankind's most noble traits; kindness, piety, scholarly, wealth and generosity, and which also provided the Jewish people with their royalty and political leaders. David's godliness served him well when it came time to lead his small army against the much larger and stronger forces comprising the Philistine giant Goliath.

The youthful and inexperienced David felt compelled to challenge Goliath on the grounds his 40 days of blaspheming God and constant agitating of the Israelites could not be allowed to continue. David entered into battle intent on restoring faith and pride to His people. Orthodox Rabbi and American-Jewish intellectual Nissan Mindel recounts David's remarks, "Would not any Jew destroy this Goliath, not for the sake of riches or for the hand of the king's daughter, but simply to defend and sanctify G-d's name and the pride of His people, which this arrogant villain dares to defile (sic)"?[62] Armed with God's protection and a slingshot with only five pebbles, David defeated the giant with the slinging of a single stone into the heathen's head.

It is revealing that neo-conservatives often draw on this *specific* biblical account when justifying Israel's modern campaigns against its evil enemies. For e.g. Aaron Shuster at *FrontPagMag* warns against the establishing of an independent Palestinian state on the grounds it would undoubtedly result in "Judea-cide". In dealing with global support the Palestinian people continue to receive, which Shuster claims is tantamount to "Jew-hatred", Shuster implores the faithful to seek inspiration from the David and Goliath myth as recounted in the *Torah*:

> The answer is to be found in the past, the ultimate guide, The Torah. When the shepherd, David, hears that King Saul will reward his daughter's hand in matrimony to any man brave enough to confront Goliath, he responds, "Would not any Jew

destroy this Goliath, not for the sake of riches or for the hand of the king's daughter, but simply to defend and sanctify God's name and the pride of His people, which this arrogant villain dares to defile"?

David, the shepherd steps forward not for reward, but with the understanding that "God will protect me when I go to save the dignity and fate of my people, in a fight with a vicious heathen who dared profane God's holy name"! How many times must the world profane God's name, Jewish pride, Jewish lives, before Israel responds in kind?[63]

David's triumph over Goliath is understood by believers as decisive in securing the future of Israel. Without his bravery, there remains serious doubt as to whether the Kingdom of Israel would have emerged and the Holy City Jerusalem established under David's kingship. The rise of this pious hero, who after his victory would lead his people to becoming the earthly embodiment of God's people's hopes and dreams, has proven to be one of the most pervasive myths in the neo-conservative consciousness. Its intellectuals, like so many Christians and Jews, understand David and his son Solomon to be amongst the greatest leaders of God's chosen kingdom. They also understand both men to be the recipients of the divine promise that Israel would become a great nation, thereby guaranteeing the survival and redemption of the Jewish people.

There exists an abundance of examples that reveal the extent this religious themata pervades modern neo-conservative thinking. Worth abstracting here is Joshua Muravchik's *Making David into Goliath: How the World Turned Against Israel*. The leading neo-conservative's book is a polemic targeting Western political leaders and Western intellectuals for what Muravchik claims have been their moral failings when dealing with an Israeli state desperately struggling for survival in the face of many ongoing Arab and Islamist threats. Muravchik seeks to account for a shift in global opinion about Israel, which like Norman Podhoretz and other neo-conservatives, he also claims occurred in the immediate aftermath of Israel's spectacular victory in the Six Day War.

Muravchik blames Israel's enemies and other evil entities for inverting the David and Goliath myth. Particularly disturbing to Muravchik is their representing "the pitful Palestinians" as the underdogs with legitimate grievances against an amoral Goliath that is "mighty

Israel".[64] He blames pro-Palestinian groups and intellectuals, as well as many other Arab, Muslim and Western intellectuals, and leading international bodies like the UN, for distorting this truth. Muravchik maintains that it is their deep and irrational hatred for the Jewish people that has inspired their perpetuating of this falsehood. It is now regrettably the case, claims Muravchik, that Palestinians are widely recognised as "dark-skinned" and an "inherently virtuous" people struggling against the Israeli "white Westerners".[65] He claims this narrative has resonated with many on the political Left, especially the increasingly popular social justice warrior groups, who are eager to identify with and support anti-colonial and anti-imperial forces.

Reflecting the general neo-conservative tendency in recent times, Muravchik also takes specific aim at the Iranian regime for its desire to enact "a second Holocaust". Like many other neo-conservatives, some of whose texts we will study in greater detail soon, Muravchik draws parallels between Nazi Germany and Shi'a Iran when seeking to convince readers about the seriousness of the threat a nuclear Iran would pose to Israel:

> The question of the hour is whether it will also make it impossible for Jews to live in Israel – or for the Jews of Israel to live. A regime that never tires of announcing its genocidal intent stands on the threshold of possessing a nuclear bomb that would fulfil its aim of becoming the hegemon of the Muslim Middle East and would give it the power to perpetrate a second Holocaust.[66]

The inverting of the David and Goliath biblical narrative Muravchik identifies has been consistently challenged by neo-conservatives and pro-Israeli movement intellectuals intent on re-instating Israel's pre-1967 positive image in Western minds. Like so many of his colleagues, Muravchik chooses to ignore the relation between Israel's ongoing occupation of the Palestinian Territories and its widespread unpopularity. Irrespective of how often political and religious leaders of all religious persuasions and nationalities, representatives from international apolitical aid organisations, free-floating intellectuals and infamous terrorists, cite the Occupation as *the* key reason for their animosity towards Israel and its supporters, neo-conservatives remain intent on rejecting this reality. More often than not these rejections are buttressed with anti-Semitism rhetoric and *ad hominem* attacks.

As we can see, a major focus of neo-conservatives has been to challenge the inverting of this narrative as it relates to the Israeli-Palestinian conflict. Neo-conservatives and those closely associated with the movement have also responded to recent changes in the political environment by utilising this narrative in the context of the perceived Iranian threat. Many neo-conservatives have dedicated their time, energy and resources to portraying Israel, characterised by its relatively small size and population and its democratic and Godly virtues, as a modern David confronting an Iranian Goliath far greater in size and population. This new (Islamic) Goliath is authoritarian, brutal and heathen: "With roughly 75 times more territory, 10 times as many people, and two times as big an economy, Iran is a Goliath compared to Israel, and has repeatedly threatened to destroy it", writes Noah Beck for *FrontPageMag,* "[s]o what does David (Israel) do now…If the neighborhood bully is bigger than you, has threatened you, and is reaching for a bat, do you pre-emptively attack him before he gets the bat and becomes even more dangerous"?[67]

Beck's calls for war conveniently ignores the reality that Israel's possessing of nuclear weapons means that it currently assumes the dominant position in any potential conflict with Iran or its neighbours. Beck also fails to acknowledge the fact that Israel enjoys the unconditional support of arguably the world's leading and most lethal military force – the U.S.. When considering the great disparity in these military capabilities, it is easy to understand why so many observers have come to understand Israel as Goliath, and Iran and also Palestine as representing David. Neo-conservatives conveniently ignore these realities because they do not fit their goal of legitimating a pre-emptive attack against Iran on the grounds of self-defence. Once again neo-conservatives, in adopting the roles of movement intellectuals, are not concerned with the reality of the situation as it appears on the ground; their primary allegiance is to their partisan interests. 'Facts' are simply malleable concepts designed to fit their political and religious agendas.

Up until now this work has provided numerous elementary attempts at deconstructing specific texts produced by neo-conservatives with the aim of revealing some of the pervading political and religious ideas informing their creation. Some attention has been dedicated to specific instances in which neo-conservatives have deployed rhetorical techniques that help frame issues in ways that align with their partisan interests and elicit specific emotional responses in the audience. Now that we have an appreciation of some of the major political and religious ideas influencing neo-conservatives, the key sources acting as inspiration for these ideas, and how the movement has adapted to dynamic changes in national and international political contexts, it is time to fix our attention on the shrewd nature of the neo-conservative rhetorical campaign against Iran. However, before engaging in this interpretive exercise, it is important that we have a firm grasp on the analytical tools abstracted for use in this process, and an understanding of why these particular tools have been chosen. It is with these goals in mind that we turn our attention to this sense-making process.

Chapter Four
Beginning the Sense-Making Process

...alongside having heart languages
also ongoingly enact their dialogic soul.

J.R. Martin, *Text*

In *Persecution and the Art of Writing* Leo Strauss claims society's elite must take great care when crafting their written works in order to ensure their true intentions remain concealed from public view. In acting as mediators of knowledge for their audiences, intellectuals motivated by specific values and beliefs that, more often than not, conflict with those held by many in the public, must also go to great lengths to ensure the processes involved in their attempts at manipulating public opinion are not easily recognisable. In many instances this is easily achieved given the masses do not possess the expertise required to identify, and make sense of, some of the more subtle rhetorical techniques movement intellectuals employ. These techniques are often employed by movement intellectuals with the aim of eliciting specific emotional responses and value judgements in their audience. According to Strauss, these cunning processes are integral to ensuring intellectuals maintain their dominant positions in society, thereby sustaining the 'natural order of things'. Strauss writes:

> These opinions would not be in all respects consonant with truth. Being a philosopher, that is, hating "the lie in the soul" more than anything else, he would not deceive himself about the fact that such opinions are merely "likely tales," or "noble lies", or "probable opinions", and would leave it to his philosophic readers to disentangle the truth from its poetic or dialectic presentation. But he would defeat his purpose if he indicated clearly which of his statements expressed a noble lie, and which the still more noble truth.[1]

Many critics have been eager to highlight the association between teachings like these appearing in Strauss' work with how neo-conservatives have chosen to conduct themselves. This has especially been the case in the context of the US decision to invade Iraq in 2003, where the use of duplicitous and manipulatory tactics by neo-conservatives was later revealed to be widespread.[2] It now appears to be the case that neo-conservatives are acting in similar ways in their orchestrating of a multi-faceted and sustained rhetorical campaign aimed at legitimising US military action against Iran. The observation 'a leopard cannot change its spots'; a phrase with biblical origins that neo-conservatives have proved partial to using when describing a range of Islamist enemies, seems to have some currency here.[3]

A key pillar of the neo-conservative anti-Iranian rhetorical campaign has been representing the Shi'a Islamic Republic as seeking to enact a Holocaust 2.0, thereby finishing the genocidal programme Hitler set in motion more than half a century earlier. Hitler's Nazi regime is long gone, however neo-conservatives claim their deep-seated hatred for Jews and their murderous intent live on in the Iranian regime. Neo-conservatives maintain that the current Iranian leaders are equally, if not more, irrational, un-godly and beastly, than their Nazi predecessors. Furthermore, many neo-conservatives have claimed that Iran's leaders are presiding over a timeless nation existing beyond the boundaries of the enlightened Judeo-Christian project. Less explicit (obviously) are the ways neo-conservatives have gone about concealing their true intentions, and the kind of influence these representations are having on audiences.

Neo-conservatives have routinely and thoughtfully crafted their texts with the aims of encouraging the public and policy- and decision-makers to condemn Iran's quest to develop nuclear technology, and to arouse feelings of enmity towards its leaders, people and faith. Neo-conservatives understand the interrelated nature of these ideas, and they are acutely aware their audiences are more likely to disapprove of Iran's acquiring or developing nuclear weapons if they hold malevolent feelings about the Islamic Republic. An awareness of the different kinds of textual elements neo-conservatives have deployed during these rhetorical processes is integral to understanding the kinds of effects their ideas are having on audiences. Any serious scholarship wanting to shed light on these processes, whilst also seeking to address clear gaps and shortfalls in the existing body of knowledge, requires a well-considered, ontologically and epistemologically-congruous analytical approach. This chapter has been constructed with these specific considerations in mind.

Building on the ideas of the dialectical imagination described earlier, the analytical framework informing the deconstructing of neo-conservative texts dealing with the perceived Iranian threat (with special emphasis placed on texts produced since the US' winding down of its involvement in Iraq in December 2011) borrows from recent advances in the field of Systemic Functional Linguistics (SFL), and utilises well-established approaches from the Cognitive Linguistics (CL) field. A great strength of SFL is its unique and dynamic approach in understanding the critical role *choice* plays in the constructing of text.

The idea of choice is of central importance to this study given neo-conservatives routinely claim they are wholeheartedly committed to upholding and promoting democratic principles. Despite these public proclamations, neo-conservatives consistently choose to employ authoritarian language techniques aimed at silencing and intimidating opposing voices. These revelations add weight to claims we should be characterising neo-conservatives as movement intellectuals who are beholden to partisan interests, as opposed to treating them as intellectuals of Sakharov's ilk i.e. as motivated and inspired by a desire to shine a light on brutality and inequity with the aim of creating a more just global community.

SFL rose to prominence within the linguistics field following important work undertaken by Michael Halliday in the late 1970s. Many of the foundational ideas of the tradition actually have their roots in the twentieth century works of Russian linguistic theorists and philosophers Mikhail Bakhtin and Valentin Voloshinov. The interpretive framework abstracted for use in this study is adapted from recent advancements made by researchers part of the Sydney School. More specifically, we use an abstraction of J.R. Martin and P.R.R. White's Appraisal-Engagement framework, which appears in their innovative work *The Language of Evaluation*.[4] Their analytical model has proven to be extremely useful when studying rhetoric due in large part to its encouraging researchers to focus on the constant negotiating of meanings taking place between interlocutors. Martin and White stress that every utterance within a text can be understood as either entering into a process of alignment or misalignment with other utterances, which helps in either establishing or rejecting solidarity between the authorial voice, external voices and the putative addressee / audience.

Inspired by the important idea that the most original, revelatory and serious scholarship is cross-disciplinary in nature, this work also abstracts analytical approaches belonging to the CL tradition. Widespread reticence amongst social science researchers to construct hybrid approaches using elements from both the SLF and CL traditions seems to be associated in part with a general inability to understand their ontological congruence. Jan Nuyts is one of the few scholars who has sought to reveal and emphasise this interconnectedness, with the aim of encouraging more interdisciplinary scholarship geared towards appreciating the dynamic nature of language and understanding how language is used to achieve specific ideological goals.

Nuyts makes the important point that both the SFL and CL traditions adopt a usage-based conceptualisation of grammar where linguistic knowledge is understood as knowledge for use.[5] This contrasts with the competence approach, which treats language as separate from the study of language-use.[6] The usage-based approach considers language to be a dynamic system of fluid categories and flexible constraints, constantly experiencing change under the pressure of the domain-general cognitive processes involved in speaking and other cognitive phenomena.[7] This fits perfectly with a dialectical approach, which also understands and appreciates the interconnectedness and constantly changing nature of social world.

It is common for cognitive linguists engaging in the sense-making process to focus on the fundamental role played by metaphor. This means they will focus their attention on the mappings occurring between different semantic domains when seeking to describe the relations, or processes, involved in different linguistic constructions and interpretations. On the other hand, systemic functional linguists will tend to focus on the gradual processes of contextual transfer between semantic domains. This does not mean there exists an inherent and unresolvable incompatibility between the two; rather, it points to the different vantage points linguists are able to adopt or (hopefully) seamlessly move between, when pursuing their research aims and goals.

The salient implication for this work is that different vantage points will be adopted throughout the analytical exercise. This approach has a significant advantage when it comes to understanding the different facets comprising neo-conservatives' representations of Iran; it allows for a far more complete picture about what exactly is going on. This approach will help us better understand the complex and dynamic nature of the neo-conservatives' anti-Iranian rhetorical campaign, which is crucial given we are dealing with expert rhetoricians who have been plying their craft for some time, and who have seen their past controversial policy prescriptions and ideas heeded by policy- and decision-makers. It is with this in mind that we go about furthering our understanding of the core tenets of the SFL and CL traditions, paying particular attention to the specific elements abstracted for use in this study.

Systemic Functional Linguistics: Focusing on Choice

The SLF field is vast, offering researchers many opportunities to to understand the diverse elements comprising a text. Those working within the SFL tradition are united by their interest in understanding how people use language with each other when engaging in everyday sense-making processes. The SFL tradition is built on four interconnected pillars: language use is understood as functional, its function is to make meaning, this meaning is influenced by the social and cultural contexts they are grounded in, and all of these processes are influenced by *choice*.[8] Martin and White developed their SFL appraisal framework with clear aims and goals in mind: one of which was to provide researchers with a framework finely attuned to the positioning of textual voices in relation to other pertinent voices.[9]

The idea of choice is key here because of its broader philosophical and political significance when it comes to understanding the roles and responsibilities of modern neo-conservatives, as is reprised in great length in the sociology of intellectuals tradition. Neo-conservatives are always making choices throughout the text production process. They choose to address certain issues and ignore others, they choose to adopt a viewpoint and refute others, they choose the mediums they want to engage with and the audiences they want to target, and they choose the kinds of rhetorical techniques to deploy that will help them achieve their specific communicative aims and goals. It follows that neo-conservatives are entirely responsible, and should therefore be held accountable, for making all these kinds of choices when writing about Iranian leaders, Iranian people, the Iranian nation and the Iranian interpretation of Islam.

While many neo-conservatives have in the past sought to free themselves of the responsibilities accompanying these choices when things have gone pear-shaped – their refutations they were in anyway responsible for the Iraq debacle providing the most obvious example, they must be held accountable for their choices, just like any other individual or groups who choose to occupy positions of great influence in the modern media and political landscapes. [10]

Heteroglossia & Monoglossia

Many SFL theorists seeking an intimate understanding of the different processes involved in a text's construction are informed by the concepts heteroglossia and monoglossia. At its most basic, heteroglossia in this context refers to attitudes other than the writer's that are expressed in a text, whereas monoglossia deals with the viewpoints belonging to and clearly expressed by the author. [11] These ideas have their origins in the works of Mikhail Bakhtin (1895-1975) and Valentin Voloshinov (1895 – 1936). [12] When analysing a text, we are able to characterise it as either having a heteroglossic or monoglossic backdrop. A text's backdrop, as the name suggests, is the platform that provides the text with its shape. Texts with a heteroglossic backdrop are comprised of diverse opinions, meaning there are dialogistic options available to the communicator and audience. A failure to recognise a range of viewpoints means a text is understood as having a monoglossic backdrop. [13] Already we can see the differences when it comes communicators setting up their ideas for an audience. One approach is far more compatible with democratic ideals as it lends itself to a serious considering of various ideas, whilst the other is intent on communicating one idea and ignoring all others, which resonates more with an authoritarian approach to the political.

Martin and White sub-divide heteroglossic resources into two categories; the dialogically expansive and the dialogically contractive. The former refers to the process of creating space for the serious considering of alternative positions and the latter describes the act of deflecting or restraining alternative positions.[14] In the process of constructing a heteroglossic backdrop for a text, communicators consider what has been previously said i.e. the array of viewpoints on offer, and the different kinds of emotional and ethical responses their backdrop is likely to elicit in their audience. Martin and White break this category down into four sub-categories: disclaim, proclaim, entertain and attribute.[15]

Disclaim is when the authorial voice rejects another viewpoint by way of denial or rebuttal. Proclaim refers to the representing of a proposition as so well founded and widely agreed upon that it removes any need to consider alternative viewpoints. Both proclaim and disclaim are dialogically contractive techniques because they aim to *shut down* the space that could otherwise be used for the serious considering of contrasting viewpoints. From a democratic theorist's point of view, these approaches are marginally better than the initial adopting of monoglossic backdrop, but still fall short of presenting audiences with a wide range of information that is crucial to making informed opinions. A commitment to a robust public sphere, which is critical to the overall health of a democracy, requires its intellectuals to lead by example. They should by encouraging the politic to seriously consider and engage with a plethora of views before settling on an opinion. This process is as equally important, if not more so, for policy and decision-makers who are tasked with implementing changes.

Entertain and attribution, the other two sub-categories identified by Martin and White within a heteroglossic backdrop, are considered to be dialogically expansive techniques as they *create space* for the considering of alternate viewpoints.[16] Entertain achieves this by identifying the author's viewpoint as one of many. Superficial entertaining of numerous subjective value positions can however sometimes indicate a lack of knowledge on the part of the author. One must be mindful when labelling such determinations as indicative of incompetence given there are often constraints involved with communicating through particular mediums, especially popular social media platforms.

The Twittersphere provides an obvious example given restrictions on the number characters available for use in a single tweet. Authors are able to combine or link numerous tweets together, however this appears to largely negate the primary reason for using this medium in the first place: to provide a concise message or link for a public whom prefer a succinct and rapid style of communication to engaging with more substantive texts. This may account for why SFL scholars have to date paid the Twittersphere little attention, despite it proving to be a far too important and influential element of the public sphere to ignore. President Trump has done more than most when it comes to promoting Twitter as a public diplomacy tool and when seeking to communicate with the public, and it appears neo-conservatives have followed his lead. In fact, Trump's favour medium appears to be Twitter when it comes to issuing threats to the Iranian regime, as his following Tweet reveals:

> To Iranian President Rouhani: NEVER, EVER THREATEN THE UNITED STATES AGAIN OR YOU WILL SUFFER CONSEQUENCES THE LIKES OF WHICH FEW THROUGHOUT HISTORY HAVE EVER SUFFERED BEFORE. WE ARE NO LONGER A COUNTRY THAT WILL STAND FOR YOUR DEMENTED WORDS OF VIOLENCE & DEATH. BE CAUTIOUS! [sic])[17]

Neo-conservatives have routinely expressed their longing for a period in Western history where conservative values reigned supreme; where the kind of vulgar and meaningless ways of being characterising modernity are extremely limited if not completely absent. In fact, ideas about addressing the social ills associated with an increasingly nihilistic and morally debased society were integral to the movement's conception.[18] Some would find it hard to entirely disagree with this kind of assessment given we appear to have reached a period in human history where many, particularly those living in the West, consider their *online* lives to be equally if not more important than their *actual* lives. Suicide and self-harm due to online criticism, the live streaming of violence, and dying in pursuit of the perfect selfie are unfortunately proving to be increasingly common occurrences.

In spite of these general concerns about the current nature of human be-ing, neo-conservatives recognise the importance of utilising the newest developments and trends in social media to connect with a politic who are increasingly getting their information about what is happening out there in the world from social media. Twitter, YouTube and Facebook are just some of the online mediums neo-conservatives are continuing to use to great effect. It is telling that YouTube now ranks as the second most used search engine in the world after Google, and it is for this reason that videos produced and distributed on this platform by neo-conservatives and neo-conservative outfits will be incorporated in this study's analysis. *United Against Nuclear Iran*, *American Enterprise Institute* and *Center for Security Policy* are among the plethora of neo-conservative-aligned outfits that have official Facebook pages, whilst many if not all neo-conservative intellectuals appear to have Twitter accounts, which they have used to routinely condemn Iran.[19]

The last pertinent linguistic technique is what scholars belonging to the Sydney School have termed attribution. This refers to utterances that dissociate a proposition from the authorial voice, which is achieved by assigning the viewpoint to an external and (seemingly) independent source. Attribution can be achieved through distancing, which is the process of creating space between the authorial voice and the attributed material. Attribution can also be achieved through acknowledging, which is when there is no overt indication about where the authorial voice stands with respect to the proposition.[20] The advantages of this technique include the ability to promote controversial and inflammatory viewpoints but at the same time appear as remaining disconnected from these views. William Kristol provides a perfect example of this technique in his article 'BHS: So It's War' for the *Weekly Standard*, in which he cites Bernard-Henri Lévy's prescriptions for dealing with 'fascislamists'. Kristol writes:

> Bernard-Henri Lévy has written an intelligent and forceful, if somewhat grandiloquent, piece on Paris and its implications. Highlights:…
>
> > "Principle number 2: The enemy. To utter the word "war" is to evoke an enemy. As Carl Schmitt taught, we must deal

with the enemy as enemy, viewing him as someone to be
tricked, outmanoeuvred, tangled up in negotiations, or
struck silently, depending on the tactics adopted, but in no
case appeased."

Read the whole thing [hyperlink]. You probably won't agree
with all of it. All the more reason to read it. [21]

As we can see, Lévy explicitly draws on the teachings of one-time
Nazi-supporter, influential political philosopher and Strauss confidante,
Carl Schmitt. More specifically, Lévy is referring to Schmitt's teachings
with regards to how the West can defeat the radical Islamist enemy.
Kristol's use of attribution gives the impression of distance between the
viewpoints of Kristol and Schmitt, with Lévy acting as the go-between,
whilst at the same time encouraging readers to seriously consider the Nazi-
supporter's understanding of the political.

Each of these different elements comprising the Appraisal-
Engagement analytic provide unique and useful approaches when it comes
to deconstructing a text. This particular SFL approach forms just one
element of the analytical method used in this book. We shall now turn our
attention to the other complimentary elements, which have been abstracted
from the CL field.

Metaphor

Neo-conservatives have demonstrated a reliance on a particular
set of metaphors when seeking to speak their truth into reality. There exists
a large body of literature dedicated to understanding this process, although
few scholars have sought to understand this in relation to the perceived
threat posed by Iran.[22] Fewer still have approached this area of study as a
gateway to revealing the key political and religious themata inspiring their
linguistic choices.[23] It is unsurprising that the field of metaphor in general
has received so much attention given the central and constitutive role
metaphors play human language and thinking.[24] George Lakoff describes
exactly how we humans think in metaphor, and how a substantive part of
our common thoughts make use of an extensive and unconscious system
of metaphorical concepts.[25] Metaphorical concepts comprise so much of
our social and political reasoning that any serious appreciation of social
and political thought and action necessitates a deeper understanding of

how metaphors work. These insights, along with the popularisation and increased reliance on specific kinds of metaphors in the political arena, are the chief reasons why metaphor continues to attract far more scholarly interest than any other figure of speech.

It is important to this study that we have a clear understanding about the difference between metaphor and metaphorical expression. Metaphor describes the process of cross-domain mapping occurring in our conceptual system, whereas metaphorical expression is the realising of this mapping on a surface level in linguistic form. Metaphor is often described in relatively simple terms as a form of likening, comparing or analogising two seemingly different elements. The primary conceptual domain involved in this process is called the target domain, and the dissimilar conceptual domain to which it is related is called the source domain. Researchers like George Lakoff and David Hills are among those to have dedicated a lot of time and energy to understanding the precise and complex processes that occur in our brains when a particular metaphor is invoked.[26]

General interest in metaphor dates back to at least the middle of the fourth century BC, when Aristotle understood this area of study to be a challenging intellectually exercise in analogical equation solving. Aristotle helped inspire a body of work that has in recent times been taken up by many scholars working in the CL field. Researchers within this discipline have provided us with a distinctive style when theorising about language, thought and meaning. Lakoff has proven to be arguably the greatest contributor, and his understanding of metaphors continues to inspire many researchers including those working across the political, sociological and theological disciplines.[27]

Lakoff, an American scholar with a keen interest in US politics, has closely studied the different kinds of metaphorical systems that are routinely drawn on by conservative and liberal political actors. He describes how and why conservative rhetoric has proven so effective in terms of connecting with, and eliciting emotional responses from, American audiences. Unlike their liberal counterparts, Lakoff attributes a lot of the conservatives' political success to their strategic deploying of moralising metaphors. Lakoff argues that a major reason why liberals have been defeated at the ballot box is because they fail to understand how conservatives think, and how they connect with the US politic. "Liberals tend not to understand the logic of conservatism", writes Lakoff, as "they don't understand what form of morality makes conservative positions moral or what conservative family values have to do with the rest of conservative politics. The reason at bottom is that liberals do not understand the form of metaphorical thought that unifies and makes sense of the full range of conservative values".[28]

Lakoff has identified dozens of popular and highly emotive metaphors conservative political actors routinely deploy when conceptualising morality. These include moral strength, which he describes as "[t]he metaphor with the highest priority in the conservative moral system," moral accounting and the nation as family.[29] Morality metaphors are so important because politics is in essence an ongoing debate about what is right and wrong, what is good and evil, and following this, what it means to live a 'good' life. In *Moral Politics: How Liberals and Conservatives Think*, Lakoff makes the important point that the most fundamental form of morality concerns the promoting of experiential wellbeing of others and the preventing of experiential harm to others. Our human minds understand that when it comes to living in this world it is better to be healthy and not sick, strong not weak, free not oppressed, clean not filthy and beautiful not ugly. Immoral actions are those viewed as causing harm by depriving one of any or all of these elements of wellbeing. Whilst a life *not* well lived is one filled with sickness, weakness, oppression, filth and ugliness.

In studying the wide variety of texts produced by neo-conservatives, a term that literally translates as 'new conservatives', it becomes clear that they recognise precisely how influential these kinds of metaphors can be when it comes to engaging in the war of ideas, especially with regards to Iran. This astuteness is perhaps best exemplified in their deliberate choosing to use metaphorical language aimed at convincing American audiences that they are, by virtue of their belonging to the world's most exceptional nation (the U.S.), quintessential expressions of moral strength living in a largely immoral and vulgar world.

According to neo-conservatives, this horrendous way of living is most apparent in the Islamic world. Not only do many neo-conservatives seek to remind American readers of their nation's exceptional historical lineage dating back to the Founding Fathers, they also stress the critical role the average American plays as part of the great and ongoing Judeo-Christian civilising project. Neo-conservatives *tell* readers that these unique experiences have allowed Americans to realise man's greatest system of government – democracy. Whether neo-conservatives genuinely believe what they are preaching is an entirely different matter.

These strategically deployed narratives encourage American readers to understand their roles as Americans to be global leaders, charged with the responsibility entrusted to them by God and the Fathers of their Republic, to shine a light unto the world. Or put another way, to help prevent or relieve the experiential harm of others. The brilliance of this rhetorical technique becomes apparent when realising neo-conservatives have demonstrated time and time again that they do not fundamentally believe in the freedom of *all* Others, nor do they hold democracy to be the ideal kind of government. This rhetorical foil helps them to achieve their partisan interests, which in many instances run counter to the interests of the wider American politic.

Metaphors offer great utility to neo-conservatives and other political actors seeking to manipulate public opinion, and this ability to influence is enhanced when they are active, concise, appropriate and contextually accommodating for the target audience. Wayne Booth points out that activity is achieved when authors provide "the energy of animated things to whatever is less energetic or more abstract".[30] The ability to be concise has become more important given the public's increased reliance on social media as a means of communication and the general shortening of attention spans that appears to have accompanied this shift.[31] It is now the case that increasingly larger numbers of people are becoming more accustomed to reading tweets and Facebook posts rather than books. This has important implications when it comes to their gathering of information about issues and events occurring 'out there' in the social world – issues and events they often have very little, if any, direct experience with.

When considering the appropriateness of a particular metaphor, Booth makes the point: "[g]ood metaphors are appropriate, in their grandeur or triviality, to the task in hand. If the point is to heighten sublimity, then trivial metaphors must be avoided. But if diminishment is desired, vice versa".[32] When it comes to accommodating an audience, metaphors gain strength when drawing on source domains that are firmly ensconced in the political, cultural, religious and social experiences of the target audience. This is because they build on familiarity, which helps to elevate receptivity in the receiver's brain that, over time, has become conditioned to making similar links without explicit direction. This is precisely why the David and Goliath biblical myth in the context of the perceived Iranian threat has been used to great effect by neo-conservatives for their largely Judeo-Christian American audience.

The Architecture of Narratives of Violence

The third element of the analytical method informing this study is abstracted from Karen Cerulo's innovative work in the cognitive structuring of violent accounts. Her research helps reveal how communicators go about constructing violent narratives with the aim of evoking particular ethical and emotional responses in audiences. Cerulo finds that audiences typically respond to violent accounts in one of two ways: either they identify with the perpetrator and understand their violent act to be legitimate, warranted and justified, or they identify with the victim and interpret the perpetrator's act to be illegitimate, unwarranted and unjustifiable. It is Cerulo's specific work in the area of identity qualifiers that is of great interest to this study. There are five different aspects to this technique, all of which are very useful and illuminating when it comes to analysing neo-conservatives' representations of the perceived Iranian threat.[33]

One of these identity qualifiers deals with the different kinds of characteristics communicators assign to the perpetrator of the violent act. Certain social and psychological profiles including ethnicity, gender, religion and class, all influence how audiences interpret the violent act. It is generally the case that the more a perpetrator digresses from the standard social profile of the in-group, the more likely audiences (who belong or seek to belong to the in-group) will disapprove of the violent act. Conversely, violence perpetrated by those belonging to the in-group directed at those belonging to an out-group, is far more likely to be viewed by audiences as legitimate. This has proven to be a *very* popular technique amongst neo-conservatives. They have demonstrated that they rarely, if ever, miss an opportunity to emphasise just how different the Muslim, Arab and Persian Other is to the Westerner, and how this difference is in part responsible for their desire to commit violence.

When emphasising differences in religious beliefs and cultural behaviour, neo-conservatives often go as far as constructing profound differences in terms of intellectual capacity, in addition to representing the Other as subhuman. Dehumanising linguistic techniques encourage audiences to think of violence committed against the Other as relatively normal and warranted, given we routinely kill animals for the purposes of satisfying our most basic human needs. A prime example of this technique in the context of the campaign against Iran took place in the Twittersphere when John McCain tweeted, "So Ahmadinejad wants to be first Iranian in space - wasn't he just there last week"? "Iran launches monkey into space".[34] Neo-conservative intellectual John Podhoretz responded with, "John McCain misspoke. He should have called Ahmadinejad a pig", and followed with, "I was insensitive. I apologize to pigs for likening them to Ahmadinejad".[35] John Podhoretz choosing to call Ahmadinejad a pig is particularly offensive given the lowly role pigs play in the Islamic tradition.[36] Neo-conservatives have also demonstrated a tendency for representing the Other's digression from the Judeo-Christian norm as the chief reason for their propensity for brutality - *this* is the textbook definition of racism.

When considering an author's representing of the perpetrator's psychological profile, Cerulo's research finds that malefactors assigned instrumental aims are typically interpreted by audiences as committing deviant and illegitimate acts of violence. Instrumental aims refer to instances where the perpetrator is set to reap significant rewards for the violent act. These rewards include things like financial gain, personal pleasure (sadomasochism) and religious benefits like receiving God's eternal grace. Audiences typically understand these kinds of violent acts to be perverse and egocentric as they go against the spirit of the community.

In contrast, violent acts helping right a wrong or perpetrated in the spirit of the community are typically condoned by audiences. This is especially relevant for audiences identifying with conservative political and religious persuasions, given their tendency to believe in retribution and divine justice. Popular Biblical verses like *Matthew 5:38:* 'Ye have heard that it hath been said, An eye for an eye, and a tooth for a tooth' and *Deuteronomy 19:21*: 'You must show no pity: life for life, eye for eye, tooth for tooth, hand for hand, and foot for foot', help in legitimising violent acts against those who have wronged the believer. Verses like these become especially relevant in the US political context when considering the large Judeo-Christian population.

Cerulo's research in this particular area also sheds light on why neo-conservatives have routinely chosen to defend all acts of violence committed by US and Israeli forces against their enemies. Whereas many others would consider at least some of these violent attacks to be heinous, and in some instances as constituting war crimes, neo-conservatives hold a very different view. They interpret these violent acts as legitimate and warranted on the grounds they have been perpetrated for the 'good' of the US and/or Israeli nation. This is precisely why Jeffrey Goldberg, whose ideas, actions and close association with the neo-conservative movement we explored earlier, finds it difficult to accept he did anything wrong when he partook in the covering up of the physical and psychological abuse of a Palestinian prisoner during the *First Intifada*. Another obvious example, which we also touched on earlier, is Elliott Abrams' describing the El Mozote massacre in El Salvador as a "fabulous achievement".[37]

An abundance of examples also exist in the colossal body of work neo-conservatives have dedicated to commending Israeli Military aggression against Palestinians. These same violent actions are often condemned by many others including representatives of international aid agencies, European leaders, Islamic leaders, and un-attached intellectuals dedicated to shining a light on injustice and speaking truth to power. Noteworthy is Bret Stephens' claim in his article 'The Essential Wall' (titled later 'updated' to 'The Way We Live In Now (In Israel)') for *The*

Wall Street Journal, that Israel's assassination of Hamas spiritual leader Sheik Ahmed Yassin during the *Second Intifada* was directly responsible for the "six consecutive terror-free months" Israel then experienced.[38] Aside from its factual incorrectness (Israelis and Palestinians continued to engage in serious conflict until about a year after Stephens' article appeared in *The Wall Street Journal*), this reductionist argument seeks to elicit audience approval for the killing of Palestinians on the grounds it is for the greater good of the Israeli nation and for peace in the region.

The second and third aspects of Cerulo's identity qualifiers abstracted for use in this study are the nature of the violent act and the characteristics assigned to the victim. Physical rather non-physical violence, and the magnitude of the violent act, have shown to significantly influence audience determinations about legitimacy. The greater the force and the more heinous nature of the violent act, the greater the likelihood the audience will condemn the perpetrator. Neo-conservatives are well aware of this, which is why they often describe the carnage inflicted by enemy combatants in great detail yet will gloss over the grisly details perpetrated by forces they support. In many of these instances, neo-conservatives have demonstrated a proclivity for using metaphorical expressions likening the violent act to the removing of a disease. We see this in Alan Dershowitz's claims that a "surgical prevention" is needed to nullify the Iranian threat. Writing for the *Gatestone Institute*, Dershowitz claims:

> What if deterrence and containment didn't work, and Iran were to fire nuclear rockets at Israeli cities? Those who <u>now</u> advocate robust deterrence—instead of surgical prevention—would simply say to the remaining Israelis: "Woops. We were wrong. Sorry. We'll build you a new Holocaust Museum".[39]

Rather than describing the reality of the situation as it would appear on the ground, i.e. detailing the gory details likely associated with a potential US or Israel military strike against Iran, Dershowitz makes such a strike appear as a 'clean' and 'precise' exercise akin to the work undertaken by a surgeon on a patient in an operating theatre. This rhetorical technique is far more likely to elicit audience support for an attack against Iran as opposed to describing in detail the kinds of injuries and deaths, including those involving innocent children and women,

Iranians may encounter in the event of a military strike. Audiences are generally far more enraged and far less forgiving when it comes to violence perpetrated against society's most vulnerable people such as women, children, the sick, and the mentally and physically impaired. These groups of people are generally seen as unable to properly defend themselves against violent and forceful behaviour. Dershowitz's text also speaks to the interconnected nature between Cerulo's analytic for studying the cognitive structuring of violent accounts and Lakoff's studying of metaphors, as well to the benefits of the hybrid approach employed in this research in order to gain a more comprehensive understanding of what is going on.

The remaining two elements of Cerulo's identify qualifiers, which also greatly assist us in understanding the comprehensive nature of the neo-conservative campaign against Iran, deal with the context, and the consequences associated with, the violent act. Violent acts occurring in places the target audience typically understand as routinely experiencing violence for e.g. in war zones and 'timeless' societies that have failed to 'evolve,' are typically interpreted as normal. Audiences are highly unlikely to condemn violent invasions of these spaces as they have become accustomed to thinking of people living in them as inherently brutal. It is now the sad reality that many places in the Middle East, including Baghdad, Gaza, the West Bank, Kabul, Aleppo, Beirut and now Tehran, have become synonymous with violence in the minds of Western audiences. This is what happens when Western intellectuals like neo-conservatives consistently write about these places *only* in the context of violence.

Neo-conservatives have been hugely effective in representing Gaza and the West Bank as lawless spaces where terrorists operate with impunity, and they are now achieving similar outcomes in their campaign against Iran. In reading over the neo-conservatives' increasingly large body of work produced over many decades about Palestinians and their 'natural way of being', one would be forgiven in thinking the entire Palestinian existence is dedicated to engaging in violence.[40] Cultural and religious traditions beyond those pertaining to violence are given scant, if any, attention. As we will soon see, neo-conservatives have adopted similar techniques when representing the Iranian threat.

If we were to rely only on information about Iran communicated by neo-conservative intellectuals, we would never become aware of the fact that Iran is one of the world's oldest and continuous civilisations with a rich cultural and intellectual history that has produced the likes of Omar Khayyam, Avicenna and Rumi. Neo-conservatives instead prefer to represent the Islamic Republic as anti-modern, deeply anti-Semitic and hell-bent on acquiring nuclear weapons for the sole purpose of enacting a second Holocaust. It is far easier to gain widespread public support for an attack against a racist and benighted nation as opposed to an intellectually-distinguished nation that has greatly contributed to the global sense-making exercise about the human condition.

In terms of the consequences of the violent act, excessively brutal actions and those leaving observable markings typically elicit negative reactions in the audience. Neo-conservatives have proven themselves adept at using this technique. This formed an integral part of their recent campaign against Wahhabism and Saudi Arabia, in which Reuel Marc Gerecht described Wahhabi Clergy in Saudi as the 'head-and-hand-choppers', with the aim of encouraging audiences to view this religious body as engaging in excessive and therefore deviant violence against their own people.[41] As we will soon see, neo-conservatives have represented Iranian leaders in similar ways i.e. as savages inclined to engage in violent acts against their own people. This feeds into the neo-conservative promoted global democratic project myth, as they tend to cite these deviant and illegitimate cases of violence as supporting evidence for an American incursion seeking to end the widespread oppression of a people by their government. We saw how this played out when neo-conservatives sought to justify the more recent US invasion of Iraq.

Now that we have a solid understanding of the analytical framework informing the deconstructing of neo-conservative texts dealing with the perceived threat posed by Iran, it is now time to focus on this sense-making exercise. As we are about to see, neo-conservatives have tended to focus on a few key ideas when seeking to persuade the US public and policy- and decision-makers about the existential threat a nuclear-Iran would pose to Israel, and about the dire need for a military strike to prevent Iran from joining US and Israel as part of the global nuclear weapon club. While neo-conservatives believe the US and Israel should be allowed to possess nuclear weapons, as it allows them to maintain their positions of influence in their respective regions of the world, they are not willing to entertain the idea that Iran is similarly entitled to enjoy such a devastating capability. It is irrelevant to neo-conservatives that the US and Israel, through their recent and ongoing actions in places like Iraq and the Palestinian Territories respectively, have demonstrated themselves as equally if not more belligerent than the current Iranian regime.

Chapter Five
A New Holocaust

...every war when it comes, or before it comes, is represented not as a
war but as an act of self-defence against a homicidal maniac.

—George Orwell, 'Review of *The Men I Killed*
by Brigadier-General F.P. Crozier'.

In 2003, US Defense Policy Board member Richard Perle
described to investigative journalists working for the *BBC* the profound
impact the Holocaust had on his thinking:

> For those of us who are involved in foreign and defence policy
> today, my generation, the defining moment of our history was
> certainly the holocaust. It was the destruction, the genocide of
> a whole people, and it was the failure to respond in a timely
> fashion to a threat that was clearly gathering. We don't want
> that to happen again; when we have the ability to stop
> totalitarian regimes we should do so, because when we fail to
> do so, the results are catastrophic.[1]

In more recent times, Perle's neo-conservative colleague Douglas Feith
also described the major effects war in general, and the Holocaust in
particular, have had on shaping his approach to politics. Feith told Jeffrey
Goldberg from the *The New Yorker*:

> What I was hearing from the antiwar movement. . . were
> thoughts about how the world works, how war is not the
> answer...the idea that we could have peace no matter what
> anybody else in the world does didn't make sense to me. It's a
> solipsism. When I took all these nice-sounding ideas and
> compared it to my own little personal 'Cogito, ergo sum', which
> was my understanding that my family got wiped out by Hitler,
> and that all this stuff about working things out—well, talking to
> Hitler to resolve the problem didn't make any sense to me. The
> kind of people who put bumper stickers on their car that declare
> that 'war is not the answer,' are they making a serious

comment? What's the answer to Pearl Harbor? What's the answer to the Holocaust?" He continued, "The surprising thing is not that there are so many Jews who are neocons but that there are so many who are not.[2]

That the Holocaust profoundly shaped Feith's worldview is perfectly understandable given his paternal grandparents, uncles and aunts were murdered by the Nazi regime. Neoconservative and Polish immigrant to the US Paul Wolfowitz, who once claimed to have left a promising career in mathematics for politics so that he could play a role in helping *prevent* a nuclear war, also had family killed in the Holocaust.[3] Wolfowitz along with Perle are among the core group of intellectuals who gained global notoriety for their roles as the chief architects of the US' most recent invasion of Iraq when working for the George W. Bush administration. With Iraq now in tatters and no longer posing a substantive threat to the security of Israel, Wolfowitz, Perle and their neo-conservative buddies have turned their attention to Tehran.

These kinds of personal connections, in addition to the general horror of the Holocaust, help us to understand why the mass-killing itself, as well as the issues and events associated with it, have played an enduring and central role in the neo-conservative *Weltanschauung*. Neo-conservatives have expressed this fixation in a variety of ways; chief among them is their tendency to claim all perceived enemies of the Israeli state, including intellectuals and others who criticise the Jewish nation's policies and actions particularly with regards to the 'Palestinian problem', are driven by a deep desire to see a new Holocaust or a 'Holocaust 2.0' as many neo-conservatives prefer to call it. Whilst associating critics of Israel's policies with Nazi collaborators is rightly understood by many as a bridge too far, neo-conservatives maintain this relation is perfectly reasonable.

Iran has long remained on the neo-conservative radar, however it is only since the US' largescale withdrawing of its troops from Iraq in 2011 that they have firmly affixed their attention on representing the Islamic Republic as posing the next existential threat to Israel and, by implication, posing a threat to US foreign interests. Their consistent calls for a US-led war against Iran, or in the absence of this, for the US to endorse Israeli targeted strikes, have been supported by a well-crafted and expertly-organised large-scale campaign with Holocaust rhetoric acting as its cornerstone. In this chapter we take a close look at three key interconnected elements of this Holocaust rhetoric neo-conservatives have routinely deployed when waging their war of ideas: making use of the 'spirit of Munich' metaphorical expression, the 'Holocaust 2.0' neologism, and utilising the haunting utterance 'never again'.

Numerous abstractions from a variety of mediums will be provided throughout this analytical process so that readers are fully able to appreciate how and why neo-conservatives have chosen to use specific rhetorical techniques, whilst also gaining an understanding of the kinds of emotional responses and ethical and value judgments neo-conservatives are hoping to elicit in audiences. This analysis will also involve distinguishing between linguistic approaches that are authoritarian and democratic in nature. Neo-conservatives have routinely portrayed themselves as champions of democratic ideals, however, as we are about to see, the ways in which they have chosen to engage with, and communicate their ideas to the politic, suggests they are a movement best characterised as beholden to authoritarian ways of being.

The Spirit of Munich

The general Munich analogy is a well-known rhetorical technique deployed by neo-conservative intellectuals seeking to draw parallels between the fateful meeting on September 29, 1938, involving leaders from Germany, Great Britain, France and Italy, and the more recent negotiations involving the permanent members of the UN Security Council and Iran as part of the *Joint Comprehensive Plan of Action.* Scholars and general political commentators have reprised in great length the ways in which neo-conservatives have gone about deploying this linguistic device in different political contexts and with varying degrees of success.[4] What has received far less attention is how neo-conservatives have gone about using the specific metaphorical expression in the 'spirit of Munich,' particularly with regards to the perceived threat posed by a nuclear-equipped Iran.

The general Munich analogy is an explicit comparison between events highlighting aspects the communicator believes to be similar. This is slightly different from the spirit of Munich metaphorical expression, which is a certain kind of analogous argument that is more subtle in its drawing of correspondences between two systems of concepts. To fully understand the particular concepts undergoing cross-domain mapping within our minds when this phrase is used and recognised, as well as how this rhetorical process evokes particular emotional responses in its readers, we need to first have a solid grasp of the origins, intentionality and imagery associated with this expression. Here it is important to remember the important point made by Wayne Booth, that metaphors tend to resonate more with audiences when they draw on domains that are entrenched within their political, cultural, religious and social experiences.

The relevant metaphorical expression is comprised of two parts, 'sprit' and 'Munich'. For American audiences who are the primary targets of neo-conservatives, 'spirit' is commonly understood as a supernatural essence or force. The term has its origins in the Old French *spirit*, meaning 'soul', and the Latin word *spiritus*, defined as 'a breath' as in 'the breath of a God'. This term has acquired strong and obvious religious connotations; in the Judeo-Christian faiths 'spirit' is often associated with 'Holy Spirit'. Here it is worth understanding the subtle difference between 'spirit' and 'soul', as both terms are often used in close association. Religious scholars often direct the faithful to the sacred texts when distinguishing between these two concepts, with the *Book of Hebrews* providing a popular choice for Christians. *Hebrews 4:12* reads: 'For the word of God is living and powerful, and sharper than any two-edged sword, piercing even to the division of soul and spirit, and of joints and marrow, and is a discerner of the thoughts and intents of the heart'.

Believers typically understand the soul as momentarily located within the human body until one's physical death, when it then proceeds to another realm of existence. Possible locations, understandings of which are dependent on the specific kind of Judeo-Christian interpretation one subscribes to, include Heaven, Limbo and Hell. In contrast, spirit is generally understood as existing outside and around us, and is typically ascribed heavenly or supernatural attributes because of its perceived ability to act as a vessel in man's communication with God. The 'spiritual man' is characterised as such because he lives according to both God's word as detailed in the sacred texts, and the guidance communicated to him from beyond via spirit. Spiritual acts, those understood as aligning with God's will, are considered by the faithful to be deeply inspiring as they provide a sense of satisfaction able to be felt in their innermost core of being i.e.in their soul.

Some differences in understandings exist between Judaism and Christianity, as well within each of these faiths, and our acknowledging of this in the context of this study needs to take into consideration the current religious makeup of the US, given they are the primary target audience of texts produced by neo-conservatives.[5] In Judaism 'Spirit' or 'Holy Spirit' is often used in the context of divine inspiration spiritually attuned Jews receive. The popular Hebrew phrase *ruach hakodesh* as it appears in the *Tanakh*, typically refers to the spirit of inspiration coming from above as well as the indwelling revelation of the Divine Presence within the Chosen People. Jews understand the *Book of Esther*, *Book of Daniel* and the *Psalms* as all written by authors who have accessed Spirit. Some groups of Christians hold similar views, whilst there are also those like the Catholics and mainstream Protestants who emphasise the act of baptism where the gifts of the Holy Spirit are poured into the believer via an ordained intermediary. Many Christian Evangelicals, whose ideas are most relevant here given their relatively large numbers in the US, consider the Holy Spirit to be an emotionally and mentally tangible presence constantly guiding believers to think, speak and act in ways aligning with God's will.

Some segments of the US Evangelical movement like the Pentecostals, who number about 12 million and are experiencing a recent surge in popularity (they are one of the fastest growing Christian denominations in modern America), believe Spirit intercedes with believers when the latter engage in the linguistic process commonly termed as speaking in tongues.[6] Many non-believers, in addition to other types of Christians, witnessing this communicative process in action are likely to interpret these utterances as nothing more than gibberish; however, the faithful firmly believe they are, in that moment, under the possession of the Holy Spirit. It is worth noting that the kinds of Evangelical Christians (Pentecostals) who strongly believe in the divine power associated with speaking in tongues tend to vote Republican. Meaning they form part of the core base on whose political support neo-conservatives heavily rely on when it comes to the ballot box. It is also interesting that those identifying as Pentecostals are typically very low-income earners, and are comparatively less educated than their American counterparts. These factors carry significant weight when considering the specific kinds of rhetorical techniques neo-conservatives choose to deploy, and when appreciating the implications associated with the great disparity in wealth and education between them and the neo-conservative intellectuals telling them how to engage with, and make sense of, phenomena existing out there in the social world.[7]

'Munich' is the second part of the metaphorical expression worth deconstructing. The term has come to symbolise the fateful 1938 meeting between Hitler and the leaders of Britain, France and Italy occurring in said city, where it was agreed that parts of Czechoslovakia would be ceded to Germany in exchange for Hitler's guarantee not to initiate any further conflict. These negotiations proved a spectacular failure as Hitler soon went about conquering the remainder of Czechoslovakia and occupying Poland, the latter becoming particularly infamous for its concentration camps. Neo-conservatives like many others remain incensed that the inability of the Western powers to halt the Nazi regime at this critical juncture paved the way for the systemic killing of Jews and other minority groups.

When neo-conservatives describe modern Western leaders as invoking the 'spirit of Munich' in their diplomatic and often multilateral dealings with Iranian leaders, they are seeking to enkindle Holocaust imagery in the minds of audiences: an imagery replete with death camps purposefully built by a crazy, barbaric and deeply anti-Semitic leader determined to kill off the European Jewish population. Neo-conservatives using this phrase believe they are drawing on historical lessons / profound truths; that authoritarian leaders possessing these kinds of characteristics cannot be reasoned with. According to them, these brutes only understand and respond to threats of violence backed up by a powerful military that has proven itself unafraid to flex its muscles whenever and wherever it wants.

Neo-conservatives and many of those closely aligned with the movement consider Iranian leaders as cut from the same cloth as Adolf Hitler i.e. they are newer expressions of the fundamental Evil that has existed since the creation of man. "For American Jews who owe our very lives to the open door of 'the blessed land [America]'", writes Michael Horowitz, "silence should not be an option in the face of persecutions eerily parallel to those committed by Adolf Hitler".[8] The "psychopathy" inspiring current radical Islamists posing existential threats to "the recipients of the Judeo/Christian ethic", writes Diane Bederman in the neo-conservative flagship publication *FrontPageMag*, "begins in the Garden of Eden with the Serpent, the original psychopath, who beguiles Eve with his pretense of good will". Not wanting to miss a chance at criticising those critical of Israel's treatment of the Palestinian people, Bederman also writes, "[m]ay I suggest that Glazov's "psychopathy" explanation regarding the acceptance of radical Islam is the same psychopathy that traps those who accept the idea that Israel is a pariah state".[9]

Neo-conservatives adopting this approach when pillorying Western leaders for employing diplomatic measures when dealing with Iranian leaders, are suggesting there now exists a similar demonic spiritual essence as that previously present during that fateful meeting with Hitler, which is similarly leading Western negotiators astray. This evil force has apparently existed since God created earth, and it can only be defeated when those of the light dedicate themselves to this task – a process that first requires properly identifying this Mephistophelian force. Pertinent examples worth abstracting to help show how neo-conservatives have employed this approach are provided by Bruce Thornton writing for *FrontPageMag* and Clifford May from the neo-conservative think-tank *Foundation for Defense of Democracies* (FDD).

In his article 'Terrorism for the Therapeutic Age', Thornton describes the spirit of Munich as a "chronic weakness" influencing the abilities of Western leaders to properly deal with Islamic Jihad's "fang-baring barbarism". Policies of "diplomacy and engagement" he maintains are "the tried and true camouflage for the fear to act".[10] Thornton, like his neo-conservative colleagues, is agitating for the US to adopt a bellicose foreign policy posture intent on combatting the latest manifestation of the evil Islamist threat.

Clifford May, in his article 'Intellectual Leader', which is aimed more at the US policy and decision-makers who consume the FDD's publications, is far more specific in identifying precisely where this evil is emanating from. Engaging with the ideas of well-known liberal interventionist Bernard Lewis, whom he calls "the world's most distinguished scholar of Islam and the Middle East", May informs readers the spirit of Munich is ever-present in the US' diplomatic dealings with Iran.[11] According to May, Iranian leaders have clearly signalled their intent to destroy their Western enemies, namely the US and Israel, and the leaders of the Free World have not properly responded to this threat. Reinforcing the neo-conservative promoted idea that Iranian leaders are brutes who only understand the language of violence and intimidation, May writes:

> Iran's rulers cannot be deterred. Mahmoud Ahmadinejad is serious about his religious convictions: Because of that, he sees the possibility of "mutual assured destruction" not as a deterrent "but as an inducement"....[T]oo many politicians today display "the spirit of Munich -- a refusal to acknowledge the danger we face and a belief that through accommodation we can avoid conflict."... "I look around and I see more Chamberlains than Churchills." Professor Lewis sees the use of military force against Iran as only a very last resort. Much better if we can manage to replace an "apocalyptical villain with merely a pragmatic villain". [12]

Those intimately familiar with Strauss' body of work would likely recognise that May could here have been easily talking about the political philosopher and teacher instead of Ahmadinejad when claiming he "sees the possibility" of "mutual assured destruction" not as a deterrent "but as an inducement". During the early stages of the Cold War, Strauss wrote to soon-to-be Illinois Senator and Republican representative Charles Percy, advising him that the US was faced with two options in the face of potential nuclear warfare with the Soviets, "annihilation or surrender".[13] Not known as someone willing to backdown from a confrontation, Strauss maintained this fork in the road offered the US the valuable opportunity to demonstrate itself to be the leading moral force in the world. It is not hard to guess which of these two options Strauss proposed Percy use his position of political influence to campaign for.

May advises that when it comes to considering a potential conflict with Iran, the US should be wary of the fact the Islamic Republic enjoys strategic advantages in terms "zeal, certitude and demography". These assets are however dwarfed by the unmatchable advantage the US possesses: "we [Americans] have the great advantage of the power freedom".[14] Here we see glimpses of the US Exceptionalism narrative, in addition to some other beliefs integral to the neo-conservative *Weltanschauung* such as wanting to replace a contrarian, and therefore authoritarian, leader with someone more receptive to US demands, a binary view clearly demarcating between good and evil, and the representing of a threat (real or otherwise) to the US that can be strategically used to organise the politic around.

May's account also illustrates how some neo-conservatives have made specific use of identity qualifiers when constructing narratives of violence that seek to elicit widespread condemnation of the Islamic Other. May ascribes what Karen Cerulo terms 'instrumental aims' to Iranian leader Mahmoud Ahmadinejad when describing him as inspired by religious "zeal", and when claiming the consequence of his "serious religious convictions" is the welcoming of death before defeat. Structuring the violent account in this way encourages audiences to think of the Iranian leader as perverse and egocentric, and by implication, his regime's motivations for violence as deviant, illegitimate and unwarranted in kind. This architecture of violence constructed by May also plays on two well-known conflict-related narratives that continue to pervade the US consciousness.

Neo-conservatives like May, who have long revealed themselves to the American and global public to be warmongers, are acutely aware of the integral role war narratives play in the American historical tradition. In this particular instance, May has constructed a violent account that takes advantage of specific cognitive associations ingrained in the American mindset. One of the pertinent narratives, which has gained huge traction in the US and the Western world at large, especially since 9/11, concerns the relatively insignificant value radical Islamist martyrs are perceived as attributing to human life. Not only are Islamic terrorists understood by many as prioritising heavenly or rather, placing what they consider to be God's plan, above their own material / worldly concerns, they are also typically viewed as subordinating the lives of non-believers (infidels) who are usually, but certainly not always, non-Muslim Westerners.

Despite many Islamic scholars contesting the theological soundness of these ideas, neo-conservatives and those closely associated with the movement routinely blame these radical Islamists for helping create a culture of death within the nations they live, and the institutions and groups they are part of. Neo-conservative darling and *New York University* academic Thane Rosenbaum, whose works have appeared in neo-conservative publications like *Commentary Magazine* and who has collaborated with leading neo-conservatives such as Bret Stephens, is among those to have offered a detail description of this quietus radical Islamist tradition in the context of the perceived Iranian threat.

Rosenbaum declared to his audience at *Congregation B'nai Tikvah* in New Jersey in 2015, that Islamic extremism, with its pre-occupation with the afterlife, has helped create a "culture of death". Rosenbaum claimed Western leaders responsible for designing and implementing the *Iran Nuclear Deal* have failed to properly recognise and understand this ghastly aspect of Islamic culture: "There is no compromise in the Muslim mindset. To come to terms is to lose". Iranians in particular "are not interested in debate and negotiation" claimed Rosenbaum, "the only submission acceptable to them would be to Allah or God".[15] It is worth noting that Rosenbaum is (in)famous in the US intellectual milieu for his anti-Palestinian rhetoric, which has included the dehumanising of the Islamic Palestinian Other with the aim of legitimating Israeli violence perpetrated against them. Following the *democratic* electing of Hamas in Gaza, Rosenbaum wrote in his Op-Ed for *The Wall Street Journal*:

> ...you forfeit your right to be called civilians when you freely elect members of a terrorist organization as statesmen, invite them to dinner with blood on their hands and allow them to set up shop in your living room as their base of operations. At that point you begin to look a lot more like conscripted soldiers than innocent civilians. And you have wittingly made yourself targets.[16]

Neo-conservative intellectual Jennifer Rubin at the *Washington Post* has also used her prominent position as an Op-Ed writer to offer detailed descriptions for her predominantly American readership about the Iranian expression of this longstanding radical Islamist culture of death. "Radical Islam is no fleeting fad but a relentless force", Rubin tells readers, "[t]hough at times stateless, Radical Islam is also supported by radicalized nations such as Iran…[it] makes up for its lack of conventional armies with unlimited zeal". Rubin declares that to fully grasp the mindset of these radical Islamists, we in the West must realise they are stuck in the past, mulling over tragedies that occurred hundreds of years ago. "[U]ntil we understand at least a modicum of what animates our enemies, we cannot defend ourselves and we cannot contain our enemies. Because radical jihadism is a culture of death and religious zealotry, containment doesn't work. Israel knows this. The entire Western world knows this".[17]

While Rubin clearly believes it is acceptable to criticise Iranians and other Muslims for not moving on from past atrocities, making similar insensitive remarks about the neo-conservative obsession with the Holocaust would no doubt fall beyond her arbitrary assessment about what is, and is not, acceptable speech within the public sphere. It is precisely this kind of hypocrisy pervading the neo-conservative and wider pro-Israeli movements that concerns many unattached intellectuals seeking to shine a light on injustice and speak truth to power. The only instances in which we do not hear neo-conservatives detailing how instrumental aims like religious convictions are corrupting particular Islamic and other groups and nations, is when these parties are engaging in conflicts aligning with their partisan interests. Exactly how many neo-conservatives have recently chosen to view and write about the *People's Mujahedin of Iran* (MEK) serves as a case in point.

Despite the MEK revealing itself to be an Islamic- *and* Marxist-inspired militant organisation, its dedication to overthrowing the Islamic Republic of Iran has meant its activities have been endorsed and supported by many neo-conservatives. The successful campaign for its reclassification (achieved when the US State Department removed the group from its designated terror list in 2012) from terrorist organisation to a legitimate, popular and democratic Iranian opposition group, with the ability to help transform the Islamic Republic into the kind of democracy neo-conservatives would be comfortable with, was supported by leading neo-conservative intellectuals like former CIA Director James Woolsey and National Security Advisor John Bolton, as well as by neo-conservative darling and Republican heavyweight Rudolph Giuliani. Despite experiencing no qualitative change in terms of ideology and behaviour, neo-conservatives came to view MEK as now having the ability "to play the critical role in derailing an Iranian bomb".[18] Editors at Rupert Murdoch's *New York Post*, a mainstream news media publication that is a key part of the neo-conservative echo chamber in New York City, even declared the MEK to "be far more deserving of a Nobel Peace Prize than a certain president of the United States we could mention" – they are obviously referring to Obama, who played an integral role in implementing the *Iran Nuclear Deal*.[19]

Returning to Clifford May's article 'Intellectual Leader' for the FDD, which has been reproduced by various other outfits within the expansive neo-conservative network such as David Pipes' *The Middle East Forum*, we also find clear evidence of May tapping into a second key narrative firmly ensconced within the American consciousness: the kamikaze myth. May draws on this when seeking to rouse support for a military strike against Iran. This myth assumed a prominent position in the American mindset following the devastating and daring attack by the Japanese on US forces at Pearl Harbor in 1941. Etched into the memories of many Americans as *the* most destructive attack by foreign forces on US soil until the 9/11 terrorist attacks in New York and Washington D.C., this event has been replayed and reconstructed many times over in the US by popular filmmakers, scriptwriters, playwrights and novelists.[20]

The extent to which this cataclysmic event continues to profoundly affect the American mindset, including the integral role it has played in providing a frame of reference for subsequent violent acts including the 9/11 terrorist attacks, has been reprised in great length by Emily Rosenberg in *A Date Which Will Live: Pearl Harbor in American Memory*. Rosenberg makes the important point that Pearl Harbor has experienced a memory boom in recent times due to a renewed interest in uncontextualised personal accounts provided by popular American personalities and writers like Tom Brokaw and Stephen Ambrose, in addition to the release of the 2001 Hollywood blockbuster *Pearl Harbor*. Nominated for four *Academy Awards* and winning one, the US$140 million budget movie is estimated to have grossed nearly 200 million dollars domestically, and an additional further $250 million worldwide (as of August 2019).[21] Within the pilot and aviation movie genre, *Pearl Harbor* remains the number one in terms of lifetime gross for theatre patronage, besting other popular films like *Top Gun*, *Black Hawk Down* and *The Aviator*.[22] In the romantic drama genre, it sits at number three for lifetime gross, behind only *Titanic* and *Ghost*.[23] This provides a clear indication of just how popular this movie has been with American audiences.

The standard narrative about the Pearl Harbor attacks is well-known and goes like this: Japanese pilots engaged in combat with US forces inspired by the idea they would welcome death in the event they could successfully strike against the American enemy or to avoid capture by American forces. The Japanese pilots considered their deaths a small price to pay in their desire to inflict as much damage as possible on their foe. First Lieutenant Fusata Iida is widely reported to have told his fellow Japanese airmen before setting off on this suicidal mission, "in case of trouble I will fly straight to my objective and make a crash dive into an enemy target rather than make an emergency landing".[24] Whilst The kamikaze myth has been popularised by the Japanese war effort, however many people remain unaware that the myth has its roots in the 13th century. More specifically, during the time of Kublai Khan, who was the great Mongol conqueror and grandson of Genghis Khan.

Khan had amassed a sizeable navy with the intention of annexing Japan. As the end of the conflict appeared imminent, a gigantic typhoon unexpectedly emerged destroying Khan's 900-strong fleet. This cataclysmic storm was named Kamikaze, meaning 'divine wind,' because its unexpectedness led many to believe it had been heaven-sent. This spiritual / otherworldly connation stuck with the term and associated wartime narratives. In more recent times however, the kamikaze myth has been used to refer to any kind of violent perpetrator whose unshakeable belief about the moral correctness of their murderous mission as well as their favourable position in the afterlife, encourages their embracing of the suicidal-nature of their attack against their enemies. This idea has proven incomprehensible for many Western audiences, particularly Americans, due in part to their relative attachment to the hedonistic pleasures of *this* world – a general condition reprised in great length by Strauss, and which helped inspire the conception of the neo-conservative movement.

The Campaign Beyond Washington & New York: Jacoby in Boston

There are many other instances where neo-conservatives, and those with intimate ties to the movement, have deployed the spirit of Munich metaphorical expression when seeking to convince US policy- and decision-makers and the politic about the existential threat Iran poses both to Israel, and by association, US interests abroad. It has often proven the case that these representations are intimately bound to the other major issue preoccupying neo-conservatives, the ongoing Israeli-Palestinian conflict. Here it is worth abstracting some of Jeff Jacoby's work for the *Boston Globe*.

Jacoby proves an interesting test case because he has largely escaped the attention of those writing about the neo-conservative movement. His position beyond the spotlight focused on the neo-conservative echo-chamber located in the Washington D.C. and New York areas certainly appears to have contributed to his relative anonymity amongst critics of the movement. There are benefits associated with expanding our attention beyond intellectuals operating in these two metropolises. Chief among these is the ability to gain an appreciation of the reach the neo-conservative movement has within the US, which has obvious implications both for the public-opinion making and the policy and decision-making processes. Having the ability to reach more of the US politic as well as law and policy makers throughout the nation is hugely beneficial for a neo-conservative movement seeking to impose both its ontological understanding of the social world, as well as its ideas about specific issues and events occurring within it, like the perceived threat posed by Iran.

The outcome of the 2016 US Presidential election highlighted some of the major issues associated with focusing on the hubs of intellectual and political activity in the Washington D.C. and New York areas, and neglecting the happenings throughout the rest of the nation. Granted Boston is not Boise, Montgomery, Raleigh, Salt Lake City or a city or town considered by some of the liberal elite to be largely populated by 'the Deplorables' (a phrase coined by Hilary Clinton when describing Trump's supporters in traditionally Republican areas), however it is an auxiliary location of intellectual activity that provides for a more complete picture of the reach of the neo-conservative network and the neo-conservative-inspired anti-Iranian campaign.[25]

Jacoby's demonstrated foreign policy beliefs and religious ideas, and his parroting and endorsing of the viewpoints of prominent neo-conservative intellectuals, suggests he should at the *very least* be characterised as existing on the fringes of the movement.[26] Jacoby's long list of pro-neo-conservative actions include his public championing of leading neo-conservative Daniel Pipes' bid for a position on the board of directors at the *United States Institute of Peace* - an institute created by US Congress to promote international peace and help resolve global conflicts in a non-violent way. Pipes is well-known for his extreme anti-Islam rhetoric and warmongering; not attributes one would normally associate with peacemaking.[27]

Similar to neo-conservatives, Jacoby is unwavering in his support for Israel. He believes Israel has a theological right to Palestinian land, and despite clear evidence to the contrary, dismisses Israel's Occupation as playing any kind of role in inspiring modern Islamic terrorism. We need only refer to Bin Laden's infamous *Letter to the American People* in order to gain a basic grasp of how Israel's brutalising of the Palestinian people inspired his, and his group's (al-Qaeda) virulent anti-Americanism.[28] This is to say nothing about the formative role the Occupation has also played in inspiring pro-Palestinian movements and groups such as Hamas, Fatah, Hezbollah, Palestinian Liberation Organization and Palestinian Islamic Jihad, all of whom have at times resorted to violence. Each organisation's founding charter explicitly states that Palestinian self-determination was *the* primary goal motivating their conception.[29] Nevertheless, it is Jacoby's ideas about Iran, which he shares with Bostonian readers as well as online visitors to his blog *Pundicity*, that are of primary concern here.

Jacoby characterises Iran as a radical Islamist state that, along with Bin Laden's ideas and networks, is chiefly responsible for inspiring "some of the world's worst conflicts". Like many other neo-conservatives, Jacoby treats prominent liberal intellectual Bernard Lewis, in addition to leading neo-conservative Daniel Pipes, as an authority on both the volatile political situation in the Middle East and the Islamic faith. In his writings about Iran, Jacoby expands the dialogic spaces to the extent that he seriously engages with Lewis' and Pipes' opinions, representing them both as experts on the Iranian situation and Middle Eastern politics. At the same time he keeps the dialogical space closed enough that contrasting views offered by intellectuals not aligned in some way with neoconservatism are ignored. Jacoby conveniently decides against describing both Lewis' and Pipes' long history of advocating for war against Islamic regimes, as well as their relations with the modern neo-conservative movement.

In his article, 'The Smell of Irresolution', which appears in both the *Boston Globe* and the *Jewish World Review*, Jacob is extremely critical of the US' decision to withdraw its forces from Iraq, claiming this manoeuvring has sent the clear message to US enemies in the Middle East that it has become fair-weathered in terms of its commitment to eliminating the global Islamist threat. Jacoby blames this specific failure of US foreign policy for Iran's increasingly bold behaviour in the international arena, which he claims has recently culminated in Iran's daring capture of Western Coalition forces during the Iraq war and subsequent ransom demands that the US must fully retreat from the region. "This is how totalitarian aggressors react to faintheartedness", laments Jacoby, who, in adopting an objectivist viewpoint of the social world that is characteristic of the neo-conservative *Weltanschauung*, expresses his bemusement as to why "so many people still refuse to absorb this fundamental fact of life".

Jacoby also writes:

> The barbarians pocket their gains and go on killing...Bernard Lewis, the renowned scholar of Islam and the Middle East, was recently quoted as saying that too many political leaders today exemplify "the spirit of Munich - a refusal to acknowledge the danger we face and a belief that through accommodation we can avoid conflict." He added, sadly: "I look around and I see more

Chamberlains than Churchills."... The enemy hasn't changed...Nor have the stakes in this war, nor the courage and commitment of the American troops fighting it. What has changed is control of Congress, and the air is heavy with the smell of irresolution.

Jacoby's message is clear: the spirit of Munich has taken hold of US policymakers, mesmerising them into implementing foreign policy measures that have encouraged radical Islamist forces like Iran to freely pursue their geopolitical interests. Not only is this not in the best interests of the US as the world's sole superpower, Jacoby also maintains that falling under this spell has threatened the security interests of Israel. According to Jacoby, Israel's leaders have at times been similarly afflicted by this spiritual malaise, which he claims was clear for all to see when Israeli forces previously "abandoned Gaza to the Palestinians" allowing them to turn it "into a launching pad for increased terror". That Israel's withdrawal from the Palestinian Territories, thereby allowing its people to make some kind of progress toward achieving self-determination, will result in the region becoming a haven for terrorists is a common trope employed by many neo-conservatives and pro-Israeli intellectuals. Frank Gaffney and Caroline Glick are among those to have commonly employed this technique, and have in fact devised the term 'Palestan' to describe this kind of independent Palestinian state.[30]

It is also worth drawing attention to just how easily Jacob goes about dehumanising the Iranian Other. This is explicit in his claims that US reticence to remain militarily engaged in the Middle East has allowed the Iranian "barbarians [to] pocket their gains and go on killing". This gives readers the impression that violence is an inherent part of the Iranian Muslim's being. In characterising the Iranian enemy as "barbarians" with a thirst to kill, they are stripped of the feelings and reasoning abilities 'we' humans enjoy. Jacoby is supporting the general neo-conservative motif that Iranian leaders *only* understand and respond to intimidation and violence. The repeating of this message by neo-conservatives helps to make any future attack against Iran more palatable, as the collateral damage will only be the deaths of unfeeling sub-humans rather than people like 'us'.

This Jeff Jacoby abstraction serves a number of useful purposes. In addition to shedding light on how the spirit of Munich metaphorical expression has been used in the current campaign against Iran, it also helps demonstrate the geographical reach of the neo-conservative movement, thereby putting paid to the idea that it only targets the US public and policy and decision-makers living in and around the New York City and Washington D.C. areas. This abstraction also helps to reveal the extent to which neo-conservative anti-Iranian efforts are intimately associated with their ongoing anti-Palestinian campaign.

Holocaust 2.0

Frank Gaffney has been a leading anti-Islamic voice within the US political and intellectual scenes since the neo-conservative movement firmly fixed its attention on the perceived threat posed by radical Islam following the US' defeat of Soviet-led communism. Gaffney cut his teeth working for Senator Henry 'Scoop' Jackson, before going on to work at the Pentagon under the direction of Richard Perle during Ronald Reagan's Presidency. Since then, Gaffney has been involved with a litany of neo-conservative and pro-Israeli outfits including the *Project for the New American Century*, *Ariel Center for Policy Research*, *Committee on the Present Danger* and *Benador Associates*. This is in addition to regularly writing Op-Ed pieces for numerous US mainstream news media organisations including *The Washington Times* and *The Wall Street Journal*, as well as for specialised neo-conservative media outfits like the *National Review*. Gaffney's frequent claims about criminal conspiracies, like his suggesting Saddam Hussein orchestrated the Oklahoma City bombing, and his accusing New Jersey Governor Chris Christie of treason for appointing a Muslim-American to his state's judiciary, have only further endeared him to his neo-conservative colleagues and members of Israel's Likud Party.[31]

Gaffney also founded, and is President of, the think tank *Centre for Security Policy* (CSP), which is located in Washington D.C.. His activities at CSP include publishing 'research' like foreign policy and national security briefs aimed at influencing those on Capitol Hill. Gaffney has been somewhat successful in this endeavour, which is perhaps best illustrated by Trump citing CSP's research findings as supporting evidence for his travel ban on individuals from select Islamic nations from entering the US.[32] Since its founding 1988, Gaffney's CSP has also provided a media platform for a host of right-wing militarists, white nationalists, pro-Israeli movement intellectuals, neo-conservatives, prominent members from Judeo-Christian religious organisations and Republicans, to express their views. White nationalists and Jewish intellectuals are not typically regarded as natural bedfellows, which is precisely why Gaffney constructs, or rather limits, his exchanges with the former in such a way that they only speak about issues both them and the pro-Israeli Jewish intellectuals that Gaffney has an affinity with, have in common. These topics include a shared disdain for Islam, and more specifically, their special hatred for radical Islam.

As mentioned earlier, Gaffney also hosts his own podcast and local Washington radio program *Secure Freedom Radio*, where he invites guests to discuss the latest perceived threats to US and Israeli security. Reflecting the general neo-conservative concern to remain engaged with a US politic that is increasingly using new media to get their information, Gaffney has made a podcast of his radio show available on popular sites like *iTunes* and *Stitcher*. This means consumers are able to download Gaffney's anti-Islamic rants as well as insights provided by the occasional white nationalist, whilst also perusing popular audiobooks like the *Life of Pi* and *Harry Potter*. Notable participants on Gaffney's program have included Newt Gingrich, John Bolton and Jared Taylor. Taylor was an especially interesting choice given his known associations with the white nationalist movement and Gaffney's staunch pro-Israeli posture – again this union only makes sense in the context of their shared contempt for all things Islamic, as well their supporting for the Republican Trump administration.

Pertinent to this study is how Gaffney and his guests have regularly employed the neologism 'Holocaust 2.0' in the context of the threat a nuclear-equipped Iran poses to Israel. This phrase does lend itself to slightly different interpretations. The most obvious is understanding it as a combination of the term 'Holocaust' with the appellation '2.0'. 'Holocaust' is typically defined as the destruction or slaughter on a mass scale, especially caused by fire or nuclear war. It has its origins in the Old French term *holocaust*, and in the Greek term *holokauston*, which is an amalgamation of *holos* 'whole' and *kaustos* 'burnt'. Since the middle of the twentieth century, the term Holocaust has taken on a narrower understanding, typically referring to the mass murdering of approximately six million European Jews by the German Nazi regime from 1941-1945. Despite arguments from a range of international political commentators, intellectuals and historians to expand the use of the term to also include other mass-killings like those in Armenia in the early twentieth century, 'Holocaust' has largely retained its Nazi Germany and Jewish character.[33] This is perhaps best reflected in how popular English language dictionaries continue to define the term.

The appellation '2.0' is derived from the phrase 'Web 2.0', which was first used by Darcy DiNucci in her 1999 article 'Fragmented Future', and later popularised by Tim O'Reilly.[34] O'Reilly used the term to describe the post-dotcom bubble World Wide Web with its emphasis on cloud computing, social networking and user-generated content.[35] 'Web 2.0' broke out of the information technology (I.T.) realm and gained widespread attention when *Time Magazine* named it *2006 Person of the Year*. The term has since been taken up by those working in other fields, and is now commonly understood as something that is second edition, corrected or improved on. The term's popularity has waned in recent times within the I.T. domain as the features of Web 2.0 have become increasingly common. The 2.0 appellation has however remained in vogue amongst Gaffney and his *confrères*.

From the vantage point of neo-conservative intellectuals like Gaffney, 'Holocaust 2.0' refers to the expanding of the systematic method the Nazi Germany regime designed and implemented in its mass murdering of European Jewry, so that the new approach better meets the rigours associated with contemporary operating conditions. In the current global climate, nuclear weaponry is widely considered the most lethal and effective way of committing mass murder. Once nuclear capability is developed or acquired by a regime or group, it requires relatively little manpower to use, particularly when contrasted with the human effort involved in the deploying of military forces. This task become especially arduous when sending military forces to far flung foreign lands, as is the case with both US and Israel vis-à-vis Iran.

Gaffney has done his part in helping inject the Holocaust 2.0 neologism into the debate about US foreign policy in relation to Iran. 'Holocaust 2.0' is actually the title of his 2014 article published by the CSP, in which he writes:

> Israel's top military intelligence officer put friends of the Jewish State, as well as Israelis, on notice this week: Preparations are far advanced for what some hope will be a second Holocaust. Major General Aviv Korchavi warned that Israel is now "surrounded 360 degrees with active enemies"...there's the Syrian incubator for jihadists, incessant cyber-attacks and the now-unchecked nuclear threat emerging from Iran...Under these circumstances, it's simply outrageous that Team Obama is trying to force Israel to become still more vulnerable by surrendering territory vital to our ally's survival. We must stand with Israel, not encourage its destruction.[36]

The territory Gaffney is referring to includes what neoconservatives commonly term Judea and Samaria, and what many others, especially those who do not interpret the Christian and Hebrew Bibles as expressing literal truths, call the Israeli-occupied West Bank.[37] The "Team Obama" plan refers to the multilateral negotiations aimed at giving Palestinians the right to self-determination; a decolonisation initiative only becoming more important as living conditions in Gaza and the West Bank deteriorate.[38] Again we see another neo-conservative representing the Israeli-Palestinian conflict, more specifically the terrorist threat Palestinians pose to the Israeli state, as intimately bound to the perceived threat Iran poses to Israel.

Gaffney also employs the neologism 'Holocaust 2.0' during his *Secure Freedom Radio* program. In one particular episode, Gaffney invites Mark Helprin - whom he calls "the greatest mind in the security policy business", to discuss Former Arkansas Governor (1996-2007), Republican heavyweight and popular Evangelical Christian Minister, Mike Huckabee's assessment of the Iranian-Israel situation as "a Holocaust 2.0 in the making". Helprin shares both Gaffney and Huckabee's concern, telling listeners Iran's developing of nuclear technology must be thwarted so that Israel can maintain the upper hand in the likely event of a war between the two nations:

> If the Iranians, as they will, get nuclear weapons, that will neutralize Israel's nuclear deterrent so in a conventional war Israel will have nothing to fall back on as it did in '73 [in its conflict with Egypt] when the only thing that saved it were its nukes…So I think that it is more than likely than in the future if the United States does not change its policies and back Israel instead of Iran…in that case, either by conventional war or one lucky shot with an Iranian nuke, Israel will be destroyed and that will be a **new Holocaust…if anyone thinks that it is not going to be a Holocaust they are wrong. Huckabee was right…it is shameful that people attack him for saying the truth** including the Jewish organisations…not just J-street but the more centrist Jewish organisations. It is **equivalent to when Hitler came to power** and if someone warned about the future for the Jews in Europe, of that person being attacked in the 30s by others Jews, it is just crazy [Emphases added].[39]

After praising Helprin for his valuable contributions to the national security debate via popular mediums like the Op-Ed section in the *The Wall Street Journal*, Gaffney questions Helprin about the possibility of Israel finding strange bedfellows amongst their enemies in the region "who have a shared enmity of Iran and are presumably also on its target list". Gaffney asks: "Is there in your judgement a possibility that Israel may yet stave off the **Holocaust 2.0**, if you would call it that, by the *modus vivendi* at the minimum that might enable them to deal with this Iranian threat with help from unlikely quarters like the Saudis [Emphasis added]? Helprin's response: "Absolutely".

Before abstracting the highlighted text for closer analysis, it is worth recalling the key SFL idea about authors *choosing* to expand the dialogic space so as to include and expose readers to specific voices and viewpoints. This SFL method of inquiry encourages us to ask: What is the communicator trying to achieve? What linguistic devices are they deploying from their toolbox of rhetorical techniques? And on what basis are they making these choices?[40] Remembering it is the notion of *choice* that is at the heart of the SFL tradition, as A.K. Halliday points out: "Text is meaning and meaning is choice, an ongoing current of selections each in its paradigmatic environment of what *might have* been meant (but was not)".[41]

In his discussion with Helprin, Gaffney chooses to expand the dialogical space to the extent it includes previous utterances that contribute to the *appearance* of a consensus with regards to the neo-conservative view; that a nuclear-Iran unquestionably poses an existential threat to Israel. Here it is worth referring to another part of the exchange between Gaffney and Helprin:

> Gaffney: "I am anxious to get your strategic vision of what Obama has wrought with this deal with Iran. There is much controversy at the moment as to whether parallels being drawn by some like Governor Mike Huckabee to a **Holocaust, well, 2.0** I guess in the making, are overblown or inappropriate? What are your thoughts on first the deal and second that possible parallel?
>
> Helprin: Well it is one and the same thing because **I think that he is absolutely right**.
>
> Gaffney: He meaning Barak Obama?
>
> Helprin: No, no, no, Huckabee (laughs)
>
> Gaffney: (laughs) just checking
>
> Helprin: I mean Huckabee is not my candidate of choice but...I think he is correct and **I am astounded that so many people are offended at his rhetoric, which is merely the truth**...
> [Emphases added]

Huckabee is an avowed Christian Evangelical (in)famous for declaring all Americans should become God-fearing people. According to his peculiar logic, a healthy fear of God is a prerequisite for non-Americans learning to fear America: "I never want this country to get to the place where people do not fear the United States of America. But I don't want to get to the place where this country does not fear God because if we don't fear God, nobody will fear us".[42] Huckabee subscribes to the particular kind of US Exceptionalism that traces its origins all the way back to the Pilgrims arriving from Europe under the directive of divine providence: "God help us all when we cannot understand that a nation that has turned its back on our Founder—and I'm not talking about George Washington, I'm talking about the fact that this nation would not exist apart from the intervention and providence of a Holy God".[43]

Gaffney's choosing to engage with Huckabee's viewpoint in a meaningful and respectful way during his discussions with Helprin gives his audience the impression the Christian Evangelical Minister and former Republican Presidential aspirant (he contested both the 2008 and 2016 Republican primaries) is some kind of authority on the issue. Gaffney's choosing to engage with Huckabee also helps to provide the appearance of a consensus with regards to how best to deal with Iran; an unanimity that transcends US intellectual, political and religious movements and traditions. On closer inspection, we find that Gaffney is utilising a linguistic technique popular amongst neo-conservatives that is also geared towards embracing / solidifying their political relationship with the US Christian Zionist community.

As we learnt earlier, neo-conservatives enjoy a very important and delicate relationship with American Evangelical Christians under the banner of the Republican Party. There always exists that potential for the fracturing of this relationship, given their fundamental disagreements about important biblical narratives like those pertaining to the End Times and the role Jesus Christ plays as Saviour. However, concerted efforts by leading neo-conservatives like Gaffney to include and promote the viewpoints of such popular figures within Christian America like Huckabee, help to solidify this relationship by demonstrating that neo-conservatives value their contributions. That needing to feel valued and respected is important for many political actors operating in a political game where egos are often big and fragile.

Helprin, who has proven himself to be a darling of the neo-conservative movement because of his strong pro-Israeli beliefs and his demonstrated willingness to use his prominent standing within the literary and intellectual communities to promote these, is added to this community of shared belief through both his explicit supporting of Huckabee's viewpoint and his characterising Iran's intentions as wanting to perpetrate a Holocaust 2.0.[44] When considering the important notion of choice, it matters that Helprin proclaims their shared proposition to be valid, well-founded and 'truthful': "I think he is absolutely right", "I am astounded that so many people are offended at his rhetoric, which is merely the truth" and "if anyone thinks that it is not going to be a Holocaust they are wrong.

Huckabee was right...it is shameful that people attack him for saying the truth".

When considering the kind of influence this commentary has on the audience, it soon becomes apparent this exchange is not about engaging with different viewpoints in any kind of meaningful way. Instead the aim is to portray their shared interpretation as fact and provide the illusion of uniformity across the intellectual and political spectrum. This is precisely the same approach the vast network of neo-conservative outfits deployed when they went about manufacturing consent for the US-led invasion of Iraq, which as we now know, was an intellectual and political exercise that remains unparalleled in the modern Western liberal democratic world in terms of duplicity.

The accusation that Iran aims to be equally, if not infinitely more, murderous than the Nazi Regime in its desire to perpetrate a new Holocaust, has also been a cornerstone of Bret Stephens' political commentary. Stephens, in his article 'Worse Than Munich', urges readers to appreciate both the existential threat a nuclear-Iran would pose to Israel, and recognise the flawed logic informing Western leaders' multilateral peace negotiations with Iran.[45] Stephens maintains the *Joint Comprehensive Plan of Action* brokered by the Obama administration is substantially worse than the Munich Betrayal, which ultimately paved the way for the Holocaust: "the interim nuclear agreement...has many of the flaws of Munich and Paris. But it has none of their redeeming or exculpating aspects...The U.S. and its allies have given Iran more time to stockpile uranium and develop its nuclear infrastructure".

Stephens also identifies what he perceives to be clear similarities between Hitler and Iranian President Hasan Rouhani:

What they [the Munich Agreement and the Iranian Deal] have in common is that each deal was a betrayal of small countries— Czechoslovakia, South Vietnam, Israel—that had relied on Western security guarantees. Each was a victory for the dictatorships: "No matter the world wants it or not", Iranian President Hasan Rouhani said Sunday, "this path will, God willingly, continue to the peak that has been considered by the martyred nuclear scientists." Each deal increased the contempt of the dictatorships for the democracies: "If ever that silly old man comes interfering here again with his umbrella," Hitler is reported to have said of Chamberlain after Munich, "I'll kick him downstairs and jump on his stomach".

Stephens is here inviting readers of *The Wall Street Journal* article to view Rouhani as existing on the same moral and ethical plane as Hitler, and as equally if not more murderous in his intent. The kicker is that the Rouhani quote abstracted by Stephens represents Rouhani's, and by implication his nation's, desire to acquire nuclear weapons as primarily driven by instrumental aims, specifically religious convictions. In juxtaposing these instrumental aims with Hitler's *relative* benign threat of violence: "I'll kick him downstairs and jump on his stomach", we begin to see how Stephens strategically positions Rouhani as far more homicidal in his intent than Hitler. Hitler was responsible for orchestrating the murdering of six million Jews; Stephens is suggesting Rouhani will do far more damage if allowed to.

Stephens' article, which gained traction with mainstream US news media like *MSNBC* and with many groups part of the US Jewish-Christian alliance like the *Unity Coalition for Israel*, also helps reveal another key element of the neo-conservative rhetorical campaign against Iran: exposing the public to the idea Israel will strike against Iran in the absence of decisive action by the US administration.[46] Stephens writes:

> As for Israel, it cannot afford to live in a neighborhood where Iran becomes nuclear, Assad remains in power, and Hezbollah—Israel's most immediate military threat—gains strength, clout and battlefield experience. The chances that Israel will hazard a strike on Iran's nuclear sites greatly increased since Geneva. More so the chances of another war with Hezbollah.

Stephens and his neo-conservative colleagues are sensitive to the reality that Israeli military aggression has routinely drawn widespread condemnation. The Israel Defence Forces' heavy-handed responses to impoverished Palestinian children throwing stones, and its frequent use of lethal force against Palestinians protesting their dire economic situation and the constructing of new Israeli settlements, are typically understood by the global politic, aid agencies, and leading international intellectual and political figures, to be excessive and beyond the bounds of what is morally and ethically acceptable.

The US public and the wider intellectual and political communities for the most part rightly acknowledge Israel's right to defend itself. However, disproportionate numbers of 'enemy' casualties, and inflammatory and revengeful public statements made by leading Israeli military and key Israeli religious and political figures, often prove public relations nightmares for neo-conservatives and other pro-Israeli supporters, who then task themselves with rationalising these violent responses for their predominantly American readership. This is an especially important task in image management in the US context given the government provides Israel with billions of dollars in 'aid' each year, a large chunk of which it uses to improve its military capability.[47]

Neo-conservative Dov Zakheim, who has held numerous Department of Defense and Foreign Policy positions in both the Reagan and George W. Bush Republican administrations, and has worked as a scholar at institutions like the National War College, Columbia University and Yeshiva University, has emphasised just how crucial this US funding is to Israel. The "Offshore Procurement (OSP) program" wrote Zakheim in 2016, "currently totals $815 million, more than twice what the United States spends on any other country, bar Egypt". In addition to providing Israel the ability to invest in its own military capability, Zakheim claims the OSP "has enabled Israel to become a major international arms supplier, at times even competing with American firms for third-country contracts".[48] It is also worth noting that Zakheim has helped lead the campaign for US 'aid' to be divided between military projects *and* helping fund new Israeli settlements in the West Bank.[49]

The task of justifying Israel military action would certainly pose neo-conservatives and pro-Israeli movement intellectuals serious challenges should Israel's leaders unilaterally decide to launch a daring military attack far beyond its borders in Iran. The great distance between Israel and Iran means any attack by air would require the violating of both Jordanian and Iraqi airspace (assuming the direct route), meaning both nations would be well within their rights to shoot down any foreign fighter jets. Bret Stephens understands this, which is part of the reason why he seeks to provide the illusion that Iran and Israel exist in close proximity.

He achieves this by deploying the metaphorical expression describing both nations as 'living in the same neighbourhood'.

Whilst US public opinion regarding a potential Israeli strike against Iran is of primary concern to neo-conservatives, they are also worried about European opinion, which has proven increasingly hostile to Israel. Neo-conservatives acknowledge the integral role Europe's economic and diplomatic relations with Israel plays in the latter's ability to remain prosperous and globally-connected. The last thing neo-conservatives want is for Israel to acquire the kind of pariah status similar to Apartheid South Africa. This is precisely why campaigns aimed at boycotting Israeli goods as part of the global Boycott, Divestment and Sanctions (BDS) campaign, and international initiatives like the Academic Boycott of Israel (ABI), have infuriated neo-conservatives to no end.[50]

Neo-conservatives are concerned an Israeli attack against sovereign Iran that does not at the most have Europe's blessing, or at the least is met with muted indifference, could help increase the popularity of the BDS, ABI and similar campaigns. Unfortunately for neo-conservatives, they do not possess anywhere near the kind of clout in Europe as they do in the US. The only real influence the movement exerts is through the global appeal of its websites and online US newspapers where its intellectuals frequently publish Op-Ed articles (*The Wall Street Journal* for example has a European arm), via its many social media accounts and also guest appearances like John Bolton's speaking at Oxford Union, which we studied in some detail earlier.

A Network Mobilised

In taking stock of the different aspects of the neo-conservative rhetorical campaign aimed at convincing policy and decision-makers that a nuclear Iran would seek to enact a Holocaust 2.0 against the Jewish people in Israel, it is important to recognise the significant role played by the vast network of well-resourced and well-funded neo-conservative think tanks and organisations. While Stephens and his colleagues writing in mainstream US news media publications have mainly targeted the general public, the network of think tanks focuses its attention on policy- and decision-makers on Capitol Hill. The *American Enterprise Institute* (AEI) and *Gatestone Institute* (GI) are two of the outfits that have led the charge in convincing US politicians through lobbying, policy briefs, conferences and seminars, that Iranian leaders are inherently evil and deeply anti-Semitic, and must therefore be attacked before they are able to develop nuclear weapons. Both AEI and GI also provide platforms to many intellectuals closely associated with the movement, allowing them to also spout their anti-Iranian rhetoric. Jonah Goldberg and Alan Dershowitz are two such intellectuals who have been utilised in this way.

The AEI claims its purpose is to build a "more prosperous, safer and more democratic nation and world".[51] It enjoys a long and storied history with the neo-conservative movement, having provided a temporary home to a host of its intellectuals including John Bolton, Paul Wolfowitz and Richard Perle, while they eagerly awaited their next official political appointments within a governing Republican administration. The opinions of those working at AEI have proven to carry significant weight with the upper echelons of the US political class, particularly amongst Republican movers and shakers, meaning their viewpoints certainly possess the ability to shape the US foreign policy-making process. During a speech at a dinner celebrating neo-conservative godfather Irving Kristol in 2003, President George W. Bush praised the work of AEI for having "some of the finest minds in our nation". Bush also told his audience, "[y]ou do such good work that my administration has borrowed twenty such minds".[52]

Jonah Goldberg is among the intellectuals working at the AEI to have spearheaded the modern anti-Iranian campaign. To help understand the nature of his contribution, it is worth here abstracting his work 'Huckabee's Hitler comparison that wasn't', in which he tells readers the advice of eloquent and serious thinkers like Israeli PM Benjamin Netanyahu must be heeded by Americans and the wider Western world in order to effectively eliminate the Iranian threat. "In countless speeches", writes Goldberg, "Bibi Netanyahu and other Israeli leaders have stressed that the legacy of the Holocaust is such that Israel cannot take a chance on Iran having a nuclear weapon". Goldberg claims engaging Iran in multilateral diplomatic negotiations, such as those initiated by the Obama administration, is tantamount to committing the same mistakes that paved the way for the first Holocaust.

After strategically positioning right-wing Israeli PM Netanyahu as an expert on this issue, Goldberg engages with his views to support his own assessment of the situation:

> In his address to [US] Congress... Netanyahu movingly singled out Holocaust survivor and Nobel Prize–winner Elie Wiesel..."I wish I could promise you, Elie, that the lessons of history have been learned. I can only urge the leaders of the world not to repeat the mistakes of the past." What mistakes? Precisely the mistakes...Obama is making. It's the same argument...listen to the Iranians...Iranian civil, military, and religious leaders have for years **vowed** to "wipe Israel off the map," deliver a new Holocaust (while denying the first one happened), etc [Emphasis added].[53]

Especially revealing here is Goldberg's use of the term "vowed" when he describes the Iranian commitment to "wipe Israel off the map". 'Vow' means a 'solemn promise', and the term comes from the Latin *votum* meaning 'a promise to a god, solemn pledge, dedication; that which is promised; a wish, desire, longing, prayer'. *Votum* has roots in the Greek term *eukhe*, understood as the 'solemn engagement to devote oneself to a religious order or life'. This brief etymological foray helps in uncovering the strong religious connotations associated with the term; something that the highly intelligent and crafty Goldberg would no doubt be aware of.

In *choosing* to describe Iran's commitment to destroy Israel in this particular way, Goldberg has represented Iranian enemy leaders as motivated by instrumental aims. Karen Cerulo's research helps to demonstrate how audiences typically view these kinds of motivations for violence as deviant, unwarranted and illegitimate. Not only does Goldberg's cognitive structuring of this violent account feed into the wider neo-conservative narrative framing Israel's potential conflict with Iran as part of the ongoing Global War on Terror, this construction encourages audiences to identify with the intended victim of the violence - Israel. At the same time this technique conveniently ignores the viewpoint that Iranian animosity toward Israel *could* be motivated by a range of non-religious factors such as its support for the Palestinian plight for self-determination. Again, as has proven to be indicative of the typical neo-conservative approach when discussing the Israeli-Palestinian situation, the dialogic space has not been constructed in such way that it includes,

and engages with in any serious way, ideas pertaining to the ongoing
Palestinian struggle for their own state.

Shifting our attention from the AEI in Washington D.C. to
GI in New York, we find similar representations offered by the Nina
Rosenwald-founded organisation. Rosenwald has been revealed as a major
financial contributor of neo-conservative and Israel lobby organisations,
using some of the fortune she inherited as heiress of the Sears Roebuck
empire to help (re)recreate the social world in ways that many find deeply
troubling. Major studies into the nature and funding of the anti-Islamic
network conducted by *The Council on American-Islamic Relations* and
Center for American Progress (their reports titled *Hijacked by Hate* and
Fear Inc. respectively) have revealed Rosenwald's extensive financial and
professional links with a range of pro-Israeli and neo-conservative outfits,
including the *Washington Institute for Near East Policy*, *American Israel
Public Affairs Committee*, *Hudson Institute*, *Jewish Institute for National
Security Affairs* and Daniel Pipes' *The Middle East Forum*.[54]

Among the more controversial of Rosenwald's political activities
include her organising of numerous functions in the US for well-known
anti-Islam Dutch MP Geert Wilders. For non-European readers not aware
of Wilders' political behaviour, his long list of inflammatory rhetoric and
objectionable claims includes comparing the *Koran* to *Mein Kempf* and
maintaining "Israel is the West's first line of defence" against radical
Islam:

> If Jerusalem falls into the hands of the Muslims, Athens and
> Rome will be next. Thus, Jerusalem is the main front protecting
> the West. It is...an ideological battle, between the mentality of
> the liberated West and the ideology of Islamic barbarism. There
> has been an independent Palestinian state since 1946, and it is
> the kingdom of Jordan.[55]

Rosenwald's associations with these various outfits speaks to the
inter-connected nature of the neo-conservative and the US-based pro-
Israeli movement, whilst her promoting of Wilders as a legitimate political
authority whose ideas are worth endorsing, especially those about Islam
and the Israel-Palestinian conflict, speaks to kind of political actor she has
revealed herself to be. It easy to understand why free-floating intellectual

and close observer of the neo-conservative movement Max Blumenthal has described Rosenwald as "the sugar mama of anti-Muslim hate".[56]

Before looking at the leading role intellectuals working for the GI have played in the anti-Iranian campaign, it is worth having a basic understanding of the Institute's long list of deceptive political activities. These include a propaganda campaign that claimed the influx of radical Muslims into Europe had resulted in the establishing of "no-go zones" that are "off limits to non - Muslims". The Institute's reports about these "miscrostates governed by Islamic Sharia law" flourishing throughout Europe were picked up and circulated by many outfits in the neo-conservative echo chamber, including by *FrontPageMag* and *The Washington Times*. The idea of no-go zones actually originated with Daniel Pipes - the neo-conservative Jeff Jacoby considered the best candidate for a position with the *United States Institute of Peace*.[57] Pipes' 'study' would later be exposed as yet another act in neo-conservative chicanery, and many mainstream news organisations, including the hugely popular *Fox News* network, would later apologise for publicising these false claims.[58]

Gatestone's contribution to the anti-Iranian campaign has included publishing the work of Alan Dershowitz. Relevant here is his article 'Why deterrence won't work against Iran', in which he claims policies of deterrence and containment employed by Israel and the US when dealing with Iran will undoubtedly result in another Holocaust:

> What if deterrence and containment didn't work, and Iran were to fire nuclear rockets at Israeli cities? Those who now advocate robust deterrence—instead of surgical prevention—would simply say to the remaining Israelis: "Woops. We were wrong. Sorry. We'll build you a new Holocaust Museum (sic).[59]

The metaphorical expression "surgical prevention" is worth abstracting, given the role it plays in dehumanising the Iranian Other. In describing an attack against Iran in this way, Dershowitz is portraying the Iranian commitment to developing nuclear technology as a disease needing to be cut out from the Iranian body. It gives readers the impression any future attack against Iran will be 'clean' and 'precise'. In light of the relatively recent 'messy' and 'imprecise' strikes against Saddam Hussein's regime in Iraq, where sickening images of the 'collateral damage' were broadcasted throughout the world for all to see, Dershowitz clearly understands the implications associated with advocating a similar attack against another Islamic nation so soon. Dershowitz is seeking to allay fears about a similar result occurring this time around.

Continuing our sense-making journey from the *Gatestone Institute* back to Washington D.C., where the *Foundation for the Defense of Democracies* (FDD) is based, we find its intellectuals like those at United Against Nuclear Iran, have campaigned for the barring of Iranian leaders from entering the US to attend meetings at the UN. FDD writer Claudia Rossett argued that then President of Iran Mahmoud Ahmadinejad should be prevented from entering the country on the grounds his nation is "a self-advertised hub of genocidal desires regarding the democratic state of Israel, and ultimately the United States".[60] Rossett and her fellow intellectuals at the FDD, have expressed no similar concern about the allowing of Israeli leaders, who have proven themselves committed to forcibly acquiring Palestinian land, from entering the US.

Rossett takes specific aim at the private sector in New York for failing to unite behind attempts by neo-conservatives and pro-Israeli intellectuals at preventing the Iranian reader from attending meetings at the UN. In constructing her argument, Rossett chooses to strategically deploy Holocaust rhetoric:

> In recent years he [Ahmadinejad] has migrated from one plush New York hotel to another…But it seems there is always another willing establishment. This year it appears to be the Warwick New York Hotel, on West 54th Street. There…Ahmadinejad can enjoy fat pillows on which to lay his Holocaust-denying head and dream his radioactive dreams of a new Holocaust.

Either unaware, or choosing to remain wilfully ignorant of, the fundamental belief governing modern neo-liberal capitalist systems that the free-market is amoral and apolitical, Rossett is unable to fathom why her group's attempts at convincing private US businesses to reject Ahmadinejad's patronage have been ignored in light of the "public outcry from organizations such as United Against Nuclear Iran (UANI)".[61]

Rossett represents the UANI, an important part of the neo-conservative network we explored in some detail earlier, as a barometer for the measuring of US public opinion about Iran. As we have learnt from our explorations so far, the opinions of neo-conservative-aligned organisations are not typically reflective of US public opinion. Rather they reflect the partisan interests of a small but influential segment of American society. Remembering that the UANI's stated *modus operandi* is the promoting of a confrontational U.S. foreign policy posture when dealing with Iran, and not conducting extensive ethnographic research with the aim of giving voice to the US politic. Again we are witnessing deliberate attempts to provide the illusion of a consensus when it comes to how the US should deal with Iran. In this particular instance this has been achieved by expanding the dialogic space just enough to include the opinions of neo-conservative outfits whose links and ulterior motives are conveniently hidden from public view.

One of the major revelations to emerge from Herman and Chomsky's seminal work on the manufacturing of consent within the US media and intellectual landscape was that moneyed special interest groups often go about establishing a network of organisations, think tanks and policy institutes, that provide its movement intellectuals with the significant resources they need to undertake, publish and disseminate their 'research'. [62] Movement intellectuals then cite each other's work and purposefully exclude or decide against seriously engaging with contrasting viewpoints, with the aim of portraying to the wider public the existence of a consensus about a particular issue. These political actors also offer themselves as 'experts' for television and radio programs, podcasts, and the like. This is an accurate depiction of what we are witnessing with the neo-conservatives and their anti-Iranian campaign.

Despite Chomsky and Herman's study taking place some time ago, things do not appear to have changed much at all with regards to the political economy of the mass meda in America– if anything the networks they focused on have only grown thereby increasing their influence. It is worth mentioning that Chomsky's body of work has not been well received by neo-conservatives who, rather than engaging with *any* of his ideas in a meaningful way, have dismissed them on the grounds he is a 'self-hating Jew'. [63] 'Self-hating Jew' is an expression of the anti-Semitism rhetorical tool specifically tailored for Jewish intellectuals whom neo-conservatives and their pro-Israeli counterparts consider to be traitors to the Jewish and Israeli causes. "Jew-haters may be Christian, Muslim or atheist. Some of the most destructive Jew-haters have themselves been Jewish or of Jewish descent" writes leading neo-conservative Clifford May for the *Washington Times,* "[i]t's an expression of an ancient and widespread pathology, one that has never been dormant for long".[64] It is an expression Norman Podhoretz was convinced Hannah Arendt was promoting throughout twentieth century America, which is precisely why he dedicated considerable time and energy and also publishing space in *Commentary Magazine* (which he was the long-time editor of) to deploying *ad hominem* attacks similar to those used by many neo-conservatives today.[65]

In more recent times Bernie Sanders has been the focus of similar rebukes for his condemning of Israel's Occupation of the Palestinian Territories and his association with the 'anti-Israeli' Democratic Party.[66] Sanders has made it clear his identifying as a Jew has not led to his favouring of the Israeli state over the welfare of Palestinians when it comes to doing what he thinks is right. Much to chagrin of neo-conservatives, Sanders has repeatedly identified with the oppressed and marginalised rather than any specific cultural, religious or ethnic group. Sanders has also been extremely critical of Israeli PM and neo-conservative favourite Benjamin Netanyahu, and maintained that diplomacy and not military action nor economic sanctions is the best course of action when dealing with Iran.[67] These opinions deeply concern neo-conservatives given Sanders is popular amongst the younger generations of Americans, including liberal Jews, and is a legitimate contender for the 2020 US Presidency.[68] These abstractions regarding the situations of prominent Jewish-Americans (Chomsky, Arendt, and Sanders) as targets of neo-conservative wrath, also helps to illustrate the important point that no one is beyond the reproach of a neo-conservative movement fiercely committed to promoting its partisan interests and imposing its understanding of what it means to be a 'good' Jew and a 'good' American.

Americanisation of the Holocaust

Working from within a dialectical imagination means serious consideration must be dedicated to understanding abstractions in terms of their connectedness within the larger whole. It is not enough to just abstract some elements for closer analysis, we must also fit this abstraction from whence it came with the aim of gaining an understanding of the larger puzzle. This process is particularly illuminating when it comes to treating the neo-conservatives' use of Holocaust rhetoric as part of a much larger effort employed by American rhetoricians. These efforts by neo-conservatives can be understood as part of a wider tendency Phillip Lopate has identified as the "the Americanization of the Holocaust".[69] The using of Holocaust rhetoric is not limited to Jewish- and Christian- neo-conservatives who remain profoundly affected by these tragic events, but is also employed by intellectuals influenced by a range of religious and political ideas.

The Americanisation of the Holocaust acknowledges the process where many users of Holocaust rhetoric are not explicitly referring to the historical events that took place in Auschwitz-Birkenau, Bełżec, Chełmno, Janowska and other extermination camps on European soil according to the twentieth century Nazi Germany programme. Rather these language users see great political, cultural and religious utility in this horrific event; they are seeking to capitalise on its misery to further their own partisan interests. Some intellectuals, including some of those who have directly experienced the effects of the Holocaust, have argued this mass killing is such a uniquely terrible event that its truth or essence should not be appropriated for the pursuing of more recent political aims and goals.

Neo-conservative darling Jonah Goldberg is certainly aware of this debate, and he has provided a brief meditation on the implications associated with this linguistic technique for both readers of the *National Review Online* and policy and decision-makers who consume the AEI's publications. "I think, as a general rule, one should pretty much always avoid talking about Jews and ovens unless discussing the actual Holocaust", writes Goldberg in his article 'Huckabee's Hitler comparison that wasn't'.[70] However, the glaring issue is that Goldberg does not follow his own advice. In reality, he has proven to be a consistent user of Holocaust rhetoric, especially when writing about the perceived threats posed by 'radical Islamists' and political Liberals to US and Israeli interests.[71] Again, what is good for the goose is definitely not good for the gander.

Many of those using Holocaust rhetoric in seemingly unrelated contexts clearly do not consider the Holocaust a catastrophic event needing to be considered in relation to its specific historical context. These individuals appear to be of the view the Holocaust should be understood as an embodiment of Jewish hatred by an individual or group possessing the desire and means to achieve their anti-Jewish genocidal fantasies. Obviously there is no universally agreed upon moral or ethical standard intellectuals and politicians need to abide by when engaging in the war of ideas within the public sphere. This is part of the reason why Iranian leaders are often unobstructed when speaking in inflammatory ways at the UN. The same principle applies for how President Trump has chosen to engage with his audience.

In the US context there exists some semblance of hate speech laws, however the right of free speech as ingrained in the constitution and fiercely defended by many Americans, particularly Conservatives, more often than not trumps the sensitivities of others. When recognising that all of this is taking place within the context of the modern liberal democratic state, whose one of many problems is its inability to clearly demarcate in any reasonable and successful fashion between the sacred and the profane, we begin to understand why Holocaust rhetoric is thought of by some as an acceptable form of speech. Whether or not this is 'good' or ethical remains highly contested.

It is easier to understand why neo-conservatives relied on this kind of rhetoric in the mid to late twentieth century America. At its conception the movement was fundamentally a Jewish-American expression. During this time American-Jews were engaging in a struggle with other minority groups with the aim of establishing their own identities. Victim culture was pervasive, which helped to create fertile ground for the use Holocaust rhetoric. Novick makes the point Jewish-Americans as a group were far wealthier, better educated and more politically influential than any other minority groups at this time – a viewpoint that continues to resonate with many observers today and which is often proudly proclaimed by many as a sign of their success.[72] Jewish-Americans did not typically suffer from the kinds of economic, societal and health disadvantages experienced by many other minority groups, yet they still struggled in establishing a distinct identity separate from these groups and the pervasive all-American identity. Novick argues the Holocaust offered Jewish-Americans "a 'certification' both for the Jewish competition for recognition and for primacy".[73]

Novick's assessment resonates with claims made by prominent Jewish-American figures like Elie Wiesel, who has spoken at great length about the uniqueness of the Holocaust and the cult of the survivor. Wiesel, a Nobel Peace Prize winner for his lifelong political and cultural activism, is among the most renowned advocates of the idea that the *Shoah* cannot and should not be represented outside of its specific temporal, political and cultural context. He stresses the uniqueness of the Holocaust, arguing that ownership rights of the event and its memory should be limited to its immediate victims and survivors. According to Wiesel, no words nor images are sufficient to re-create the unimaginable.[74]

Wiesel's calling for a taboo on Holocaust representation has not been heeded by neo-conservatives, who remain adamant they are putting its memory to good use when using it to agitate for war against Iran. It is with this in mind that we will now abstract another key aspect of Holocaust rhetoric acting as a key pillar for the current neo-conservative anti-Iranian campaign, the strategic deploying of the haunting phrase 'never again'.

Never Again

On July 22, 2015 in Times Square, New York City, a who's who of the neo-conservative and pro-Israeli movements gathered for the *Stop Iran Rally*. The event was heavily promoted on social media (mainly Facebook and Twitter), by neo-conservative websites, publications and think-tanks. It featured the likes of Frank Gaffney, James Woolsey, Caroline Glick, Monica Crowley and Alan Dershowitz. One after the other, speakers took to the makeshift stage to criticise the *Iran Nuclear Deal*. In light of Iraq and Syria's recent dismembering, the speakers warned the crowd and those watching via live streams online, about the existential threat this latest manifestation of Islamist evil posed to Israel, whilst at the same extoling the virtues of the US and Israeli 'special relationship'. New York Democratic Senator Chuck Schumer was called out by name for his perceived failure to adopt a hard-line approach when dealing with Iran, signalling the speakers' intent to directly affect the policy- and decision-making processes, in addition to their wanting to rouse public support for a military strike against Iran.

What was very interesting and appeared to have struck a chord with many in the audience, was how the orators went about deploying Holocaust rhetoric to help achieve their communicative aims and goals. Particularly compelling was how some speakers chose to use the phrase 'never again', which has strong and obvious associations with the Holocaust. Mikhail Bakhtin and Valentin Voloshinov's notions of dialogism and heteroglossia remind us that modern users of phrases like this are not the first to disturb the eternal silence of the universe in such a way, but instead are parts of a never-ending linguistic chain comprised of previous and future utterances. It was Voloshinov who stressed that verbal communication "invariably orients itself with respect to previous performances in the same sphere", whilst also engaging "in ideological colloquy of a large scale: it responds to something, affirms something, anticipates possible responses and objects, [and] seeks support".[75]

'Never again' belongs to the Holocaust memorial sphere; it is from here that it harvests its powerful ability to influence by evoking the shocking imagery associated with the German Nazi programme. A close review of the history associated with this utterance reveals it gained widespread prominence in the US in the late 1960s largely thanks to the ideas and actions of Jewish-American Meir Kahane. It was Kahane who devised the slogan 'never again' when establishing the US-based *Jewish Defense League* in response to what he perceived to be an impending threat of another Holocaust. Whilst Jews would again be targeted, this time the perpetrators would not be Nazis or a similar totalitarian political group. Instead Kahane was concerned about the inner-city Black and Hispanic populations, namely those living in and around New York City, whom he deemed capable and willing to commit such atrocities.

This idea seems ludicrous now, and many at the time no doubt shared this view, however we need to consider the relevant spatial and temporal contexts as well as the vantage points of Kahane and other

Jewish-Americans at that moment in time. Many had only recently arrived in the US after fleeing the Nazi hunting ground in Europe. This was a period in US history in which minorities were competing against each other in order to establish their identities separate from the mainstream white Christian American, and it was *only* two decades after the Holocaust. It is worth noting that many of the individuals who were on the precipice of their neo-conservative journeys at this time were not generally as sensationalist nor paranoid as Kahane when it came to perceiving threats posed by their fellow Americans. Some neo-conservatives such as Norman Podhoretz and Patrick Moynihan certainly appeared to hold a deep resentment towards Black Americans, however the kind of 'never again' rhetoric we see many neo-conservatives using now was not nearly as widespread nor vociferous.[76]

On this particular day in *Times Square* New York, Monica Crowley proved to be one of the chief users of the 'never again' utterance popularised by Kahane. Her speech was live-streamed and recorded on social media, and continues to remain on popular streaming websites like YouTube. Crowley made her message explicit from the very beginning of her speech:

> Two words to begin tonight, '**never again**'. Seventy years after the Holocaust, have we forgotten already? Have we already forgotten what it means to say and live the phrase '**never again**?' It seems so. How else can we interpret a deal that legitimises as a threshold to nuclear power, the world's most fearsome state sponsor of terror, the key exporter of the Islamic revolution, one of the most defiant traffickers of deadly weapons, an unapologetic denier of the Holocaust bent on Israel's destruction, the passionate believer of death to America and death to Israel, and a killer of thousands of Americans. ... Of the countless dangerous and destructive things this President has done, this deal is literally the worst of all. We are here today because we all know this to be true... this is a potential death sentence for the West and for Israel... President Obama says that he can basically do whatever he wants because quote "he has got a pen and phone." Well guess what Mr. President we've gone pens and phones too. And with our pens and phones, we are going to put them to work to defeat this deal [Emphases added].

Crowley concluded her speech in similar fashion: "Stop the deal, stop Iran, before it is too late. Because as we have long told ourselves **'never again'**. Now is the time to bring those words to life. Thank you, God bless you. God bless the state of Israel and God Bless America [Emphasis added]".[77]

Crowley serves as an interesting test case for the fuzzy category that is neo-conservatism. As we can see from these abstracts, she subscribes to many of the core beliefs distinguishing the neo-conservative *Weltanschauung*: a binary good vs. evil view of the world, understanding US and Israel's interests as intertwined, an unwavering support for Israel, a general antipathy for Islamic nations and the Democratic Party, and strongly influenced by Christian-Judeo religious beliefs. Her large body of work put together over many years also reveals a firm commitment to these ideas.[78]

Her professional associations also reveal she has been heavily involved with numerous neoconservative outfits. Crowley worked for the neo-conservative organisation *Family Security Matters* (FSM), a Washington D.C. based organisation whose mission is "...to inform all Americans...about the issues surrounding national security...to highlight the connection between individual safety and a strong national defense...and to empower all Americans to become proactive defenders of our national security".[79] FSM's political activities have included echoing wider neoconservative calls for the adopting of hawkish US foreign policies when dealing with Iran, championing the US' most recent invasion of Iraq, the exclusive endorsing of Republican Presidential candidates, and promoting preferential treatment of Israel on the basis of its exceptional nature. FSM also has strong links to Gaffney's CSP.[80]

Crowley has been a frequent guest on Gaffney's *Secure Freedom Radio* program (between 2010 and 2013). She has publicly idolised leading neo-conservative thinkers including Gaffney, for their anti-Islamic and pro-Israeli views, and she has been recognised by the movement for her general contribution to their cause by the way of awards and funding by neo-conservative outfits. Amongst the most notable is Crowley receiving the CSP's *Mightier Pen Award*, which recognises an intellectual's "commitment to a robust national security and their efforts to educate our countrymen and women about the need to practice the philosophy President Reagan called 'peace through strength'".[81] Previous winners include neo-conservative stalwarts Charles Krauthammer and Norman Podhoretz, which should provide readers with some idea about the kind of political actor the CSP values.

Crowley has also worked as online opinion editor for the *Washington Times*, a proven popular neoconservative haunt, and has plied her trade at many other mainstream news media outlets that have proven themselves to be key proponents of the neo-conservative worldview like the *New York Post, The New Yorker* and *The Wall Street Journal.* Crowley identifies as a Republican, and her contribution to their political cause has included speaking at the 2016 Republican National Convention, where she used a substantive part of her allotted time to remind fellow Republicans about the importance of the US properly distinguishing between friends and foes. Despite all of these activities, Crowley perhaps remains most recognisable to the US general public and international viewers for her regular appearances on *Fox News* and her hosting of *The Monica Crowley Show*.

Crowley does not fit the physical neoconservative archetype; she is relatively younger, female and less irascible than many neo-conservatives. This *could* account for why she has received scant attention by observers of the movement. It is also possible the pervasiveness of gender stereotyping where foreign policy has generally been understood in masculine terms and the foreign policy arena as 'a man's game', has meant women like Crowley are sometimes overlooked for their substantive intellectual contributions. Crowley is an intellectual demanding serious attention given her ability to reach many in the US public as well as her demonstrated political clout, which is perhaps best exemplified by President Trump's appointing her to the National Security Council (a post she soon had to relinquish due to allegations of plagiarism. One might say her alleged intellectual dishonesty adds additional weight to her characterisation as a neo-conservative).[82]

It is worth re-iterating that many emerging scholars have tended to focus their analysis of the neo-conservative movement on established intellectuals operating in long-standing neo-conservative outfits. Whether or not this is because they see this as a safe-bet, not wanting to upset the apple cart so early in their academic career, or have allowed themselves to be guided in this way by previous prominent research projects dedicated to understanding neo-conservatism, is open for debate. It is easy to understand why so many observers and researchers have tended to focus on the big names, however it is important we recognise the movement's dynamic nature i.e. its constant adapting to changes in the national and international political, religious and intellectual climates. Crowley along with Nikki Haley, are two intellectuals who should be treated as members of the movement or, at the very least, as having strong ties to it.

It also remains important that observers of the movement continue to appreciate its influential Jewish and masculine nature, especially when considering its earliest expressions, however critics must not become wholly fixated on these elements nor treat the movement as fixed in nature. Claims like those made by Jacob Heilbrunn: "Indeed, as much as they may deny it, neo-conservatism is in a decisive respect a Jewish phenomenon, reflecting a subset of Jewish concerns", may have been accurate in the past, however continuing to treat the movement *only* in this way ensures valuable contributions made by newer, non-stereotypical intellectuals, including female self-proclaimed Christians like Haley and Crowley, are largely ignored.[83]

Refocusing our attention to the deploying of the slogan 'never again' when representing the perceived Iranian threat, a review of the large body of works produced by neo-conservatives reveals that Crowley is not the only intellectual to use this particular rhetorical technique. The late Charles Krauthammer (1950-2018) also demonstrated a proclivity for using this utterance. His article 'Never Again', which appeared in the *Washington Post* almost a decade prior to the *Stop Iran Rally*, illustrates the sustained effort by neo-conservatives when it comes to deploying this aspect of Holocaust rhetoric. Krauthammer used his Op-Ed column to persuade readers the modern Iranian regime should be understood as the "successor" to Hitler's Nazi Germany:

> He [Hitler] demonstrated that modern anti-Semitism married to modern technology -- railroads, disciplined bureaucracies, gas chambers that kill with industrial efficiency -- could take a scattered people and "concentrate" them for annihilation

> ...[Israel is] a tempting target for those who would finish
> Hitler's work.

> His successors now reside in Tehran. The world has paid ample
> attention to President Mahmoud Ahmadinejad's declaration that
> Israel must be destroyed. Less attention has been paid to Iranian
> leaders' pronouncements on exactly how Israel would be
> "eliminated by one storm", as Ahmadinejad has promised...

Krauthammer routinely made use of the phrase 'never again' right up until
his death in 2018. In his 2015 article for the *Oakland Tribune*, he described
the Iranian threat to Israel for his Californian readers as "[d]irect,
immediate and mortal":

> The Iranian bomb is a [US] national security issue, an alliance
> issue and a regional Middle East issue. But it is also a uniquely
> Jewish issue.

> On the 70th anniversary of Auschwitz, mourning dead Jews is
> easy. And, forgive me, cheap. Want to truly honor the dead?
> Show solidarity with the living – Israel and its 6 million Jews.
> Make "**never again**" more than an empty phrase. It took Nazi
> Germany seven years to kill 6 million Jews. It would take a
> nuclear Iran one day [Emphasis added].[84]

Krauthammer's use of rhetoric bears a striking resemblance to that
routinely used by popular right-wing Israeli political figures, particularly
Benjamin Netanyahu. When considering the linguistic and ideological
similitudes between the Israeli Likud Party and the US neo- conservatives,
it is telling that Netanyahu has used the same kind of Holocaust rhetoric
when addressing US policy and decision-makers in Washington. He
declared in his 2011 address to the joint meeting of US Congress:

> The tyranny in Tehran brutalizes its own people. It supports
> attacks against American troops in Afghanistan and Iraq. It
> subjugates Lebanon and Gaza. It sponsors terror worldwide... A
> nuclear-armed Iran would ignite a nuclear arms race in the
> Middle East. It would give terrorists a nuclear umbrella. It
> would make the nightmare of nuclear terrorism a clear and
> present danger throughout the world. ... Now the threat to my
> country cannot be overstated... Less than seven decades after
> six million Jews were murdered, Iran's leaders deny the
> Holocaust of the Jewish people, while calling for the
> annihilation of the Jewish state... When we say **never again**,
> we *mean* **never again**! Israel always reserves the right to defend
> itself... In Judea and Samaria, the Jewish people are not foreign

occupiers…This is the land of our forefathers, the Land of
Israel, to which Abraham brought the idea of one God, where
David set out to confront Goliath, and where Isaiah saw a vision
of eternal peace… No distortion of history can deny the four
thousand year old bond, between the Jewish people and the
Jewish land…[Emphases added].[85]

It is worth here briefly reflecting on the general neo-conservative
response to Netanyahu's landmark speech to US Congress. Alvin
Felzenberg, a member of the *Committee on the Present Danger*, bizarrely
described Netanyahu's commanding address as a prime example of
speaking truth to power.[86] Whether Felzenberg is seeking to invert how
the sociology of intellectuals tradition has long characterised movement
intellectuals or he is engaging in Orwellian rhetoric (seeking to convince
citizens to "reject evidence of your eyes and ears" in favour of party
propaganda) is open for debate.[87] Those with some kind of grasp on the
conceptualisations of the modern intellectual provided by writers like
Benda, Chomsky, Hitchens, Havel, Mannheim and Said, would
undoubtedly be aware that Netanyahu's past actions and speech preclude
him from assuming the mantle of speaking truth to power and shining a
light on injustice.

Setting aside Netanyahu's federal indictment for bribery, fraud
and breach of trust committed during his time as Israeli PM, all of which
point to an abuse of power, his long list of offensive and inflammatory
rhetoric include the following remarks about Palestinians: "beat them up,
not once but repeatedly, beat them up so it hurts so badly, until its
unbearable", and "we must defend ourselves against the wild beasts".[88]
Netanyahu's general disdain for the Other also includes African migrants
to Israel, some of whom are Jewish.[89] In late 2017, Netanyahu pledged to
the Israeli politic to "return south Tel Aviv to citizens of Israel" from the
African "infiltrators".[90] The term 'infiltrator' is common to military and
pathology contexts, where it refers to 'enemy combatants who have broken
through ones defences' and 'undesirable substances or group of cells that
have made their way into the body' respectively. It is certainly a peculiar
way of describing black African economic migrants / refugees.

'Never again' is such a powerful phrase because of its ability to
evoke Holocaust imagery. This utterance works by building ideological

solidarity between the communicator and the putative addressees, the former signalling to the latter that Iran's desire to acquire nuclear technology should be viewed through the lens of Jewish victimhood. Neo-conservatives want readers to understand the modern Iranian regime as an incarnation or rather a continuation of Hitler's Germany, and they want to pressure US policy- and decision-makers into adopting aggressive foreign policy measures aimed at snuffing out any possibility that Iran could acquire the kind of nuclear technology that would put its military capability on par with Israel.

Conclusion

There are dark shadows on the earth,
but its lights are stronger in the contrast.

Some men, like bats or owls, have
better eyes for the darkness than for the light.

—Charles Dickens, *The Pickwick Papers*

This work helps to shed light on some of the reasons why neo-conservatives have not chosen to seriously engage in discussions about why nations like Israel and the US should be allowed / are entitled to possessing nuclear weapons, whilst others like Iran should not be afforded a similar right. It is here the notions of US, Israeli and Jewish Exceptionalism are relevant, with their starting points precluding the idea that nations like Iran exist on anything approaching the same moral or ethical plane as the US and Israel. Neo-conservatives have proven that they will not expand the dialogical space of their texts so as to seriously consider the nuclear question from the vantage points of Others, especially Islamic Others, who have demonstrated an unwillingness to acquiesce to US and Israeli demands.

If the priority is to maintain a healthy and robust democratic sphere, which is what neo-conservatives claim they want, then these linguistics techniques do not pass muster. Nor are they sufficient or acceptable in light of recent and ongoing US and Israeli (highly questionable) military activities in the Middle Eastern region; the US-led invasion of Iraq on the back of manufactured evidence, and Israel's ongoing brutal occupation of Palestine, serve as ideal cases in point. These are the kinds of discussions neo-conservatives *would* seriously be engaging in if they were *truly* committed to democratic debate, and if they were to adopt the roles of intellectuals that sought to speak truth to power and shine a light on injustice. Instead, neo-conservatives have chosen to play the roles of movement intellectuals with a clear tendency for an authoritarian conceptualisation of the political.

The case can certainly be made that Israel's ongoing brutalisation of Palestinians, which appears to be on par if not worse than some of the atrocities committed by the Iranian regime against its own people, provides valuable evidence as to why it should not be trusted with nuclear weapons. In light of these actions, many observers are left wondering what is it exactly about Israel that makes it inherently trustworthier than Iran when it comes to possessing a nuclear arsenal that could bring about widespread devastation? Could not the case be made that Israel's awful treatment of many secular, Muslim and Christian Palestinians is indicative of the same kinds of racist and violent tendencies that neo-conservatives claim makes Iran so untrustworthy and unpredictable? These are all serious considerations for the kind of intellectual whose principal allegiances are to speaking truth to power and shining a light on injustice, rather than to Jerusalem, Washington, Tehran, God, Yahweh or Allah.

It is deeply regrettable we find ourselves in a situation where Iranian leaders have decided that it is a matter of political and military necessity to go about acquiring nuclear weapons. It is equally regrettable there exists intellectual movements like neo-conservatism whose members dedicate so much time, energy and financial resources to dividing the people and nations of the world through the using of specific linguistic techniques that emphasise, embellish and/or manufacture differences, and promote feelings of antipathy about the Other. In light of global advancements made by the hugely successful anti-colonial struggle in the twentieth century, it is tragic that the Occupation of Palestine continues, and that neo-conservatives have thought it necessary to combine their ongoing anti-Palestinian campaign with their current anti-Iranian campaign.

With Iraq and Syria now in tatters, neo-conservatives have capitalised on that space in their mindscapes by dedicating their energies to convincing the US public and policy- and decision-makers about the dire need to wage war against Iran. The lamentable reality is that we currently find ourselves living in a period in history where neo-conservatives have made it their mission to convince others that the Iranian regime, and the Iranian nation by implication, is inherently evil and sadistic, and that the only way to deal with these brutes is by threatening violence and using other forms of intimidation. One cannot but help to wonder if and when the US or Israel effectively 'deal' with Iran, which nation will be next on their hit-list?

Given the nature of the relationship between the neo-conservatives and the Republican Party, one can say with some confidence that a return of the Democratic Party to government would go a long way in preventing the neo-conservatives from realising their desire for war. However, should the Republican Party be successful in the 2020 general election, and should neo-conservative influence in the US administration continue to expand (following on from the appointments of John Bolton and Elliot Abrams), it is very likely given recent history that we will soon be talking about another potential US invasion of the next (Islamic) nation or a co-ordinated attack against whichever (Islamic) group next takes the fancy of the neo-conservatives.

This study has dedicated itself to revealing some important aspects of the current anti-Iranian rhetorical campaign, whilst also revealing some of the key religious and political ideas motivating and inspiring these choices. There is no doubt these revelations will sit uneasy with neo-conservatives, pro-Israeli movement intellectuals, many of those who identify with Judeo-Christian faiths, and supporters of these groups. However, the reality is their conceptualisations of the political and their understanding of truth do not sit well with many of those who do not want their society organised around the idea of political enmity, and who do not want their government making important political decisions based on literalist interpretations of religious texts.

It is hoped this research helps inform readers about some of the major factors at play in this ongoing war of ideas about Iran, which are not immediately apparent or rather are largely concealed from public view. It is also hoped future researchers adopt more dynamic understandings about the nature of the neo-conservative intellectual movement both in terms of personnel and ideas, and are willing to draw attention to linguistic devices, especially the more controversial techniques such as the rhetorical uses of anti-Semitism, with the aim of further revealing some of the more duplicitous and totalitarian aspects of the movement. These tasks would not be so important if neo-conservatives admitted their commitment to authoritarian ideas and practices, however it appears that this is not something that we can expect anytime soon.

A major problem is neo-conservatives continue to portray themselves as fundamentally committed to upholding and practicing democratic ideals. Whether these actions are inspired by the ideas of prominent political theorists like Leo Strauss, are more generally related to their development as humans constantly making sense of their place in the world, or is a combination of these elements and others, remains open for debate. This research certainly offers suggestions, however stops short of making the kinds of claims to truth that neo-conservatives are more than happy to make when it comes to making sense of the social world and the nature of man.

Hannah Arendt was right when she claimed some time ago that the newer generations living on earth will only ever know a world in which there exists nuclear weapons, meaning they will forever live with an acute awareness about the very real possibility of a nuclear doomsday scenario.[1] This is even more worrying for those who do not believe there is a supernatural being waiting to save us all if, or when, such a time arrives. This is precisely why issues like those explored in this work remain of great interest to those who do not consider inflammatory rhetoric as the ideal way of resolving disagreements.

Many people would no doubt feel uncomfortable with Iran possessing nuclear weapons, similar to how they feel about the US and Israel also having access to such devastating weapons. Some of us also see similarities between the current anti-Iranian campaign and previous neo-conservative efforts aimed at manipulating public opinion and influencing US policy- and decision- makers about the nature of Iraqi threat, and this makes us very, very scared.

Bibliography

Abrams, Elliott. *Faith or Fear: How Jews Can Survive in a Christian America.* New York: Simon & Schuster, 1999.

Abrams, Elliott. "Joining the Jackals: The Obama Administration Abandons Israel." *Washington Examiner,* June 2, 2010. https://www.washington examiner.com/weekly-standard/joining-the-jackals

Abrams, Elliott. "Two Words." *Mosaic,* October 13, 2013. https://mosaic magazine.com/ response/ uncategorized / 2013 / 10 / two-words/

Abunimah, Ali, Nigel Parry and Laurie King. "Republican Party leader calls for ethnic cleansing of Palestinians on prime time talk show.' *The Electronic Intifida.* May 1, 2002. https://electronicintifada. net/content/republican-party -leader- calls-ethnic-cleansing-palestinians-prime-time-talk-show/ 4033

Adib-Moghaddam, Arshin. "Manufacturing War: Iran in the Neo-Conservative Imagination." *Third World Quarterly* 28, no. 3 (2007):635-653.

The Algemeiner. "Livid Giuliani Contrasts Obama with Netanyahu: 'That's a Man Who Fights for His People, Unlike Our President." February 17, 2015. https://www.algemeiner.com/ 2015 / 02 / 17 /livid – Giuliani - contrasts-netanyahu - with-obama-thats-a-man-who-fights-for-his-people-unlike-our-president-video/

Ali, Wajahat, Eli Clifton, Matthew Duss, Lee Fang, Scott Keyes, and Faiz Shakir. "Fear, Inc." *Center For American Progress*, August 2011, https://cdn. American progress.org / wp-content / uploads / issues / 2011 / 08 / pdf/ islamophobia.pdf

American Enterprise Institute. "AEI's Organization and Purpose." 2019. http://www.aei.org/about/

American Israel Public Affairs Committee. "A Light Unto the Nations." *Israel Connection* 5, no.3. https://www.aipac.org/-/media/publications/policy-and-politics/aipac-periodicals/israel-connection/2011/03/israelconnection_general_yh5771_.pdf

American Israel Public Affairs Committee. "Oppose Boycotts of Israel." 2019. https://www.aipac.org / learn/legislative-agenda / agenda-display/2019-oppose-boycotts-of-israel

Anderson, Benedict. *Imagined Communities: Reflections on the Origins and Spread of Nationalism.* London: Verso, 1983.

Arendt, Hannah. *On Violence.* New York: Harcourt, 1970.

Arendt, Hannah. *The Origins of Totalitarianism: Imperialism.* New York: Harcourt, Brace & World, 1968.

Atran, Scott. "Interview with Ramadan Shallah, Secretary General, Palestinian Islamic Jihad (Damascus, Syria, December 15, 2009)". *Perspective on Terrorism* 4, no.2 (2010). http://www.terrorismanalysts.com/pt/index. php/pot/article/view/95/html ISSN: 2334-3745

Bakhtin, Mikhail. "Discourse in the Novel." In *The Dialogic Imagination: Four Essays*. 259-422. Translated by Michael Holquist and Caryl Emerson. Austin: University of Texas Press, 1981.

Bakhtin, Mikhail. *Speech Genres and Other Late Essays.* Austin: University of Texas Press, 1986.

"The Battle for Iran, 1953: Re-Release of CIA Internal History Spotlights New Details about anti-Mosaddeq Coup." *The National Security Archive.* Released June 27, 2014. https://nsarchive2.gwu.edu/NSAEBB/NSAEB B476/

Beck, Noah. "Can Israel Survive Obama?" *The Times of Israel,* November 15, 2013. https://blogs.timesofisrael.com/can-israel-survive-obama/

Bedermen, Diane. "The Troubling Influence Of The 'Jihadist Psychopath.' *FrontPageMag,* January 18, 2019. https://www.frontpagemag.com/fpm/ 272601/troubling-influence-jihadist-psychopath-diane-bederman

Bell, David A. "Not Everything Is Munich and Hitler." *The National Interest,* April 25, 2016. https://nationalinterest.org/feature/not-everything-mun ich-hitler-15929

Benda, Julien. *The Treason of the Intellectuals.* New York: W.W. Norton and Company, 1969.

Bennis, Phyllis. "John Bolton Loves War and Detests Diplomacy – Even More Than Trump." *Newsweek,* March 30, 2018. https://www.newsweek.com/ john – Bolton – loves - war-and-detests -diplomacy – even - more-trump- 864469

Bercovici, Vivian. "The Corruption Scandal that Could Upend Israeli Elections: Who is to blame?" *The Weekly Standard,* January 10, 2019. https:// www.commentarymagazine.com / politics-ideas / corruption-scandal- upend-israeli-elections-benjamin-netanyahu/

"Bernie Sanders on Iran." 2019. *FeeltheBern.org*

Bever, Lindsey. "Report: Rudy Giuliani tells private dinner 'I do not believe that the president loves America.'" *The Washington Post – Weblog Post,* February 19, 2015. ProQuest document ID: 1656268287.

Biale, David. *Power & Powerlessness in Jewish History.* New York: Schocken, 1986.

"Blockade turns Gaza into 'big open air prison.'" March 5, 2010. http://www. china.org.cn/opinion/2010-03/05/content_19534342.htm

Blumenthal, Max. "The Sugar Mama of Anti-Muslim Hate." *The Nation,* July 14, 2014. https://www.thenation.com/article/sugar-mama-anti-muslim-hate/

Bogost, Ian. *How to Do Things with Videogames.* Minneapolis: University of Minnesota Press, 2011.

Bohbot, Amir and Yaakov Katz. *The Weapon Wizards: How Israel Became a High-Tech Military.* New York: St. Martin's Press, 2017.

Booth, Wayne C. "Metaphor as Rhetoric: The Problem of Evaluation." *Critical Inquiry* 5, no.1 (1978): 49-72. https://www.jstor.org/stable/1342977

Box Office Mojo. "Pearl Harbor." August 29, 2019. https://www.boxofficemojo.com/movies/?id=pearlharbor.htm

Box Office Mojo. "Pilot / Aircraft." August 29, 2019. https://www.boxofficemojo.com/genres/chart/?id=pilot.htm

Box Office Mojo. "Romantic Drama." August 29, 2019. https://www.boxofficemojo.com/genres/chart/?id=romanticdrama.htm

British Broadcasting Commission. "Clinton: Half of Trump Supporters 'basket of deplorables.'" September 10, 2016. http:// www . bbc . com / news/av/election-us-2016-37329812/clinton-half-of-trump-supporters-basket-of-deplorables

British Broadcasting Commission. "Panorama: The War Party." May 18, 2003. https://www.youtube.com/watch?v=2fBVvSvUawE

Brooks, David. "The Era of Distortion." *The New York Times,* January 6, 2004. A23.

Buber, Martin. "Dialogue Between Heaven and Earth." In *Wrestling with God: Jewish Theological Responses During and after the Holocaust.* Edited by Steven T. Katz, Shlomo Biderman and Gershon Greenberg. 372-374. Oxford: Oxford University Press, 2007.

Buber, Martin. *Two Types of Faith.* Translated by Norman P. Goldhawk. New York: The MacMillan Company, 1951.

Burack, Emily. "How 'Never Again' evolved from Holocaust commemoration slogan to universal call." *The Times of Israel,* March 9, 2018. https://www.timesofisrael.com/how-never-again-evolved-from-holocaust-commemoration-slogan-to-universal-call/

Burgers, Tobias and Scott Nicholas Romaniuk, "How the US military is using 'violent, chaotic, beautiful' video games to train soldiers." *The Conversation.* March 7, 2017. https://theconversation.com/how-the-us-military-is-using-violent-chaotic-beautiful-video-games-to-train-soldiers-73826

Caputo, John. *Truth.* London: Penguin, 2014.

Center for American Progress. "Fear Inc.: The Roots of the Islamophobia Network in America." August 2011. https://cdn.americanprogress.org/wp-content/uploads/issues/2011/08/pdf/islamophobia.pdf

Center for Security Policy. "2013 Mightier Pen Award: Honoring Diana West." November 22, 2013. https://www.centerforsecuritypolicy.org/2013/11/22/2013-mightier-pen-award-honoring-diana-west/

Cerulo, Karen. *Deciphering Violence: The Cognitive Structure of Right and Wrong.* New York: Routledge, 1998.

Chabad-Lubavitch Media Center. "June 9: David and Goliath." 2019. https://www.chabad.org/multimedia/timeline_cdo/aid/525338/jewish/David-and-Goliath.htm

Chait, Jonathan. "The Neocons Have Gone From GOP Thought-Leaders to Outcasts." *New York Media: Intelligencer.* August 21, 2016. http://nymag.com/intelligencer/2016/08/neocons-outcast-trump.html

Chang, Kuang-Kuo and Geri Alumit Zeldes. "Three of Four Newspapers Studied Favor Israeli Instead of Palestinian Sources." *Newspaper Research Journal* 27, no.4 (2006): 84-90 https://doi.org/10.1177/073953290602700407

The Charter Of Allah: The Platform of the Islamic Resistance Movement (HAMAS). Translated and annotated by Raphael Israeli. Jerusalem: Harry Truman Research Institute at The Hebrew University. https://fas.org/irp/world/para/docs/880818.htm

Child, Ben. "New Zealand points to its diplomat's diary as proof that Argo got it wrong." *The Guardian,* April 4, 2013. https://www.theguardian.com/film/2013/apr/04/argo-new-zealand-diplomat-diary

Chomsky, Noam. "The Responsibility of Intellectuals." *The New York Review of Books,* February 23, 1967. http://www.nybooks.com/articles/archives/1967/apr/20/the- responsibility-of-intellectuals-4/.

Chomsky, Noam and Edward Herman. *Manufacturing Consent: The Political Economy of the Mass Media.* New York: Pantheon, 1988.

Christians United for Israel. "Pastors' Briefings Events." 2019. http://support.cufi.org/site/PageServer?pagename=events_pastors_luncheons_landing

Christians United for Israel. "Who We Are." 2019. https://www.cufi.org

Chughtai, Alia. "Understanding US military aid to Israel." *Al Jazeera,* March 8, 2018. https:// www . aljazeera . com / indepth / interactive / 2018 / 03 / understanding-military-aid-israel-180305092533077.html

Clay, Jenny Strauss. "The Real Leo Strauss." *The New York Times,* June 7, 2003. A15.

Clifton, Eli. "A Great Little Racket: The Neocon Media Machine." *Right Web.* March 19, 2007. https://rightweb.irc-online.org/a_great_little_racket_the_neocon_media_machine/

Clifton, Eli. "Billionaire's sketchy Middle East gamble: Meet the man betting on war with Iran." *Salon,* August 11, 2014. https://www.salon.com/2014/08/11/billionaires_sketchy_middle_east_gamble_meet_the_man_betting_on_war_with_iran/

Clifton, Eli. "Following Paul Singer's Money, Argentina, And Iran (Continued)." *Lobe Log,* May 8, 2015. https://lobelog.com/following-paul-singers-money-argentina-and-iran-continued/

Clifton, Eli. "Trump's Muslim Ban: Thanks To Supreme Court Decision, Bogus Polling, And AIPAC Funding." *Lobe Log,* June 26, 2018. https://lobelog.com / trumps - muslim - ban-thanks - to-supreme-court -decision-bogus-polling-and-aipac-funding/

Cody, Edward. "GOP leaders criticize Obama's Iran policy in rally for opposition group." *Washington Post,* December 23, 2010. http://www.washingtonpost.com/wpdyn/content/article/2010/12/22/AR2010122205180.html.

Cohen, Roger. "Obama's American Idea." *The New York Times,* December 10, 2007. https://www.nytimes.com/2007/12/10/opinion/10cohen.html

The Connecticut Forum. "God: Big Questions…Bigger Questions." January 29, 2009. https://www.youtube.com/watch?v=Xx_ov2NiNo4

Cortellessa, Eric. "Norman Podhoretz, the last remaining 'anti-anti Trump' neoconservative." *The Times Of Israel,* September 7, 2016. https://www. timesofisrael.com / norman - podhoretz-the - last-remaining - anti-anti-trump-neoconservative/

Council of Foreign Relations. "A Conversation with Senator Marco Rubio." May 31, 2012. https://www.cfr.org/event/conversation-senator-marco-rubio

Council on American-Islamic Relations. "Hijacked by Hate: American Philanthropy and the Islamophobia Network." 2019. http://www. islamophobia.org/images/IslamophobiaReport2019/CAIR_Islamophobi a_Report_2019_Final_Web.pdf

Cramer, Jane K. and A. Trevor Thrall. *Why Did the United States Invade Iraq?* London: Routledge, 2011.

Critchley, Simon. *Infinitely Demanding: Ethics of Commitment, Politics of Resistance.* London: Verso, 2013.

Crowley, Monica. "Monica Crowley: Syrian airstrikes show Trump has learned from history." *The Hill*, April 16, 2018.

Crowley, Monica. "Speech Delivered at Stop Iran Rally in Times Square, New York." *Jewish Broadcasting Service*, July 22, 2015. https://www.you tube.com/watch?v=4U-Qhbfuzqs

Crowley, Monica. "The Holy War Begins: Interview with Bill O'Reilly." *O'Reilly Factor*, New York, February 17, 2015. Transcript available via ProQuest Database, ProQuest Document ID: 1795946165.

Crowley, Monica. *What The (Bleep) Just Happened? The Happy Warrior's Guide to the Great American Comeback.* New York: Broadside, 2012.

Csillag, Ron. "Bret Stephens: U.S. Jews Are Not Single-Issue Voters." *The Canadian Jewish News,* April 29, 2019. https://www.cjnews.com/news/ international/bret-stephens-u-s-jews-are-not-single-issue-voters

Curtis, Richard H. "You Don't Have to be Jewish to Be a Neo-con: John Bolton." *Washington Report on Middle East Affairs,* October 2003. https://www. wrmea.org/ from - our- archives/you-don-t- have-to-be-jewish-to-be-a-neo-con-john-bolton-and-james-woolsey.html

Daileda, Colin. "Take a wild guess what Trump's favorite hashtag was in his first 100 days." *Mashable,* April 29, 2017. https://mashable.com/2017/04/ 28/donald-trump-twitter-favorite-hashtags-words/

Damavandi, Samira. "Why Iranian students in US are crowdfunding to pay their tuition." *Al Jazeera,* April 5, 2019. https://www.aljazeera.com/news/ 2019/04/iranian-students-crowdfunding-pay-tuition-190404140457051. html

Daou, Marc. "John Bolton's dangerous 'obsession' with Iran." *France24*, May 24, 2019. https://www.france24.com/en/20190524-john-bolton-nuclear-iran -military -trump-usa-ayatollah-khamenei

Davis, Rohan. *Western Imaginings: The Intellectual Contest to Define Wahhabism.* Cairo: American University in Cairo Press, 2018.

Dehghan, Saeed Kamali and Richard Norton-Taylor, "CIA Admits Role in 1953 Iranian Coup." *The Guardian,* August 20, 2013. https://www. theguardian.com/world/2013/aug/19/cia-admits-role-1953-iranian-coup

Deleuze, Gilles. *Negotiations.* New York: Columbia University Press, 1995.

Dershowtiz, Alan M. "Bernie Sanders: Knave or Fool?" *Gatestone Institute*, June 10, 2017. https : // www.gatestoneinstitute.org / 10508/bernie – sanders -knave-or-fool

Dershowitz, Alan M. "Chomsky Calls Russian Interference a Joke - Blames Guess Who?" *Gatestone Institute,* August 3, 2018. https://www.gatestone institute.org/12799/noam-chomsky-russian-interference

Dershowitz, Alan M. "Why deterrence won't work against Iran." *Gatestone Institute,* March 20, 2012. https://www.gatestoneinstitute.org/2958/iran-deterrence

Dexter, Helen. "Warfighting and Lifesaving: New Wars, Cosmopolitan Law Enforcement and the War on Terror." PhD Thesis, The University of Manchester, 2007.

Dorrien, Gary. *The Neoconservative Mind: Politics, Culture, and the War of Ideology.* Philadelphia: Temple University Press, 1993.

Dowd, Maureen. "I'm With Dick. Let's Make War!" August 28, 2002. *The New York Times*, https://www.nytimes.com / 2002 / 08 / 28/opinion/i-m-with-dick-let-s-make-war.html

Drury, Shadia. "Gurus of Endless War." *New Humanist,* July 11, 2007. https://newhumanist.org.uk/articles/1463/gurus-of-endless-war

Drury, Shadia. *Leo Strauss and the American Right.* London: Palgrave Macmillan, 1999.

Drury, Shadia. "Leo Strauss's Classic Natural Right Teaching." *Political Theory* 15, no.3 (1987): 299-315. DOI: 10.1177/0090591787015003001

Drury, Shadia. "Saving America: Leo Strauss and the Neoconservatives." *Evatt Foundation.* https://evatt.org.au/papers/saving-america.html

Drury, Shadia. "The Esoteric Philosophy of Leo Strauss." *Political Theory* 13, no.3 (1985): 315-337. https://www.jstor.org/stable/191234

Drury, Shadia. *The Political Ideas of Leo Strauss.* Updated Edition. New York: Palgrave Macmillan, 2005.

Dugan, Andrew. "After Nuclear Deal, U.S. Views of Iran Remain Dismal." *Gallup News*, February 17, 2016. https://news.gallup.com/poll/ 189272/ after-nuclear-deal-views-iran-remain-dismal.aspx

Duss, Matt. "Prissy Schoolmarm's Lips." *ThinkProgress,* November 2, 2009. https://thinkprogress.org/prissy-schoolmarms-lips-b3c40cba8292/

DeMuth, Christopher. "Irving Kristol Award and Lecture for 2009." *American Enterprise Institute,* March 11, 2009. http://www.aei.org/publication /irving-kristol-award-and-lecture-for-2009/

DiNucci, Darcy. "Fragmented Future." *Print Magazine* 53, no. 4: 221–222. http://darcyd.com/fragmented_future.pdf

Eggins, Suzanne. *Introduction to Systemic Functional Linguistics. 2nd Edition.* London: Continuum, 2004.

Ehrman, John. *The Rise of Neoconservatism: Intellectuals and Foreign Affairs, 1945-1994.* New Haven: Yale University Press, 1995.

Eliot, TS. *Four Quartets.* San Diego: Harcourt, 1941.

Engel, Pamela. "Krauthammer: Trump should 'put his name on' UN headquarters and 'turn it into condos.'" *Business Insider Australia*, December 28, 2016. https://www.businessinsider.com.au/krauthammer-trump-un-head quarters-condos-2016-12?r=US&IR=T

Eshman, Rob. "The Hidden Hero of the Six-Day War." *Jewish Journal,* June 1, 2017. https:// jewishjournal.com / cover_story / 219903 / hidden-hero-six-day-war/

Essa, Azad. "Israel: no country for black people." *IOL*, January 24, 2018. https://www.iol.co.za/news/opinion/israel-no-country-for-black-people-12900274

Eyerman, Ron. *Between Culture and Politics: Intellectuals in Modern Society.* Cambridge: Polity, 1994.

Fackenheim, Emile. "Faith in God and Man After Auschwitz: Theological Implications." April 2002. https://www.holocaust-trc.org/faith-in-god-and-man-after-auschwitz-theological-implications/

Fackenheim, Emile. "Jewish Faith and the Holocaust." August, 1968. http://www.blankgenealogy.com/holocaust/Concentration%20camps/Jewish%20Faith%20and%20twentiethe%20Holocaust%20by%20Emil%20Fackenheim.pdf

Fackenheim, Emile. *To Mend the World: Foundations of Post-Holocaust Jewish Thought. Reprint Edition.* Bloomington: Indiana University Press, 1994.

Feldman, Shai and Zalmay Khalilzad. "The Future of U.S.-Israel Strategic Cooperation." *The Washington Institute For Near East Policy.* May 2, 1996. https : // www.washingtoninstitute.org / policy-analysis / view/the-future-of-u.s.-israel-strategic-cooperation1

Felzenberg, Alvin. "Benjamin Netanyahu for President in 2012?" *US News*, May 26, 2011. https:// www. usnews.com / opinion/ blogs/alvin- felzenberg/ 2011/05/26/benjamin-netanyahu-for-president-in-2012

Feuerlicht, Roberta Strauss. *The Fate of the Jews: A People Torn Between Israeli Power and Jewish Ethics.* New York: Times Books, 1983.

Fisher, Max. "Gary Samore, a leading skeptic of the Iran deal, explains why he changed his mind." *Vox,* August 13, 2015. https://www.vox.com/2015/8/13/9147289/gary-samore-iran

Fisk, Robert. *The Great War for Civilisation: The Conquest of the Middle East.* London: Fourth Estate, 2014.

Flynn, Michael. "The War Hawks." *Chicago Tribune*, April 13, 2003. https://www. chicagotribune.com / news/ct-xpm -2003-04-13-0304130427-story.html

Forest, David R. "The Bush Administration and Political Rhetoric: A Mixed Methods Study." PhD Thesis, Northern Arizona University, 2017.

Frantzman, Seth. "Will Iran's Pinprick Provocations Backfire?" *The Middle East Forum,* May 22, 2019. https://www.meforum.org/58572/will-iran-pinprick-policy-call-us-bluff

Freud, Sigmund. *Civilization and Its Discontents.* Translated by James Strachey. Vienna: Verlag, 1930. https:// www. stephenhicks. org/ wp-content/ uploads/ 2015/10/ FreudS-CIVILIZATION-AND-ITS-DISCONTENTS -text-final.pdf

Friedman, Murray. *The Neoconservative Revolution.* Cambridge: Cambridge University Press, 2005.

Gadamer, Hans-Georg. "The Problem of Historical Consciousness." *Graduate Faculty Philosophy Journal 5,* no.1 (1975): 8-52.

Gaffney, Frank. "Holocaust 2.0." *Centre For Security Policy*, January 31, 2014. https://www.centerforsecuritypolicy.org/2014/01/31/holocaust-2-0/

Gaffney, Frank. "ObamaBomb: Holocaust 2.0." *Secure Freedom Radio*, July 29, 2015. https://www.centerforsecuritypolicy.org/2015/07/29/obamabomb -holocaust-2-0/

Gaffney, Frank. "Seeing the threat for what it is." *Washington Times*, May 8, 2006.   http://www.washingtontimes.com/news/2006/may/8/20060508- 091537-9132r/

Gaffney, Frank. "The Jihadist Vote." *The Washington Times,* October 14, 2008. https://www.washingtontimes.com/news/2008/oct/14/the-jihadist-vote/

Gaffney, Frank. "The National Iranian American Council (#NIAC) - always a faithful transmission belt of the mullahs' line in Tehran - calls for @AmbJohnBolton's ouster." @frankgaffney. May 16, 2019. *Tweet Since Deleted By Gaffney.*

George, Jim. "Leo Strauss, Neoconservatism and US Foreign Policy: Esoteric Nihilism and the Bush Doctrine." *International Politics* 42, no.2 (June 2005): 174-202.

Gerecht, Reuel Marc. "The New Rouhani; Same as the old Rouhani." *The Weekly Standard* 19, no.5: (2013).

Gharib, Ali and Jim Lobe. "The Project For An Anti-Trump Century." *Lobe Log,* March 5, 2016. https:// lobelog.com / the-project-for - an-anti - trump-century/

Gilbert, Alan. "Segregation: Aggression, and Executive Power: Leo Strauss and 'The Boys.'" *Nomos* 56 (2016): 407-440. https://www.jstor.org/stable/ 26387891

Glick, Caroline. "Ehud Olmert's "Convergence" Plan for the West Bank and U.S. Middle East Policy." *Centre For Security Policy*, April 1, 2006. https://www. centerforsecuritypolicy.org / 2006 /04/ 01/ ehud- olmerts-convergence-plan-for-the-west-bank-and-u-s-middle-east-policy/

Glick, Caroline. "Israel's Arab Cheerleaders." *Jerusalem Post*, April 27, 2009. https://www.jpost.com/Opinion/Columnists/Israels-Arab-cheerleaders

Glick, Caroline. "Rousing the Americans From Their Slumber." *The Jerusalem Post,* February 20, 2014. https://www.jpost.com/Opinion/Columnists/ Rousing-the-Americans-from-their-slumber-342118

Glick, Caroline. "What the Left is Really After." *Townhall*, September 27, 2010. https://townhall.com/columnists/carolineglick/2010/09/27/what-the-left-is-really-after-n749165

Goldberg, Jeffrey. "A Little Learning: What Douglas Feith knew, and when he knew it." *The New Yorker*, May 1, 2005. https://www.newyorker.com/magazine/2005/05/09/a-little-learning-2

Goldberg, Jeffrey. *Liberal fascism: The Totalitarian Temptation from Mussolini to Hillary Clinton*. New York: Doubleday, 2007.

Goldberg, Jeffrey. "More tear gas, please?" *The Jerusalem Post,* November 29, 1991.

Goldberg, Jeffrey. "Obama's tough talk is poisoning America's relationship with Israel." *Penn Live*, March 27, 2015. https://www.pennlive.com/opinion/2015/03/heres_why_we_shouldnt_take_the.html

Goldberg, Jeffrey. *Prisoners: A Story of Friendship and Terror*. New York: Vintage, 2008.

Goldberg, Jeffrey. "Who is Stephen Walt?" *The Atlantic,* December 10, 2010. https: // www.theatlantic.com/national/archive/2010/12/who-is-stephen-walt/67842/

Goldberg, Jonah. "Huckabee's Hitler comparison that wasn't." *American Enterprise Institute*, July 31, 2015. http://www.aei.org/publication/huckabees-hitler-comparison-that-wasnt/

Goldberg, Jonah. "The Term 'Neocon' Has Run Its Course." *Townhall,* January 6, 2016. https://townhall.com/columnists/jonahgoldberg/2016/01/06/draft-n2100163

Goldenberg, Suzanne. "Rioting as Sharon visits Islam holy site." *The Guardian,* September 28, 2000. https: // www.theguardian.com/world/2000/sep/29/israel

Gordon, Evelyn. "'Palestine' is a Civil War Waiting to Happen." *Commentary,* May 18, 2015. https://www.commentary magazine.com / 2015 /05/18/palestine-is-a-civil-war-waiting-to-happen/

Goulka, Jeremiah, Lydia Hansell, Elizabeth Wilke and Judith Larson. "The Mujahedin-e Khalq in Iraq: A Policy Conundrum." *RAND Corporation,* 2009. https://www.rand.org/ content/ dam/rand/pubs/monographs /2009/RAND_MG871.pdf

Gramsci, Antonio. *Prison Notebooks*. Translated and edited by Quintin Hoare and Geoffrey Nowell Smith. New York: International Publishers, 1971.

Grandin, Greg. "The Strange Career of American Exceptionalism." *The Nation,* December 6, 2016. https://www.thenation.com/article/the-strange-career-of-american-exceptionalism/

Grant of Executive Clemency. Proclamation 6518 of December 24, 1992. By the President of the United States of America. https://www.govinfo.gov/content/pkg/STATUTE-107/pdf/STATUTE-107-Pg2606.pdf

Greenfield, Susan. *Mind Change: How Digital Technologies are Leaving Their Mark on Our Brains.* New York: Random House, 2015.

Gregory, Derek. *The Colonial Present.* Oxford: John Wiley & Sons, 2004.

Griffiths, Brent D. "Giuliani: Trump is 'committed to' regime change in Iran.''
    Politico, May 5, 2018. https://www.politico.com/story/2018/05/05/
    giuliani-trump-iran-regime-change-570744

Grondin, David. "Mistaking Hegemony for Empire: Neoconservatives, the Bush
    Doctrine, and the Democratic Empire." *International Journal* 61, no.1
    (2005/2006): 227-241. DOI: 10.2307/40204140

The Guardian. "Full text: bin Laden's 'letter to America.'" 24 November, 2002.
    https://www.theguardian.com/world/2002/nov/24/theobserver

Gugliotta, Guy and Douglas Farah, "12 Years of Tortured Truth on El Salvador."
    The Washington Post, March 21, 1993.

Haaretz. "Bernie Sanders Says He Hopes Netanyahu Loses." April 9, 2019.
    https:// www.haaretz.com/us-news/israel-s-election-bernie-sanders-says
    -he-hopes-netanyahu-loses-1.7106092

Habermas, Jürgen. *The Structural Transformation of the Public Sphere: An
    Inquiry into a Category of Bourgeois Society.* Cambridge: Polity, 1989.

Halbfinger, David M. and Iyad Abuheweila. "For Gaza Protestor, Living or Dying
    is the 'Same Thing.' *The New York Times.* April 29, 2018. https://www.
    nytimes.com/2018/04/29/world/middleeast/gaza-israel-protests.html

Haley, Nikki. "Iran now saying it will violate the disastrous nuclear deal. Time
    for the Europeans to step up and join U.S. in re-imposing sanctions. The
    only way to make the radical Iranian regime truly give up their nuke
    ambitions is to put maximum pressure on them." @NikkiHaley. 10:31
    am, May 8. 2019. https://twitter.com/nikkihaley/status/1126177883809
    026048

Halliday, M.A.K. *Linguistic Studies of Text and Discourse.* Edited by Jonathan
    Webster. London: Continuum, 2002.

Halper, Stefan and Jonathan Clark. *America Alone: The Neo-Conservatives and
    the Global Order.* Cambridge: Cambridge University Press, 2006.

Harrison, Christopher T. "The developmental implications of image theory in
    inciting a population to war: A content analysis of Bush administration
    discourse leading to the Iraq War." PhD Thesis, Institute of
    Transpersonal Psychology, 2009.

Harrow, Eve. "Charles Krauthammer: A unique voice in our world." *Arutz Sheva,*
    June 26, 2018. http://www.israelnationalnews. com/News/News.aspx/
    248001

Hartman, Andrew. "The Neoconservative Counterrevolution." *Jacobin*, April 23,
    2015.

Hassan, Mehdi. "Here's Why Washington Hawks Love This Cultish Iranian Exile
    Group." *The Intercept,* July 7, 2017. https://theintercept.com/2017/ 07/
    07/mek-iran-rajavi-cult-saudi-gingrich-terrorists-trump/

Hasten, Josh. "New York State Republican Committee Chair Tours Israel."
    Jewish News Syndicate, July 15, 2019. https://www.jns.org/new-york-
    state-republican-committee-chair-tours-israel/

Havel, Vaclac. *Disturbing the Peace: A Conversation with Karel Hvizdala.* New
    York: Vintage Books, 1991.

Havers, Grant and Mark Wexler. "Is U.S. Neoconservatism Dead?" *Quarterly Journal of Ideology* 24, nos.1 & 2 (2001): 1-12. https://www.lsus.edu/... /IS%20U.S%20Neoconservatism%20Dead%20Haves%20and%20Wex ler.pdf

Healy, Gene. "Think Tanks and Iraq War." *Cato Institute*, June 8, 2015. https://www.cato.org/blog/think-tanks-iraq-war

Hekman, Susan J. "Weber's Ideal Type: A Contemporary Reassessment." *Polity* 16, no.1 (1983): 119-137. doi:10.2307/3234525.

Heidegger, Martin. *Being and Time.* Translated by Joan Stambaugh. Albany: State University of New York Press, 1996.

Heilbrunn, Jacob. *They Knew They Were Right: The Rise of the Neocons.* New York: Doubleday, 2008.

Hemmer, Nicole. "Donald Trump is Pushing Neocons into the Wilderness." *U.S. News Report*, March 8, 2016. https://www.usnews.com/opinion/blogs/ nicole-hemmer/articles/2016-03-08/donald-trump-is-pushing-neocons-into-the-wilderness

Hill, Jason D. "My 'Black Lives Matter' Problem." *Commentary,* May 14, 2018. https:// www. commentarymagazine. com / articles/black - lives - matter-problem/

Hills, David. "Metaphor." *Stanford Encyclopedia of Philosophy,* September 6, 2016. https://plato.stanford.edu/entries/metaphor/

Himmelfarb, Milton. "Is American Jewry in Crisis?" *Commentary*, June 1969. https:// www.commentarymagazine.com / articles / american -jewry-in - crisis/

History News Network. "CNN's Pearl Harbor Mistake." https://historynewsnet work.org/article/88

Hitchens, Christopher. "Machiavelli in Mesopotamia: The case against the case against "regime change" in Iraq." *Slate,* November 7, 2002. https:// slate. com/news – and - politics / 2002/11/ the- flawed - case - against-regime-change.html

Hitchens, Christopher. "The Plight of the Public Intellectual." *Foreign Policy,* April 10, 2008. http://www.foreignpolicy.com/articles/2008/04/10/the_ plight_of_the_public_intellectual.

Hobsbawm, Eric. *Nations and Nationalism Since 1780: Programme, Myth, Reality.* Cambridge: Cambridge University Press, 1992.

Holger, Diessel. "Usage Based Linguistics." October 23, 2017. http://www. personal.uni-jena.de/ ~x4diho / Usage_based_linguistics.pdf DOI: 10.10 93/acrefore/9780199384655.013.363

Horowitz, David. "Who Are Our Adversaries." *National Review,* April 28. 2014. https ://www.nationalreview.com / 2014 / 04 / who-are-our-adversaries-david-horowitz/

Horowitz, Michael. "New intolerance between crescent and cross." *The Wall Street Journal*, July 5, 1995. A1.

Horton, Scott. "Six Questions for Peter Minowitz." *Harper's Magazine: The Harper's blog,* September 29, 2009. https://harpers.org/blog/2009/09/_straussophobia_-six-questions-for-peter-minowitz/

Hosch, William L. "Web 2.0: Internet." *Encyclopaedia Brittanica,* April 25, 2018. https://www.britannica.com/topic/Web-20

Hovannisian, Richard G. *The Armenian Holocaust: A Bibliography Relating to the Deportations, Massacres, and Dispersion of the Armenian People, 1915-1923.* Cambridge: Armenian Heritage Press/National Association for Armenian Studies and Research, 1980.

Idrees, Muhammad Idrees. *The Road to Iraq: The Making of a Neoconservative War.* Edinburgh: Edinburgh University Press. 2014.

Institute for Palestinian Studies. "The Uses of Anti-Semitism." *Jerusalem Quarterly* 15, 2002. https:// www.palestine-studies.org / ar / jq/fulltext / 78021

Iran Freedom. "OIAC Holds Up, 'The Path To Freedom-The Alternative.'" September 22, 2018. https://iranfreedom.org/en/2018/09/22/oiac-ncri-rudolph-giuliani-mek/

Ish-Shalom, Piki. "'The Civilization of Clashes:' Misapplying the Democratic Peace in the Middle East." *Political Science Quarterly* 122, no. 4 (Winter 2007/2008): 533-554. https://www.jstor.org/stable/20202926

Israeli Ministry of Foreign Affairs. "11 National Covenant of the Palestine Liberation Organization- 28 May 1964- ." May 28, 1964. https://mfa.gov .il/mfa/foreignpolicy/mfadocuments/yearbook1/pages/11%20national%20covenant%20of%20twentiethe%20palestine%20liberation%20o.aspx

Israeli Ministry of Foreign Affairs. "104 Report of the Commission of Inquiry into the events at the refugee camps in Beirut," February 8, 1983. https://www.mfa.gov.il/mfa/foreignpolicy/mfadocuments/yearbook6/pages/104%20report%20of%20twentiethe%20commission%20of%20inquiry%20into%20twentiethe%20e.aspx

Jacoby, Jeff. "Pipes's effective path to peace." *Pundicity,* June 22, 2003. http://www.jeffjacoby.com/8900/pipes-effective-path-to-peace

Jaffe, Greg. "Obama's new patriotism: How Obama used his presidency to redefine 'American Exceptionalism.'' *Washington Post*, June 3, 2015. https:// www.washingtonpost.com / sf / national/2015/06/03/obama-and-american-exceptionalism/?utm_term=.d0da461605c5

Jamison, Matthew. "Donald Trump and the Demise of the Neo-Conservatives." *Strategic Culture Foundation*, December 3, 2016. https://www.strategic-culture.org / news / 2016 / 12 / 03 / donald-trump - and – demise - neo-conservatives/

Jamjoum, Lama. "The Effects of Israeli Violations During the Second Uprising "Intifada" on Palestinian Health Conditions." *Social Justice* 29, no.3 (2002): 53-72.

Jeffers, Thomas L. *Norman Podhoretz: A Biography.* Cambridge: Cambridge University Press, 2014.

The Jerusalem Post. "Charles Krauthammer Lauded by Netanyahu, 'We Were as Brothers.'" June 22, 2018. https://www.jpost.com/Diaspora/Charles-Krauthammer-lauded-by-Netanyahu-we-were-as-brothers-560635

JTA, Haaretz and Ron Kampeas. "9 Reasons Why John Bolton Is Causing a Frenzy Among U.S. Jews and Across the Middle East." March 25, 2018. https://www . haaretz.com / us-news / 9 - reasons - why - john-bolton-is-causing-a-frenzy-among-u-s-jews-1.5938717

Kampeas, Ron. "Most American Jews are concerned about anti-Semitism and disapprove of Trump, survey finds." *Jewish Telegraphic Agency*, May 22, 2019.

Karpel, Dalia. "What's Wrong With This Picture." *Haaretz*, August 7, 2002. https://www.haaretz.com/1.5036858

Kassimeris, George and Leonie Jackson. "The West, the rest, and the 'war on terror:' representation of Muslims in neoconservative media discourse." *Contemporary Politics* 17, no.1 (2011): 19-33. ISSN: 1356-9775

Keller, Bill. "The Sunshine Warrior." *The New York Times Magazine*, September 22, 2002. https://www.nytimes.com/2002/09/22/magazine/the-sunshine-warrior.html

Kellner, Douglas. "Bushspeak and the Politics of Lying: Presidential Rhetoric in the 'War on Terror.'" *Presidential Studies Quarterly* 37, no.4 (December 2007): 622-645. https://www.jstor.org/stable/27552281

Kellner, Douglas. "Lying in Politics: The Case of George W. Bush and Iraq." *Cultural Studies: Critical Methodologies* 7, no.2 (20070: 132-144. https://doi.org/10.1177/1532708606295649

Kerboua, Salim. "From Orientalism to neo-Orientalism: Early and contemporary constructions of Islam and the Muslim world." *Intellectual Discourse* 24, no.1 (2016): 7-34. ISSN: 01284878

Khoury, Jack and Barak Ravid. "Netanyahu's 'Wild Beast' Quote Was Apartheid-speak, Says Chief Palestinian Negotiator." *Haaretz*, February 10, 2016. haaretz.com/ israel -news / erekat -pm – s – wild – beast – quote - was-apartheid-speak-1.5402778

Kichik, James. "The Rise of Black Anti-Semitism." *Commentary*, May 14, 2018. https:// www . commentarymagazine . com / articles / rise – black – anti -semitism/

Kinzer, Stephen. "Is Iran Really So Evil." *Politico Magazine,* January 17, 2016. https:// www.politico.com/magazine/story/2016/01/ iran-demonize-evil-tehran-213539

Kirchick, James. "Donald Trump Is Turning Me Liberal." *Tablet Magazine*, March 14, 2016. https://www.tabletmag.com/jewish-news-and-politics /198487/donald-trump-is-turning-me-liberal

Krauthammer, Charles. "A Compassion-free Passion." *Milwaukee Journal Sentinel.* March 5, 2004. 23A.

Krauthammer, Charles. "At Last Zion." *Washington Examiner,* May 11, 1998. https://www.washingtonexaminer.com/weekly-standard/at-last-zion

Krauthammer, Charles. "Charles Krauthammer: If we really mean 'never again,' must stop Iran nukes." *East Bay Times*, January 30, 2015. https://www.eastbaytimes.com/2015/01/30/charles-krauthammer-if-we-really-mean-never-again-must-stop-iran-nukes/

Krauthammer, Charles. "Charles Krauthammer's Reflections on Israel, Zionism, Judaism, and God." *Mosaic Magazine,* June 25, 2018. https://mosaicmagazine.com/picks / israel - zionism / 2018 / 06 /charles-krauthammers-reflections-on-israel-zionism-judaism-and-god/

Krauthammer, Charles. "Charles Krauthammer: If we really mean 'never again,' must stop Iran nukes." *East Bay Times*, January 30, 2015. https://www.eastbaytimes.com/2015/01/30/charles-krauthammer-if-we-really-mean-never-again-must-stop-iran-nukes/

Kreiss, Daniel and Shannon C. McGregor. "Technology Firms Shape Political Communication: The Work of Microsoft, Facebook, Twitter and Google with Campaigns During the 2016 U.S. Presidential cycle." *Political Communication* 35 (2017): 155-177. doi:10.1080/10584609.2017.1364 814

Krieger, Hilary Leila. "Lieberman backs Hagee despite calls to cut ties." *The Jerusalem Post,* July 23, 2008. https://www.jpost.com/Jewish-World /Jewish-News/Lieberman-backs-Hagee-despite-calls-to-cut-ties

Kristol, Irving. *Neo Conservatism: An Autobiography of an Idea.* Lanham: Ivan R. Dee, 1999.

Kristol, Irving. "Obama's Israel Problem." *The Weekly Standard,* January 29, 2015.

Kristol, Irving. *Reflections of a Neoconservative: Looking Back, Looking Ahead.* New York: Basic Books, 1983.

Kristol, Irving. *The Neoconservative Persuasion: Selected Essays, 1942-2009.* New York: Basic Books, 2013.

Kristol, William. "BHL: So It's War." *The Weekly Standard,* November 17, 2015. https://www.washingtonexaminer.com/weekly-standard/bhl-so-its-war

Lakoff, George. "Metaphor, Morality, and Politics Or, Why Conservatives Have Left Liberals In the Dust." *Social Research* 62, no.2, (1995): 177-213. https://www.jstor.org/stable/40971091

Lakoff, George. *Moral Politics: How Liberals and Conservatives Think. 2nd Edition.* Chicago: University of Chicago Press, 2002.

Lakoff, George and Mark Johnson. *Metaphors We Livy By.* Chicago: University of Chicago Press, 2003.

Lamb, Brian. "Neoconservatism: Interview with Irving Kristol." *C-Span,* September 5, 1995. https: // www . c-span.org / video / ?67045-1 / neoconservatism

Langois, Jill. "McCain compares Iran's Ahmadinejad to monkey in tweet." *GlobalPost,* February 4, 2013. https://www.pri.org/stories/2013-02-04/mccain-compares-irans-ahmadinejad-monkey-tweet-video

Lebanon Renaissance Foundation. "The New Hezbollah Manifesto." November, 2009. http://www.lebanonrenaissance.org/assets/Uploads/15-The-New-Hezbollah-Manifesto-Nov09.pdf

Ledeen, Michael. "Easy Prey: Can We Even Pray? *National Review,* April 3, 2006. https:// www . nationalreview . com /2006 / 04 / easy-prey-michael -ledeen/

Leibovitz, Liel. "Fibi Netanyahu." *Tablet,* July 15, 2010. https://www.tabletmag .com/scroll/39692/fibi-netanyahu

Leo Strauss Centre at the University of Chicago. "Recollections: Leo Strauss as Teacher." April 22-23, 2014. https://leostrausscenter.uchicago.edu/rec ollections/

Lind, Michael. "Neoconservatism and American hegemony." In *Why Did the United States Invade Iraq?* Edited by Jane K. Cramer and A. Trevor Thrall. 114-128. London: Routledge, 2012.

Lior, Ilan. "Netanyahu on African 'Infiltrators:' We Will Return South Tel Aviv to Israelis." *Haaretz,* August 31, 2017. https://www.haaretz.com/israel-news / netanyahu - on-african-infiltrators-we-will - return-south-tel-aviv-to-israelis-1.5447329

Lipka, Michael. "A closer look at Jewish identity in Israel and the U.S." *Pew Research Center,* March 16, 2016. https://www.pewresearch.org/fact-tank/2016/03/16/a-closer-look-at-jewish-identity-in-israel-and-the-u-s/

Lipset, SM. "Neoconservatism: Myth and Reality." *Society* 25, no.5 (1988): 29-37. https://doi.org/10.1007/BF02695739

Logan, Justin. "Where the Neocons Went, Rubio Is Following." *Cato Institute,* March 26, 2013. https://www.cato.org/publications/commentary/where-neocons-went-rubio-following

Lopate, Phillip. "Resistance to the Holocaust." *Tikkun,* June 28, 2016. https://www.documentcloud.org/documents/2892966-4-3-19-a-Distance-From-the-Holocaust-Resistance.html.

Lynch, Timothy J. "Neoconservative Visions of Political Islam." *International Politics* 45, no.2 (2008): 182-211. ISSN: 1384-5748

Mackey, Robert. "Fox News Apologizes for False Claims of Muslim-Only Areas in England and France." *New York Times* January 18, 2015. https://www. nytimes.com/2015 / 01/19/world/europe/fox-news-apologizes-for-false-claims-of-muslim-only-areas-in-england-and-france.html

Madarasz, Norman. "Behind the neo-con curtain." *Counterpunch,* May 29, 2003. https://www.counterpunch.org/2003/05/29/behind-the-neo-con-curtain/

Malone, Linda A. "The Kahan Report, Ariel Sharon and the Sabra-Shatilla Massacres in Lebanon: Responsibility Under International Law for Massacres of Civilian Populations." *College of William & Mary Law School: Faculty Publications,* 1985. https://core.ac.uk/download/pdf/ 73972805.pdf

Malone, Scott. "Trump's profanity delights supporters, horrifies etiquette experts." *Reuters,* January 13, 2018. https://www.reuters.com/article/us-

usa-trump - language / trumps - profanity - delights - supporters-horrifies -etiquette-experts-idUSKBN1F12SR

Maltz, Judy. "Islamophobe and 'Great Friend of Israel' Frank Gaffney Reportedly Joining Trump Team." *Haaretz*, November 16, 2016. https://www. haaretz.com/world-news/.premium - islamophobe-great-friend-of-israel -frank-gaffney-to-join-trump-team-1.5462391

Mandel, Seth. "Why Bernie Sanders Doesn't Talk About Being Jewish." *Commentary*, March 2016. https://www.commentarymagazine.com/arti cles/bernie-sanders-doesnt-talk-jewish/

Mannheim, Karl. "The Sociological Problem of the 'Intelligentsia.'" *Ideology and Utopia*. Translated by Louis Wirth and Edward Shils. 153-164 San Diego: Harcourt Brace Jovanovich, 1985.

Mantyla, Kyle. "President Huckabee's Foreign Policy? 'If We Don't Fear God, Nobody Will Fear US.'" *Right Wing Watch*, January 30, 2015. http:// www.rightwingwatch . org/content/ president-huckabees-foreign-policy -if-we-dont-fear-god-nobody-will-fear-us.

Martin, J.R. and David Rose. *Working with Discourse: Meaning Beyond the Clause. 2nd Edition.* London: Continuum, 2007.

Martin, J.R. and P.R.R White. *The Language of Evaluation: Appraisal in English.* Basingstoke: Palgrave Macmillan, 2005.

Marx, Karl. *A Contribution to the Critique of Political Economy.* Translated by S.W. Ryazanskaya. Moscow: Progress, 1859.

Mason, John G. "Leo Strauss and the Noble Lie: The Neo-Cons at War." *Logos* 3, no.2 (Spring 2004). http://www.logosjournal.com/mason.pdf

Massad, Joseph. "Are Palestinian children less worthy? *Al Jazeera,* May 31, 2011. https://www.aljazeera.com/indepth/opinion/2011/05/201152911579533 291.html

May, Clifford D. "A brief history of Jew-hatred." *Israel Hayom*, March 14, 2019. https://www.israelhayom.com/opinions/a-brief-history-of-jew-hatred/

May, Clifford D. "Intellectual Leader [On Bernard Lewis]." *Foundation For the Defence of Democracies* and *Middle East Forum*, March 13, 2007. https://www.meforum.org/campus-watch/10850/intellectual-leader-on-bernard-lewis.

Mead, Corey. *War Play: Video Games and the Future of Armed Conflict.* Boston: Eamon Dolan / Houghton Mifflin Harcourt, 2013.

Mearsheimer, John and Stephen Walt. "Is It Love or The Lobby? Explaining America's Special Relationship with Israel." *Security Studies* 18, no.1 (2009): 58-78. https://doi.org/10.1080/09636410802678031

Mearsheimer, John and Stephen Walt. "Setting the Record Straight: A Response to Critics of 'The Israel Lobby.'" December 12, 2006, https:// mearsheimer.uchicago.edu/pdfs/A0043.pdf

Mearsheimer, John and Stephen Walt. *The Israel Lobby and U.S. Foreign Policy.* Chicago: University of Chicago Press, 2007.

Media Education Foundation. "Edward Said on Orientalism." 2002.

Melzer, Arthur M. *Philosophy Between the Lines: The Lost History of Esoteric Writing.* Chicago: University of Chicago Press, 2014.

Middle East Forum. "A friend's encounter with Chomsky." December 28, 2005. http://www.danielpipes.org/comments/30686

Milbank, Dana. "Prince of Darkness Denies Own Existence." *The Washington Post,* February 20, 2009. https://www.commondreams.org/news/2009/02/20/prince-darkness-denies-own-existence#

Mindel, Nissan. "David and Goliath." *Chabad-Lubavitch Media Center,* https://www.chabad.org / library/ article_cdo/aid/112517 / jewish / David-and-Goliath.htm

Mindell, Cindy. "Conversation with Dr. Richard L. Rubenstein." *CT Jewish Ledger,* August 16, 2017. http://www.jewishledger.com/2016/08/ conv ersation-dr-richard-l-rubenstein/

Mindock, Clark. "Hillary Clinton doubles down on use of word 'deplorable' to describe past two years under Donald Trump." *Independent,* May 6, 2019. https://www.independent.co.uk/news/world/americas/us-politics/hillary-clinton-donald - trump - deplorables-presidency-2016-las-vegas-a8902081.html

Minowitz, Peter. *Straussophobia: Defending Leo Strauss and Straussians against Shadia Drury and Other Accusers.* New York: Lexington Books, 2009.

Mishra, Ashutosh. "Orientalism and Media Representations of Iran in the USA." MA Thesis, Boise State University, 2012.

Monten, Jonathan. "The Roots of the Bush Doctrine: Power, Nationalism, and Democracy Promotion in the U.S. Strategy." *International Security* 29, no.4 (Spring, 2005): 112-156. https://www.jstor.org/stable/4137499

Morning Joe Staff. "Must-Read Op-Eds for Tuesday, Nov. 26." *MSNBC,* November 26, 2013. http://www.msnbc.com/morning-joe/must-read-op-eds-tuesday-nov-26

Mousa, Issam Suleiman. "The Arab Image: The New York Times, 1916-1948." *International Communication Gazette* no.40 (1987): 101-120.

Moynihan, Daniel Patrick. "Ex-Friendly Fire." *Washington Examiner* (redirected from *Weekly Standard*), February 1, 1999. https://www.washington examiner.com/weekly-standard/ex-friendly-fire-3698

Moynihan, Daniel Patrick. *The Negro Family: The Case for National Action.* United States Department of Labour, Office of Policy Planning and Research: Washington, 1965.

Mullin-Lery, Corinna. "Political Islam and the United States' New "Other": An Analysis of the Discourse on Political Islam (2001-2007)." PhD Thesis, London School of Economics and Political Science, 2008.

Muravchik, Joshua. *Making David into Goliath: How the World Turned Against Israel.* New York: Encounter, 2014.

Murray, Charles. *Curmudgeon's Guide to Getting Ahead: Dos and Don'ts of Right Behavior, Tough Thinking, Clear Writing, and Living a Good Life.* New York: Crown Business, 2014.

Murray, Charles. "Jewish Genius." *American Enterprise Institute*, April 2, 2007. http://www.aei.org/publication/jewish-genius/

Murray, Douglas. *Neoconservatism: Why We Need It.* New York: Encounter, 2005.

MacDonald, Kevin. *A people that shall dwell alone: Judaism as a group evolutionary strategy.* Bloomington: iUniverse, 2002.

MacDonald, Kevin. *The Culture of Critique: An evolutionary analysis of Jewish involvement in twentieth-century intellectual and political movements.* Bloomington: Author House, 1998.

McCain, John. "So Ahmadinejad wants to be first Iranian in space - wasn't he just there last week? "Iran launches monkey into space."" @SenJohn McCain. 7.41am, February 4, 2013. https://twitter.com/ senjohnmccain /status/298456316538662912?lang=en

McCarthy, Andy. "Is There Legitimate Doubt About Obama's Eligibility to be President?" *National Review,* July 6, 2008. https://www.nationalreview. com / corner/there - legitimate-doubt - about-obamas - eligibility-be-president-andrew-c-mccarthy/

The National. "Gaza is 'open-air prison' ? UN humanitarian chief." March 12, 2010. https://www.thenational.ae/world/mena/gaza-is-open-air-prison-un-humanitarian-chief-1.553055

The National Security Archive. "Campaign to Install Pro-Western Government in Iran Authority." Released 21, June, 2011. https://nsarchive2.gwu.edu /NSAEBB/NSAEBB435/docs/Doc%202%20-%201954-00-00%20Sum mary%20of%20Wilber%20history.pdf

Naureckas, Jim. "Three Reasons Bret Stephens Should Not Be a NYT Columnist– and the Real Reason He Is One." *FAIR,* May 2, 2017. https://fair.org/ home / three-reasons-bret-stephens-should-not-be-a-nyt-columnist-and-the-real-reason-he-is-one/

Netanyahu, Benjamin. "Israeli Prime Minister Netanyahu Address to Joint Meeting of the US Congress." *Israel Ministry of Foreign Affairs,* July 26, 2011. https://mfa.gov.il/MFA/ForeignPolicy/Iran/Pages/Iran_State ments_Israeli_leaders-May_2011.aspx

Neuchterlein, James A. "Neoconservatism & Irving Kristol." *Commentary,* August 1984. https://www.commentarymagazine.com/articles/ neocons ervatism-irving-kristol/

New York Post. "Loose lips." February 10, 2012. https://nypost.com/2012/02/10/ loose-lips-2/

The New York Times. "From the Editors – The Times and Iraq." May 26, 2014. https://www.nytimes.com/2004/05/26/world/from-the-editors-the-times -and-iraq.html

Newsmax TV. "James Woolsey to Newsmax TV: Sanctions Key to Stopping Iran." May 28, 2019. https://www.newsmax.com/newsmax-tv/sanctions-regime-change-nuclear-deal-james-woolsey/2019/05/28/id/917938/

Nolan, Hamilton. "The Best of Bret Stephens: Your Newest *New York Times* Opinion Columnist." *Splinter*, April 14, 2014. https://splinternews.com/ the-best-of-bret-stephens-your-newest-new-york-times-o-1794297718

Nossiter, Bernard. D. "Israeli's Condemned by Security Council for Attack on Iraq." *The New York Times,* June 20, 1981. https://www.nytimes.com /1981/ 06 / 20 /world/israelis-condemned-by-security-council-for-attack -on-iraq.html

Novak, William. "Commentary and the Jewish Community: The Record Since 1960." *Response* 7, no.3 (Fall 1973): 49-66.

Novick, Peter. *The Holocaust in American Life.* Boston: Houghton Mifflin, 1999.

Nuyts, Jan. *Aspects of a cognitive-pragmatic theory of language: On cognition, functionalism and grammar.* Amsterdam: John Benjamins, 1992.

Nuyts, Jan. *Autonomous vs. non-autonomous syntax.* Amsterdam: John Benjamins, 1995.

Nuyts, Jan. "Cognitive Linguistics and Functional Linguistics." In *The Oxford Handbook of Cognitive Linguistics.* Edited by Dirk Geeraerts and Herbert Cuyckens. 824-860. Oxford: Oxford University Press, 2007.

Okrent, Daniel. "The Hottest Button: How the Times Covers Israel and Palestine." *The New York Times,* April 24, 2005. https://www.nytimes.com/ 2005/04/24/ weekinreview / the-hottest- button-how-the-times - covers-israel-and-palestine.html

Ollman, Bertell. *Dance of the Dialectic: Steps in Marx's Method.* Chicago: University of Illinois Press, 2003.

Orwell, George. "Notes on Nationalism." *Polemic,* October 1945. https://ebooks.adelaide.edu.au/o/orwell/george/notes-on-nationalism/

Orwell, George. "Writers and Leviathan." *The Intellectuals: A Controversial Portrait.* Edited by George B. de Huszar. 267-71. Glencoe: The Free Press, 1960.

Orwell, George. *1984.* New York: Harcourt, Brace & World, 1949.

Osborne, Thomas. "On Mediators: Intellectuals and the Ideas Trade in the Knowledge Society." *Economy and Society* 33, no.4 (2004): 430-447. doi:10.1080/0308514042000285224.

Owens, Patricia. "Beyond Strauss, Lies and the War in Iraq: Hannah Arendt's Critique of Neoconservatism." *Review of International Studies* 33, no.2. (April 2007): 265-283. DOI:10.1093/acprof:oso/9780199299362.003. 0007

Oxford Union. "John Bolton Full Address." February 11, 2013. https://www. youtube.com/watch?v=0M1-nLUDJ0s

O'Reilly, Tim. "Web 2.0: Compact definition?" *Radar,* October 1, 2005. http://radar.oreilly.com/2005/10/web-20-compact-definition.html

Palestine National Liberation Movement. "Fatah: Internal Charter." https://fas.org/irp/dni/osc/fatah-charter.pdf

Parsons, Talcott. "'The intellectual:' a social role category." *On Intellectuals: Theoretical Studies, Case Studies.* Edited by Philip Rieff. 3-26. Garden City: Doubleday, 1969.

Paul, Darel E. "The Siren Song of Geopolitics: Towards a Gramscian Account of the Iraq War." *Millennium: Journal of International Studies* 36, no.1 (2007): 51-76. https://doi.org/10.1177/03058298070360010401

Paulin, Tom. "Writing to the moment." *The Guardian,* September 25, 2004. https://www.theguardian.com/books/2004/sep/25/society.politics

Peleg, Ilan. *The Legacy of George W. Bush's Foreign Policy: Moving Beyond Neoconservatism.* Boulder: Westview Press, 2009.

Pew Research Center: Religion and Public Life. "Pentecostals in the Evangelical Tradition." 2014. https://www.pewforum.org/religious-landscape-study/ religious – family / pentecostal – family – evangelical - trad/#social - and-political-views

Pew Research Center: Religion and Public Life. "Religious Composition by Country, 2010-2050." April 2, 2015. https://www.pewforum.org/2015/ 04/02/religious-projection-table/2010/number/all/

Pipes, Daniel. "Lessons of the War in Gaza." *National Review*, August 9, 2014. https:// www.nationalreview . com/ 2014 / 08 / lessons-war-gaza-daniel-pipes/

Pipes, Daniel. "The Case for Supporting Assad." *National Review*, April 12, 2013. https:// www.nationalreview.com / 2013 / 04 / case-supporting-assad-daniel-pipes/

PJTV Media. "Paul E. Vallely Video Interview With Paul Whittle." May 20, 2010.

Plaut, Steven. "Celebrating Rachel Corrie: Israeli Tax Dollars at Work." *FrontPageMag,* July 3, 2013, https://www.frontpagemag.com/fpm/1953 92/celebrating-rachel-corrie-israeli-tax-dollars-work-steven-plaut

Plaut, Steven. "The Truth About the 'Apartheid' Wall." *FrontPageMag*, May 1, 2012. https://www.frontpagemag.com/fpm/130357/truth-about-aparthei d-wall-steven-plaut

Plitnick, Mitchell. "AIPAC: The Essential Profile." *Lobe Log,* April 1, 2019. https://lobelog.com/aipac-the-essential-profile/

Podhoretz, John. "We're pulling out of the Iran deal and @SonnyBunch is right about something.Truly this is a historic day."@jpodhoretz. 9.31 am, May 8, 2018. https://twitter.com/jpodhoretz/status/993891271654739968

Podhoretz, John. @jpodhoretz. 4.01am, February 5, 2007.

Podhoretz, Norman. "Hannah Arendt on Eichmann: A Study in the Perversity of Brilliance." *Commentary*, September 1963. https://www.commentary magazine. com / articles/hannah - arendt-on-eichmanna-study-in-the-perversity-of-brilliance/

Podhoretz, Norman. "My Negro Problem – And Ours." *Commentary*, February 1963. https: // www.commentarymagazine.com / articles/my-negro-pr oblem-and-ours/

Podhoretz, Norman. "Norman Podhoretz - Reflections of a Jewish Neoconservative." *The Tikvah Fund*, July 14, 2014. https://tikvahfund. org/library/norman-podhoretz-reflections-of-a-jewish-neoconservative/

Podhoretz, Norman. "Why are Jews Liberals?" New York: Vintage, 2009.

Postel, Danny. "Noble lies and perpetual war: Leo Strauss, the neocons, and Iraq." *Open Democracy*, October 15, 2003, https://www.opendemocracy.net /en/article_1542jsp/

Potok, Chaim. "Martin Buber and the Jews." *Commentary*, March 1996. https ://www.commentarymagazine . com / articles / martin-buber -and-the-jews/

Power, Samantha. "Boltonism." *The New Yorker,* March 13, 2005. https://www. newyorker.com/magazine/2005/03/21/boltonism

Prange, Gordon William, Donald M. Goldstein and Katherine V. Dillion, *At Dawn We Slept: The Untold Story of Pearl Harbour*. New York: McGraw-Hill, 1981.

Ragin, Charles C. *Fuzzy-Set Social Science.* Chicago: University of Chicago Press, 2000.

Real Time with Ben Maher. "Bret Stephens: Out of the Echo Chamber." HBO. Published online on September 15, 2017. https://www.youtube.com/ watch?v=60JPl6G791E

Record, Jeffrey. "Retiring Hitler and 'Appeasement' from the National Security Debate." *Air War College Maxwell*, January 2008. https://apps.dtic.mil /dtic/tr/fulltext/u2/a597225.pdf

Record, Jeffrey. "Using (and Misusing) History: Munich, Vietnam, and Iraq." *Survival* 49, no.1 (March 2007):163-180. DOI:10.1080/0039633070125 4628

Rees, Matt. "Streets Red with Blood," *Time Magazine*, March 18, 2002. http://www.time.com/time/magazine/article/0,9171,1002012,00.html#i xzz17Cpns1Y8

Rezaian, Jason. "Jason Rezaian, 'John Bolton wants regime change in Iran, and so does the cult that paid him." *The Washington Post,* March 24, 2018. ISSN: 0190-8286.

Right Web. "Bernard Marcus." May 21, 2018. https://rightweb.irc-online.org/ profile/bernard-marcus/

Right Web. "Family Security Matters." January 27, 2012. https://rightweb.irc-online.org/profile/family_security_matters/

Right Web. "Marco Rubio." February 2, 2019. https://rightweb.irc-online.org/ profile/marco-rubio/

Right Web. "Paul E. Vallely." October 8, 2015. https://rightweb.irc-online.org/ profile/paul-vallely/#_edn7

Right Web. "Paul Singer." May 29, 2018. https://rightweb.irc-online.org/ profile/paul-singer/

Right Web. "People's Mujahedin of Iran (MEK)." January 23, 2019. https:// rightweb.irc-online.org/profile/peoples_muhajedin_of_iran_ mek/

Right Web. "Sheldon Adelson." September 28, 2018. https://rightweb.irc-online.org/profile/sheldon-adelson/

Rogachevsky, Neil. "After Netanyahu." *The Weekly Standard* (re-directs to *Washington Examiner),* October 6, 2017. https://www.washington exa miner. com/weekly-standard/after-netanyahu-2009953

Rosenbaum, Thane. "Hamas's Civilian Death Strategy." *The Wall Street Journal*, July 21, 2014. https://www.wsj.com/articles/thane-rosenbaum-civilian-cas ualties-in-gaza-1405970362

Rossett, Claudia. "For Hotel Hosting Ahmadinejad, Just Another 'International Event.'" *Foundation For Defense of Democracies*, September 21, 2011. https:// www.fdd.org/analysis/2011/09/21/for-hotel-hosting-ahmadineja d-just-another-international-event/

Rossini, Patricia, Jeff Hemsley, Sikana Tanupabrungsun, Feifei Zhang and Jennifer Stromer-Galley. "Social Media, Opinion Polls, and the Use of Persuasive Messages During the 2016 US Election Primaries." *Social Media + Society* (July 2018) doi:10.1177/2056305118784774.

RT News. "Ban the Koran? Geert Wilders speaks out on his radical views." March 7, 2010. https://www.youtube.com/watch?v=GanFV4b1wvk

Rubenstein, Richard. *After Auschwitz: Radical Theology and Contemporary Judaism*. London: Macmillan, 1966.

Rubenstein, Richard and John K. Roth, *Approaches to Auschwitz: The Holocaust and its Legacy*. Louisville: John Knox Press, 1987.

Rubin, Debra. "Author decries radical Islam's 'culture of death.'" *New Jersey Jewish News*, October 2, 2015. https://njjewishnews.timesofisrael.com/ author-decries-radical-islams-culture-of-death/

Rubin, Jennifer. "Rand Paul's Confused Foreign Policy Speech." *The Washington Post*, February 6, 2013. https://www.washingtonpost.com/blogs/right-turn/wp/2013/02/06/rand-pauls-confused-foreign-policy-speech/

Rubin, Michael. "The Middle East's real bane: corruption." *Middle East Forum*, November 18, 2005. https://www.meforum.org/790/the-middle-easts-real-bane-corruption

Rudy Giuliani Presidential Committee, Inc. "Rudy Giuliani Announces Foreign Policy Team Members." July 10, 2007. http://p2008.org/giuliani/ giuliani071007pr.html

Sahlane, Ahmed. "Metaphor as rhetoric: newspaper Op/Ed debate of the prelude to the 2003 Iraq War." *Critical Discourse Studies* 10, no.2 (2013): 154-171. https://doi.org/10.1080/17405904.2012.736397

Said, Edward. *Orientalism*. London: Penguin, 1977.

Said, Edward. *Representations of the Intellectual: the 1993 Reith Lectures*. London: Vintage, 1994.

Said, Edward. *The Public Intellectual*. Edited by Helen Small. Oxford: Blackwell, 2002.

Sakharov, Andrei. *Thoughts on progress, peaceful coexistence and intellectual freedom*. Petersham: Foreign Affairs Publishing Co., 1968.

Sanchez, Luis. "Bolton: Recognizing Jerusalem as Capital of Israel 'Enhances the chances for peace.'" *The Hill*, May 13, 2018. http://thehill.com/ homenews / sunday-talk-shows / 387477-bolton-recognizing-jerusalem-as-capital-of-israel

Schachtman, Tom. "It's Time to Abandon 'Munich.'" *Foreign Policy*, September 29, 2013. https:// foreignpolicy.com / 2013 / 09 / 29/its-time-to-abandon-munich/

Schanzer, Jonathan. "Huge Verdict Is the Price the Palestinian Authority Pays for Not Controlling the P.L.O." *The New York Times,* May 7, 2015. https:// www.nytimes.com / roomfordebate /2015/02/24/terror-and-the-palestini an-authority / huge-verdict-is-the-price-the-palestinian-authority-pays-for-not-controlling-the-plo

Schmitt, Carl. *The Concept of the Political.* Translated by George Schwab. Chicago: The University of Chicago Press, 1996.

Schmitt, Eric. "Paul Dundes Wolfowitz." *The New York Times,* March 17, 2005. https:// www.nytimes.com / 2005 / 03 / 17 / politics/paul-dundes-wolfo witz.html

Shaban, Hamza. "Playing War: How the Military Uses Video Games." *The Atlantic,* October 10, 2013. https://www.theatlantic. com/technology/ archive/2013/10/playing-war-how-the-military-uses-video-games/2804 86/

Shearer, Elisa and Jeffrey Gottfried. "News Use Across Social Media Platforms 2017." *Pew Research Center: Journalism and Media,* September 7, 2017. https://www.journalism.org/2017/09/07/news-use-across-social-media-platforms-2017/Shell, Susan. "To Share the Vanquished and Crush the Arrogant: Leo Strauss's Lecture on 'German Nihilism." In *The Cambridge Companion to Leo Strauss.* Edited by Steven B. Smith. 171-192. Cambridge: Cambridge University Press, 2009.

Shils, Edward. *The Intellectuals and the Powers and Other Essays.* Chicago: University of Chicago Press, 1972.

Shupak, Gregory. *The Wrong Story: Palestine, Israel and the Media.* New York: OR Books, 2018.

Shuster, Aaron. "Israel's Role and the Way Forward." *FrontPageMag,* December 11, 2012. https://www.frontpagemag.com/fpm/168270/israels-role-and-way-forward-aaron-shuster

Simon Wiesenthal Center. "Speech by PM Netanyahu to a Joint Meeting of the U.S. Congress." May 24, 2011. http://www.wiesenthal.com/about/news/ speech-by-pm-netanyahu-to-a.html

Smith, Anthony D. *Theories of Nationalism.* Teaneck: Holmes & Meier, 1983.

Sniegoski, Stephen J. *The Transparent Cabal: The Neoconservative Agenda, War in the Middle East, and the National Interest of Israel.* Plano: Enigma Editions, 2008.

Sokal, Sam. 'Settlers welcome Mike Huckabee to a Trump-style building dedication in Efrat.' *Jewish Telegraphic Agency,* August 1, 2018. https:// www.jta. org/2018/08/01/israel/settlers-welcome-mike-huckabee-trump -style-building-dedication-efrat

Soloveichik, Meir. "Jews and Power: Tradition, Literature and Politics." *The Tikvah Fund,* November 17, 2014. https://www.youtube.com/watch? time_ continue=6&v=ya-SXGKpRqY

Southern Poverty Law Center. "'No-Go Zones:' The Myth That Just Won't Quit." *Intelligence Report* (Summer 2015). https://www.splcenter.org/fighting-hate/intelligence-report/2015/%E2%80%98no-go-zones%E2%80%99-myth-just-won%E2%80%99t-quit

Stein, Rebecca L. "'Fake News!' The view from Israel's Occupation." *Open Democracy,* February 12, 2018. https://www.opendemocracy.net/en/north-africa-west-asia/fake-news-view-from-israel-s-occupation/

Stephens, Bret. "Liberalism's Imaginary Enemies." *The Wall Street Journal,* November 30, 2015. https: // www.wsj.com / articles/liberalisms-imagi nary-enemies-1448929043

Stephens, Bret. "Obama is Pushing Israel Towards War." *The Wall Street Journal,* September 15, 2009. https://www.wsj.com/articles/SB10001424052970 2039173045744106722271269390

Stephens, Bret. "Palestine: The Psychotic Stage." *The Wall Street Journal,* October 12, 2015. https://www.wsj.com/articles/palestine-the-psychotic -stage-1444692875

Stephens, Bret. "Stephens: Haiti, Sudan, Cote d'Ivoire – Who Cares?" *The Wall Street Journal,* January 11, 2011. https://www.wsj.com/articles/ SB100 014240 52748703779704576073593183855836

Stephens, Bret. "Stephens – Worse than Munich." *The Wall Street Journal,* November 25, 2013. https://www.wsj.com/articles/no-headline-availab le-1385420050

Stephens, Bret. "The Essential Wall (later updated to 'The Way We Live Now (in Israel)." *The Wall Street Journal,* October 14, 2004. https://www. wsj.com /articles/SB1097708285801447660

Stephens, Bret. "The Queerest Denial." *The Wall Street Journal.* October 2, 2007. https://www.wsj.com/articles/SB119129023259045999

Stephens, Bret. "What you need to know about Iran's rulers in one video." @BretStephensNYT. 9:12 am, June 23, 2019. https://twitter.com/brets tephensnyt/status/1142827808793800709

Stephens, Bret. "Who Did This to Us." *The Wall Street Journal,* August 29, 2016. https://www.wsj.com/articles/who-did-this-to-us-1472513066

Stern, Sol. "The Lies of Hannah Arendt." *Commentary,* September 2013. https: //www.commentarymagazine.com/articles/the-lies-of-hannah-arendt/

Strauss, Leo. *Natural Right and History.* Chicago: University of Chicago Press, 1965.

Strauss, Leo. *On Tyranny – An Interpretation of Xenophon's Hierod.* Glencoe: The Free Press, 1948.

Strauss, Leo. *Persecution and the Art of Writing.* Chicago: University of Chicago Press, 1988.

Suny, Ronald Grigor and Michael D. Kennedy (Eds.) *Intellectuals and the Articulation of the Nation.* Michigan: University of Michigan Press, 2001.

Supporters of People's Mojahedin Organization of Iran (PMOI/MEK). "Camp Ashraf & Liberty." 2018. https://mek-iran.com/camp-ashraf-camp-liberty/

Swaine, John and Ciara McCarthy. "Young black men again faced highest rate of US police killings in 2016." *The Guardian,* January 8, 2017. https://www.theguardian.com/us-news/2017/jan/08/the-counted-police-killings-2016-young-black-men

Tapson, Steve. "The War to Destroy Christian America." *FrontPageMag,* March 6, 2019. https:// www.frontpagemag.com / fpm / 273060 / war-destroy - christian-america-mark-tapson

Terry, Janice and Gordon Mendenhall. "1973 US Press Coverage on the Middle East." *Journal of Palestinian Studies* 4, no.1 (1974): 120-133. DOI: 10.2307/2535928

Terry Lakin Action Fund. "Interview with Major General Paul E. Vallely." June 13, 2011.

Tesich, Steve. "A Government of Lies." *The Nation* 254, no.1. (January 6, 1992): 12-14.

The Times of Israel. "Giuliani: Sanctions creating the conditions for revolution in Iran." September 23, 2018. https://www.timesofisrael.com/giuliani-sanctions-creating-the-conditions-for-revolution-in-iran/

Thomas, Cal. "For Secretary of State, John Bolton is best choice." *Chicago Tribune,* December 1, 2016. https://www.chicagotribune.com/opinion/ commentary/ ct – trump – secretary – of – state – john - bolton-20161201 -story.html

Thornton, Bruce. "Terrorism in the Therapeutic Age." *FrontPageMag,* July 21, 2016. https ://www.frontpagemag.com / fpm / 263535 / terrorism-therape utic-age-bruce-thornton

Tian, Tian. "An Analysis of the Causes of the American Invasion of Iraq." PhD Thesis, Peking University, 2010.

The Tikvah Fund. "About: What is The Tikvah Fund?" https://tikvah fund.org/about/

The Tikvah Fund. "Elliott Abrams on Reconsidering America's Democracy Agenda." March 19, 2014. https://tikvahfund.org/library/elliott-abrams-reconsidering-americas-democracy-agenda/

The Times of Israel. "Dutch populist Wilders faces huge backlash on Moroccan critique." March 21, 2014. https://www.timesofisrael.com/dutch-populist-wilders-faces-huge-backlash-on-moroccan-critique/

Tibon, Amir. "Watch - 2020 Hopeful Bernie Sanders Says Netanyahu Leads 'Racist Government.'" *Haaretz*, April 23, 2019.

Toosi, Sina. "The Best Way to Avert War with Iran? Fire John Bolton." *Newsweek,* 13 May, 2019. https://www.newsweek.com/iran-war-trump-sack-john-bolton-1423998

Torossian, Ron. "Jews Who Abandon Judaism Abandon Israel: A Glance at the Self-Hating Narcissism of the Jewish Left." *FrontPageMag,* February

25, 2014. https://www.frontpagemag.com/fpm/219703/jews-who-aban
don-judaism-abandon-israel-ronn-torossian

Trask, Robert Lawrence and Peter Stockwell. *Language and Linguistics: The Key Concepts.* New York: Routledge, 2007.

Trump, Donald. "To Iranian President Rouhani." @realDonaldTrump, 8.24pm, July 22, 2018. https://twitter.com/realDonaldTrump/status/102123452 56266096 66

Tucker, Robert. "The Middle East: Carterism Without Carter." *The Weekly Standard,* September, 1981. https://www.commentarymagazine.com/ articles/the-middle-east-carterism-without-carter/

United Against Nuclear Iran. "Coalition Information." 2019. http://www.united againstnucleariran.com/about/coalition.

United Against Nuclear Iran. "FAQ". 2019. https://www.unitedagainst nucleariran .com/about/faqs

United Against Nuclear Iran. "Our Mission." 2019. http://www.unitedagainstn ucleariran.com/about/mission.

Unity Coalition For Israel. "Stephens: Worse Than Munich." November 27, 2013. https://unitycoalitionforisrael.org/?p=11036

Unger, Craig. *The Fall of the House of Bush.* New York: Scribner, 2007.

US Congress. "S.1 - Strengthening America's Security in the Middle East Act of 2019." Bill Introduced by Senator Marc Rubio, March 1, 2019. https://www.congress.gov/bill/116th-congress/senate-bill/1

Vaïsse, Justin. *Neoconservatism: The Biography of a Movement.* Cambridge: Belknap Press, 2011.

Vice Media. "Why Evangelical Christians Love Israel." *HBO.* May 15, 2018. https://www.youtube.com/watch?v=Fo77sTGpngQ

Vlastos, Gregory, Paul Sunstein, Robert Gordis and M.F. Burnyeat. "Further Lessons of Leo Strauss: An Exchange." *The New York Review of Books,* April 24, 1986. https://www.nybooks.com/articles/1986/04/24/further-lessons-of-leo-strauss-an-exchange/

Vološinov, Valentin N. *Marxism and the Philosophy of Language.* Cambridge: Harvard University Press, 1973.

Wagner, John. "Trump national security spokeswoman Monica Crowley to forgo post amid plagiarism charges." *The Washington Post,* January 16, 2017. https:// www.washingtonpost.com / news / post-politics/ wp/2017/01/16/ trump-national-security-spokeswoman-monica-crowley-to-forgo-post-amid-plagiarism-charges/

Wald, Alan M. *The New York Intellectuals: The Rise and Decline of the Anti-Stalinist Left From the 1930s to the 1980s.* Chapel Hill: The University of North Carolina Press, 1987.

Wallace, Mark D. and Irwin Cotler. "In Case You Missed It: 'To Protect Human Rights, Companies Must Pull Out Of Iran.'" *United Against Nuclear Iran,* February 2, 2012. https://www.unitedagainstnucleariran .com/ press - releases/case-you-missed-it-protect - human-rights -companies-must-pull-out-iran

Walsh, David Austin. "The New York Times recycles John Ford Pearl Harbor footage." *History News Network*, October 28, 2013. https://history newsnetwork.org/article/153739

The Washington Times. "Appointment gratification." March 20, 2005. https://www.washingtontimes.com/news/2005/mar/20/20050320-08564 7-4816r/

Weber, Max. "'Objectivity' in Social Science and Social Policy." *The Methodology of Social Science.* Edited and translated by E.A. Shils and H.A. Finch. 49-122. New York: The Free Press, 1949.

Weinthal, Benjamin and Asaf Romirowsky. "What Americans Can Learn from Europeans about Fighting BDS." *Middle East Forum,* August 30, 2017. https://www.meforum.org/6892/banks-the-israel-boycott-movement

Wiesel, Elie. "Acceptance Speech." *The Noble Peace Prize 1986.* https://www .nobelprize.org/prizes/peace/1986/wiesel/acceptance-speech/

Wiesel, Elie. "Art and the Holocaust: Trivializing Memory." *The New York Times*, June 11, 1989. https://www.nytimes.com/1989/06/11/movies/art-and-the-holocaust-trivializing-memory.html move this up one so it appears before Wiesel's reference 'night'

Wiesel, Elie. *Night.* New York: Hill and Wang, 2006.

Woodward, Bob. *State of Denial*. New York: Simon & Schuster, 2006.

The World Bank. "Fifteen months – Intifada, Closures and Palestinian Economic Crisis." March 25, 2002. http://documents.worldbank.org/curated/pt/ 394371468049795957/ Fifteen – months – Intifada – closures – and - Palestinian-economic-crisis-an-assessment

The World Bank. "Twenty-seven months - Intifada, closures, and Palestinian economic crisis: an assessment (English)." January 5, 2003. http:// documents.worldbank.org / curated / en/616581468765333893/Twenty-seven-months - Intifada-closures-and - Palestinian - economic-crisis-an-assessment

Yasar, Abdulaziz Ahmet. "Israeli wants to be 'in Africa' but to keep Africans out of Israel." *TRT World*, January 9, 2019. https://www.trtworld.com/ mea /israel-wants-to-be-in-africa-but-to-keep-africans-out-of-israel-23196

Zadeh, Lotfi A. "Fuzzy Sets." *Information Control* 8, no.3 (1965): 338-353.

Zakheim, Dov. "Fund Israel's Military, Not Its Settlements: Washington should link part of its defense aid to Jerusalem's settlement funding." *The National Interest,* August 9, 2016. https ://nationalinterest.org/ feature /fund - israels-military-not- its-settlements-17295

Zakheim, Dov. "Obama Should Give up on East Jerusalem." *Foreign Policy*, November 10, 2010. https:// foreignpolicy.com / 2010 / 11 / 10 / obama-should-give-up-on-east-jerusalem/

Zakheim, Dov. "Practicing Jews Serving in the National Security Community." *Institute for Jewish Ideas and Ideals,* https://www.jewishideas. org/ article/practicing-jews-serving-national-security-community-dr-dov - zakheim

Zakheim, Dov. "The Iran Nuclear Agreement: Tehran 'Achieved All It Wanted.'" *The National Interests,* July 14, 2015. https://nationalinterest.org/feature /the-iran-nuclear-agreement-tehran-achieved-all-it-wanted-13334

Zuckert, Catherine and Michael Zuckert, *The Truth About Leo Strauss: Political Philosophy and American Democracy*. Chicago: University of Chicago. 2006.

Endnotes

Introduction

[1] *The Tikvah Fund*, 'About: What is The Tikvah Fund?'
[2] *The Tikvah Fund*, 'Elliott Abrams on Reconsidering America's Democracy Agenda.'
[3] Simon Critchley, *Infinitely Demanding: Ethics of Commitment, Politics of Resistance.*
[4] Some of the more interesting and revelatory accounts include Muhammad Idrees Ahmad, *The Road to Iraq: The Making of a Neoconservative War*; Craig Unger, *The Fall of the House of Bush*; Jacob Heilbrunn, *They Knew They Were Right: The Rise of the Neocons*; Stefan Halper and Jonathan Clarke, *America Alone: The Neo-Conservatives and the Global Order.*
[5] Some of the more original and engaging doctoral studies from around the world include Christopher T. Harrison, *The developmental implications of image theory in inciting a population to war: A content analysis of Bush administration discourse leading to the Iraq War*; Helen Dexter, *Warfighting and Lifesaving: New Wars, Cosmopolitan Law Enforcement and the War on* Terror; Tian, Tian, *An Analysis of the Causes of the American Invasion of Iraq.*
[6] Corinna Mullin-Lery, *Political Islam and the United States' New "Other": An Analysis of the Discourse on Political Islam (2001-2007)*; David R. Forest, *The Bush Administration and Political Rhetoric: A Mixed Methods Study*; Ahmed Sahlane, 'Metaphor as Rhetoric: Newspaper Op/Ed Debate of the Prelude to the 2003 Iraq War.'
[7] Muhammad Idrees Ahmad, *The Road to Iraq: The Making of a Neoconservative War*; Gene Healy, 'Think Tanks and Iraq War;' Bob Woodward, *State of Denial.*
[8] Shadia Drury, *The Political Ideas of Leo Strauss*; Danny Postel, 'Noble lies and perpetual war: Leo Strauss, the neocons, and Iraq,' an interview with Shadia Drury.
[9] Catherine Zuckert and Michael Zuckert, *The Truth About Leo Strauss*; Peter Minowitz, *Straussophobia: Defending Leo Strauss and Straussians against Shadia Drury and Other Accusers.*
[10] Andrei Sakharov, *Thoughts on progress, peaceful coexistence and intellectual freedom.*

---

[11] George Orwell, 'Writers and Leviathan,' Julien Benda, *The Treason of the Intellectuals*; Edward Said, 'The Public Role of Writers and Intellectuals;' Vaclav Havel, *Disturbing the Peace: A Conversation with Karel Hvizdala*.

[12] Edward Said, *Reith Lectures 1993: Representations of an Intellectual, Lecture 5, Speaking Truth to Power*, 2.

[13] Guy Gugliotta and Douglas Farah, '12 Years of Tortured Truth on El Salvador.'

[14] George Bush, 'Proclamation 6518—Grant of Executive Clemency.'

[15] George Orwell, 'Notes on Nationalism,' 1.

[16] Gilles Deleuze, *Negotiations*; Thomas Osborne, 'On mediators: Intellectuals and the ideas trade in the knowledge society.'

[17] Jonathan Chait, 'The Neocons Have Gone From GOP Thought-Leaders to Outcasts;' Matthew Jamison, 'Donald Trump and the Demise of the Neo-Conservatives;' James Kirchick, 'Donald Trump is Turning me Liberal;' Ali Gharib and Jim Lobe, 'The Project For An Anti-Trump Century;' Nicole Hemmer, 'Donald Trump is Pushing Neocons into the Wilderness.'

[18] *Right Web Policy Institute* has identified a small group of hugely wealthy individuals who are responsible for funding many neo-conservative outfits. See *Right Web*, 'Sheldon Adelson;' *Right Web*, 'Bernard Marcus;' *Right Web*, 'Paul Singer.'

[19] According to a 2016 Gallup Poll only 18% of respondents who identified as Democrats and 4% Republicans held a favourable view of Iran. See Andrew Dugan, 'After Nuclear Deal, U.S. Views of Iran Remain Dismal.'

[20] Stephen Kinzer, 'Is Iran Really So Evil?'

[21] It is worth noting that *Argo* is not a documentary meaning there exists no moral obligation nor general expectation for its makers to produce a factually correct and historically accurate account of the Iranian Hostage Crisis and associated events. For some understanding about where exactly the film digresses from historical reality see Ben Child, 'New Zealand points to its diplomat's diary as proof that Argo got it wrong.'

[22] Interesting cases of popular US war film propaganda include, *The Green Berets* (1968), which received the Pentagon's backing and President Lyndon Johnson's approval, in order to help counter pervading negative opinions about the Vietnam War. From 1942-1945 the *Office of War Information* was involved in the producing of many propaganda films (too many to list here) aimed at rousing support for the Allied Forces.

[23] Edward Said, *Orientalism*, 28

[24] Charles Krauthammer, 'A Compassion-free Passion,' 23A.

[25] For an insight into the roles violent games play in motivating and inspiring soldiers to go to war see Hamza Shaban in 'Playing War: How the Military Uses Video Games;' Corey Mead, *Video Games and the Future of Armed Conflict*; Ian Bogost, *How to Do Things with Video Games*.

[26] Scott Romaniuk and Tobias Burgers, 'How the US military is using 'violent, chaotic, beautiful' video games to train soldiers.'

[27] *Central Intelligence Agency*, 'The Battle for Iran.'

[28] Document C01384505, 'Campaign to Install Pro-Western Government in Iran.'

[29] Saeed Kamali Dehghan and Richard Norton-Taylor, 'CIA Admits Role in 1953 Iranian Coup.'

[30] Jacob Heilbrunn, *They Knew They Were Right*, 11

[31] Max Weber, '"Objectivity' in Social Science and Social Policy.'

[32] *Ibid.*, 90.

[33] Susan J. Hekman, "Weber's Ideal Type: A Contemporary Reassessment," 121.

[34] The speaking truth to power and shining a light on injustice approaches within the sociology of intellectuals tradition is reprised at great length by authors like Edward Said, Noam Chomsky, Christopher Hitchens, Karl Mannheim, Talcott Parsons and Edward Shils. See Edward Said, *Reith Lectures 1993: Representations of an Intellectual*; Noam Chomsky, 'The Responsibility of Intellectuals;' Christopher Hitchens, 'The Plight of the Public Intellectual;' Karl Mannheim, 'The sociological problem of the 'intelligentsia,'' Talcott Parsons, ''The intellectual:' a social role category;' Edward Shils, *The Intellectuals and the Powers and Other Essays.*

[35] See for e.g. Timothy J. Lynch, 'Neoconservative Visions of Political Islam;' Ashutosh Mishra, 'Orientalism and Media Representations of Iran in the USA;' Salim Kerboua, 'From Orientalism to neo-Orientalism: Early and contemporary constructions of Islam and the Muslim world;' George Kassimeris and Leonie Jackson, 'The West, the rest, and the 'war on terror:' representation of Muslims in neoconservative media discourse.'

[36] See for e.g. Scott Malone, 'Trump's profanity delights supporters, horrifies etiquette experts.'

[37] John Caputo, *Truth.*

[38] Hans-Georg Gadamer, 'The Problem of Historical Consciousness.'

[39] Mannheim, 'The sociological problem of the 'intelligentsia';' Benda, *The Treason of the Intellectuals*; Said, 'The Public Role of Writers and Intellectuals.'

[40] Many observers who have visited the Palestinian Territories, including those working for apolitical international aid organisations, have reported that its people are living in dire situations best characterised as 'open-air prisons.' John Holmes, UN Under-Secretary-General for *Humanitarian Affairs and Emergency Relief*, reported that Gaza "It is a big open air prison...Half the population is unemployed, if there is food in the shops people don't have money to buy it. It's a rather desperate, depressing situation where people are easily falling prey to despair." David Halbfinger and Iyad Abuheweila of the *The New York Times* have written that in Gaza "living and dying is the same thing...[it] is little more than an open-air prison." Their viewpoint is especially interesting given the *Times* is generally regarded as more receptive to pro-Israeli viewpoints, rather than shining a light on injustice in the Palestinian Territories. This claim is supported by serious scholarship and is perhaps best illustrated by the *Times'* recent hiring of neo-conservative Bret Stephens, who gained notoriety for amongst other things claiming "colonialism may be the best thing that could happen to at least some countries in the postcolonial world" due in part to "the depravity of the locals." See *The National*, 'Gaza is 'open-air prison'? UN humanitarian chief;' David Halbfinger and Iyad Abuheweila, 'For Gaza Protester, Living Or Dying is the

'Same Thing;' Janice Terry and Gordon Mendenhall, '1973 US Press Coverage on the Middle East;' Kuang-Kuo, Chang and Geri Alumit Zeldes, 'Three of Four Newspapers Studied Favor Israeli Instead of Palestinian Sources;' Issam S. Mousa, 'The Arab Image The New York Times;' Daniel Okrent, 'The hottest button: How The Times covers Israel and Palestine;' Bret Stephens, 'Haiti, Sudan, Côte d'Ivoire: Who Cares?'
[41] Cited in Bertell Ollman, *Dance of the Dialectic*, 45.

Chapter One

[1] Martin Heidegger, *Being and Time*.
[2] Bertell Ollman, *Dance of the Dialectic*.
[3] Karl Marx cited in Bertell Ollman, *Dance of the Dialectic*, 154.
[4] Thomas L. Jeffers, *Norman Podhoretz: A Biography*, 125.
[5] Hannah Arendt, *The Origins of Totalitarianism: Imperialism*.
[6] Karl Marx, *A Contribution to the Critique of Political Economy*, 293-294.
[7] Bertell Ollman, *Dance of the Dialectic*, 60.
[8] *Ibid.*
[9] For a more in-depth understanding of notion of fuzzy categories see Lotfi A. Zadeh, 'Fuzzy Sets;' Charles C Ragin, *Fuzzy-Set Social Science.*
[10] T.S. Eliott, *Four Quartets*, 24.
[11] Karl Marx cited in Bertell Ollman, *Dance of the Dialectic*, 100.
[12] Bertell Ollman, *Dance of the Dialectic*, 101.
[13] Gadamer, 'The Problem of Historical Consciousness.'
[14] *Ibid.*, 155.
[15] Mikhail Bakhtin, *Speech Genres and Other Late Essays*, 91.
[16] Mikhail Bakhtin, "The Problem of Speech Genres," in *Speech Genres and Other Late Essays*, 69.
[17] There is a long tradition of writers describing how intellectuals with clear connections to a particular communities and interest groups dedicate themselves to advancing their partisan interests. See Ron Eyerman, *Between Culture and Politics: Intellectuals in Modern Society*; Derek Gregory, *The Colonial* Present; Eric Hobsbawm, *Nations and Nationalism Since 1780: Programme, Myth, Reality*; Anthony Smith, *Theories of Nationalism*; Ronald Suny and Michael Kennedy (eds.), *Intellectuals and the Articulation of the Nation;* Benedict Anderson, *Imagined Communities: Reflections on the Origins and Spread of Nationalism.*
[18] Antonio Gramsci, *Prison Notebooks*, 113.
[19] Daniel Kreiss and Shannon C. McGregor, "Technology Firms Shape Political Communication: The Work of Microsoft, Facebook, Twitter and Google with Campaigns During the 2016 U.S. Presidential cycle;" Patricia Rossini, *et al*, "Social Media, Opinion Polls, and the Use of Persuasive Messages During the 2016 US Election Primaries."

[20] Elisa Shearer and Jeffrey Gottfried, "News Use Across Social Media Platforms 2017."

[21] M.A. K. Halliday, Linguistic Studies of Text and Discourse, 48.

[22] Jürgen Habermas outlines his normative account of the public sphere in his seminal work *The Structural Transformation of the Public Sphere: An Inquiry into a Category of Bourgeois Society.*

[23] For what it is worth, Trump's favourite hashtag during his first 100 days as President was #MAGA, which is an acronym of his campaign slogan 'Make America Great Again.' See Colin Daileda, 'Take a wild guess what Trump's favorite hashtag was in his first 100 days.'

[24] Michael Ledeen@MichaelLedeen, May 20, 2019; Bret Stephens@Bret StephensNYT; Nikki Haley@NikkiHaley, June 23, 2019; Frank Gaffney@ frankgaffney, May 16, 2019.

[25] For an understanding of how neo-conservatives have gone about dehumanising the 'Wahhabi' Other for specific aims and goals see Rohan Davis, *Western Imaginings: The Intellectual Contest to Define Wahhabism*, 139-176.

[26] Some of the better studies exploring the extensive and interconnected nature of the neo-conservative network in the context of their influence on US foreign policy-making include Michael Lind, 'Neoconservatism and American Hegemony;' Stephen J. Sniegoski, *The Transparent Cabal: The Neoconservative Agenda, War in the Middle East, and the National Interest of Israel*; John J. Mearsheimer and Stephen M. Walt, *The Israel Lobby and US Foreign Policy*; Muhammad Idrees Ahmad, *Road to Iraq: The Making of a Neoconservative War.*

[27] For an understanding of the function of the pro-Israel Lobby in the US see Mearsheimer and Walt, *The Israel Lobby and US Foreign Policy*; Mearsheimer and Walt, 'Is It Love or The Lobby? Explaining America's Special Relationship with Israel;' Mitchell Plitnick, 'AIPAC: The Essential Profile;' Murray Friedman, *The Neoconservative Revolution: Jewish Intellectuals and the Shaping of Public Policy.*

[28] Noam Chomsky and Edward Herman, *Manufacturing Consent: The Political Economy of the Mass Media.*

[29] These revelations have now reached the mainstream US media see for e.g. VICE on HBO, 'Why Evangelical Christians Love Israel.'

[30] Gramsci, *Prison Notebooks.*

[31] United Against Nuclear Iran, 'FAQ.'

[32] United Against Nuclear Iran, 'Our Mission.'

[33] United Against Nuclear Iran, 'Coalition Information.'

[34] Max Fisher, 'Gary Samore, a leading skeptic of the Iran deal, explains why he changed his mind.'

[35] Hilary Leila Krieger, 'Lieberman backs Hagee despite calls to cut ties.'

[36] Nicole Hemmer, 'Donald Trump is Pushing Neocons into the Wilderness.'

[37] *The New York Times*, 'From The Editors; The Times and Iraq.'

[38] Rohan Davis, *Western Imaginings: The Intellectual Contest to Define Wahhabism,* 158.

[39] George Lakoff, *Moral Politics: How Liberals and Conservatives Think*, xi.

[40] Hannah Arendt, *On the Origins of Totalitarianism: Imperialism,* 4.

[41] *Supporters of People's Mojahedin Organization of Iran (PMOI/MEK),* 'Camp Ashraf & Liberty.'

[42] Arshin Adib-Moghaddam has described some of the inner-workings and the makeup of the *Iran Policy Committee.* See "Manufacturing War: Iran in the Neo-Conservative Imagination."

[43] PJTV Media, 'Paul E. Vallely Video interview with Paul Whittle.'

[44] Terry Lakin Action Fund, 'Interview with Major General Paul Vallely;' *Right Web,* 'Paul E. Vallely.'

[45] Jeremiah Goulka, Lydia Hansell, Elizabeth Wilke and Judith Larson, 'The Mujahedin-e Khalq in Iraq: A Policy Conundrum,' 4; Mehdi Hassan, 'Here's Why Washington Hawks Love This Cultish Iranian Exile Group.'

[46] *Right Web,* 'People's Mujahedin of Iran (MEK);' Jason Rezaian, 'John Bolton wants regime change in Iran, and so does the cult that paid him.'

[47] Edward Cody, "GOP leaders criticize Obama's Iran policy in rally for opposition group."

[48] The pariah status MEK has acquired amongst many Iranians is described in some detail by Jason Rezaian in his article 'John Bolton wants regime change in Iran, and so does the cult that paid him.' Rezaian writes

> When it became clear that the MEK could no longer coexist with the ruling Islamic Republic Party, some MEK members withdrew from the group, while others were imprisoned. Those who were left fled to Iraq...Many took up arms and fought against their Iranian countrymen, earning the group the unofficial nickname monafegheen, or the "hypocrites." That title has stuck, and most Iranians inside the country...refer to them as such. The group is loathed by most Iranians.

[49] Eli Clifton, 'A Great Little Racket: The Neocon Media Machine.'

Chapter Two: Trauma & Inspiration

[1] Muhammad Idrees Ahmad, *The Road to Iraq: The Making of a Neoconservative War*; Douglas Kellner, 'Lying in Politics: The case of George W. Bush and Iraq;' Darel E. Paul, 'The Siren Song of Geopolitics: Towards a Gramscian Account of the Iraq War;' David Grondin, 'Mistaking Hegemony for Empire: Neoconservatives, the Bush Doctrine, and the Democratic Empire;' Jim George, 'Leo Strauss, Neoconservatism and US Foreign Policy: Esoteric Nihilism and the Bush Doctrine;' Justin Vaïsse, *Neoconservatism: The Biography of a Movement*; Jane K. Cramer and A. Trevor Thrall, *Why Did the United States Invade Iraq?*

[2] Grant Havers and Mark Wexler, 'Is US Neoconservatism Dead?;' Alan M. Wald, *The New York Intellectuals: The Rise and Decline of the Anti-Stalinist Left From the 1930s to the 1980s*; SM Lipset, 'Neoconservatism: Myth and Reality;'

John Ehrman, *The Rise of Neoconservatism: Intellectuals and Foreign Affairs, 1945-1994.*

[3] Jacob Heilbrunn, *They Knew They Were Right: The Rise of the Neocons*, 11.

[4] David Biale, *Power & Powerlessness in Jewish History*, 203.

[5] Elie Wiesel, *Night*, 34.

[6] Martin Buber, "The Dialogue Between Heaven and Earth," in *Wrestling with God: Jewish Theological Responses during and after the Holocaust*, 373.

[7] Buber's view of Jesus and Christianity is made explicit in his work *Two Types of Faith*, in which he writes:

> From my youth onwards I have found in Jesus my great brother. That Christianity has regarded him as God the Savior has always appeared to me a fact of highest importance which, for his sake and my own, I must endeavor to understand... My own fraternally open relationship to him has grown ever more stronger and clearer, and today I see him more strongly and clearly than ever before. I am more certain than ever that a great place belongs to him in Israel's history of faith... (12-13)

For an understanding of the general Jewish, especially Jewish-American, reaction to Buber's ideas see Chaim Potok, 'Martin Buber and the Jews.'

[8] Richard Rubenstein, *After Auschwitz: Radical Theology and Contemporary Judaism,* 151-152.

[9] Richard Rubenstein, *Approaches to Auschwitz: The Holocaust and its Legacy*, 298, 333.

[10] Charles Krauthammer, 'Charles Krauthammer's Reflections on Israel, Zionism, Judaism, and God.'

[11] Cindy Mindell, 'Conversation with Dr. Richard L. Rubenstein.'

[12] Brian Lamb interview with Irving Kristol, 'Neoconservatism.'

[13] Norman Podhoretz interview with Eric Cohen, 'Norman Podhoretz – Reflections of a Jewish Neoconservative.'

[14] Charles Murray describes the profound impact Christianity has had on his life in *Curmudgeon's Guide to Getting Ahead: Dos and Don'ts of Right Behavior, Tough Thinking, Clear Writing, and Living a Good Life.* Murray writes

> Even dabbling at the edges has demonstrated to me the depths of Judaism, Buddhism and Taoism. I assume that I would find similar depths in Islam and Hinduism as well. I certainly have developed a far greater appreciation for Christianity, the tradition with which I'm most familiar. The Sunday school stories I learned as a child bear no resemblance to Christianity taken seriously. You've got to grapple with the real thing.

[15] Christopher DeMuth, 'Irving Kristol Award and Lecture for 2009.'

[16] Charles Murray, 'Jewish Genius.'

[17] Kevin MacDonald, *The Culture of Critique: An evolutionary analysis of Jewish involvement in twentieth-century intellectual and political movements*; Kevin

MacDonald, *A people that shall dwell alone: Judaism as a group evolutionary strategy.*

[18] *The Washington Times,* 'Appointment Gratification;' Richard H. Curtiss, 'You Don't Have to be Jewish to Be a Neo-con: John Bolton.'

[19] *JTA, Haaretz* and Ron Kampeas, '9 Reasons Why John Bolton Is Causing a Frenzy Among U.S. Jews and Across the Middle East.'

[20] Josh Hasten, 'New York State Republican Committee Chair Tours Israel.'

[21] It is noteworthy that organisers of the 2018 rally chose to adopt the Trump-inspired slogan 'Build Israel Great Again' (even printed on Trump-replica 'Make America Great Again' hats with the bold-white lettering on a red background). It is precisely this kind of rhetoric that "helped the president in the United States get elected," claimed Frager, "The idea is that Judea and Samaria have to grow. The president, I think, likes to see demonstrations of that fact." See Sam Sokal, 'Settlers welcome Mike Huckabee to a Trump-style building dedication in Efrat.'

[22] *JTA, Haaretz* and Ron Kampeas, '9 Reasons Why John Bolton Is Causing a Frenzy Among U.S. Jews and Across the Middle East,' JTA, Haaretz and Ron Kampeas.'

[23] This was a favourite technique of Rachel Abrams' when writing about Palestinians on her blog *Bad Rachel* and in her articles for *The Weekly Standard.* Pertinent articles have since conveniently been removed by the *The Weekly Standard* online historical record. The rhetorical technique Abrams employs has been identified and commented on by writers like Matt Duss. See Matt Duss, 'Prissy Schoolmarm's Lips.'

[24] John Mearsheimer and Stephen Walt, *The Israel Lobby and US Foreign Policy*; Mearsheimer and Walt, 'Setting the Record Straight: A Response to Critics of "The Israel Lobby."'

[25] See for e.g. Sina Toossi, 'The Best Way to Avert War with Iran? Fire John Bolton.'

[26] Marc Daou, 'John Bolton's dangerous 'obsession' with Iran.'

[27] Elliott Abrams, 'Joining the Jackals: The Obama Administration Abandons Israel.'

[28] For a brief discussion of the appropriating of the phrase 'never again' see Emily Burack, 'How 'Never Again' evolved from Holocaust commemoration slogan to universal call.'

[29] Emile Fackhenheim, *To Mend the World: Foundations of Post-Holocaust Jewish Thought*; Emile Fackenheim, 'Faith in God and Man After Auschwitz: Theological Implications.'

[30] Norman Podhoretz interview with Eric Cohen, 'Norman Podhoretz – Reflections of a Jewish Neoconservative.'

[31] *Ibid.*

[32] For a greater understanding of this qualitative transformation of *Commentary Magazine* see William Novak, '*Commentary* and the Jewish Community: The Record Since 1960,' 58; the particular work of Emile Fackenheim's in question is 'Jewish Faith and the Holocaust,' 30-36.

[33] *Ha-satan* is the Hebrew term for Satan as it appears in the *Tanakh*. Uses of this term can be found in the *Book of Zecharia* and the *Book of Job*.

[34] Caroline Glick, 'Rousing the Americans From Their Slumber;' David Horowitz, 'Who Are Our Adversaries?;' Seth Frantzman, 'Will Iran's Pinprick Provocations Backfire?;' Shai Feldman and Zalmay Khalilzad, 'The Future of U.S.-Israel Strategic Cooperation.'

[35] Eric Cortellessa, 'Norman Podhoretz, the last remaining 'anti-anti Trump' neoconservative.'

[36] Ron Torossian, 'Jews Who Abandon Judaism Abandon Israel: A Glance at the Self-Hating Narcissism of the Jewish Left.'

[37] Roberta Strauss Feuerlicht, *The Fate of the Jews: A People Torn Between Israeli Power and Jewish Ethics.*

[38] Michael Lipka, 'A closer look at Jewish identity in Israel and the U.S.'

[39] Jim Naureckas, 'Three Reasons Bret Stephens Should Not Be a NYT Columnist–and the Real Reason He Is One.'

[40] *Ibid.*

[41] Jeffrey Goldberg, 'More tear gas, please?'

[42] Andy McCarthy, 'Is There Legitimate Doubt About Obama's Eligibility to be President.'

[43] Frank Gaffney, 'The Jihadist Vote.'

[44] Irving Kristol, 'Neo Conservatism: An Autobiography of an Idea,' 7-8.

[45] Christopher Hitchens, 'Machiavelli in Mesopotamia: The case against the case against "regime change" in Iraq;' Shadia Drury, 'Saving America: Leo Strauss and the Neoconservatives;' Shadia Drury, *Leo Strauss and the American* Right, Norman Madarasz, 'Behind the neo-con curtain;' Stefan Halper and Jonathan Clarke, *America Alone: The Neo-Conservatives and the Global Order.*

[46] Irving Kristol, 'Neo Conservatism: An Autobiography of an Idea,' 7.

[47] This point was well made by academics taking part of in an academic conference called 'Leo Strauss as Teacher,' held at the Leo Strauss Center at the University of Chicago on April 22-23, 2014.

[48] Shadia Drury was amongst the first to make this argument. See Shadia Drury, 'Leo Strauss's Classic Natural Right Teaching,' 303 – 309.

[49] Leo Strauss, *Natural Right and History,* 152.

[50] Shadia Drury's emphasies this key idea that is prevalent in Strauss' work, specifically his book *On Tyranny.* See Shadia Drury, *The Political Ideas of Leo Strauss,* 81.

[51] Real Time with Bill Maher, 'Bret Stephens: Out of the Echo Chamber.'

[52] Bret Stephens, 'Who Did This to Us;' Bret Stephens, 'Liberalism's Imaginary Enemies.'

[53] John Swaine and Ciara McCarthy, 'Young black men again faced highest rate of US police killings in 2016.'

[54] Carl Schmitt, *The Concept of the Political*, 26.

[55] Norman Podhoretz interview with Eric Cohen, 'Norman Podhoretz – Reflections of a Jewish Neoconservative.'

[56] Leo Strauss, *Natural Right and History*, 146.

---

[57] *Ibid.*, 149.

[58] Danny Postel, 'Noble Lies and Perpetual War: Leo Strauss, the Neocons, and Iraq;' John G. Mason, 'Leo Strauss and the Noble Lie: The Neo-Cons at War;' Jim George, 'Leo Strauss, Neoconservatism and US Foreign Policy: Esoteric Nihilism and the Bush Doctrine' ; Shadia Drury, *Leo Strauss and the American Right.*

[59] George Bush, 'Proclamation 6518—Grant of Executive Clemency.'

[60] Irving Kristol, 'The Neoconservative Persuasion: Selected Essays, 1942-2009.'

[61] A key theme of Freud's work *Civilization and Its Discontents* is the clash betwixt the assertions of the isolated individual and the cultural demands of the group. According to Freud, some kind of social coercion is required in order to restrict man from succumbing to his innate aggression: a society constructed in such way that allows man to develop his self in positive ways both in terms of work and love, should be this kind of coercion. He saw psychoanalysis as key to developing oneself, especially with regards to understanding and overcoming differences, notably sexual differences, between people. Freud also reveals himself to be a supporter of John Stuart Mill's conception of liberty. In *Civilization and Its Discontents* Freud states: "The liberty of the individual is no gift of civilization. It was created before there was any civilization (p.95)." He expects the individual to always prioritise his own liberty over the will of the group (p.96). This, in addition to Freuds desire for an individual to learn to accept the differences of others, stands in stark contrasts to the ideas of Leo Strauss who argues that the individual should be willing to fight and die for the betterment of the group against the Other who is profoundly different.

[62] Irving Kristol, 'Neo Conservatism: An Autobiography of an Idea,' 7.

[63] Leo Strauss, *On Tyranny*, 27.

[64] Pamela Engel, 'Krauthammer Blasts UN: Trump Should Turn Manhattan HQ 'Into Condos."

[65] Phyllis Bennis, 'John Bolton Loves War and Detests Diplomacy – Even More Than Trump;' Samantha Power, 'Boltonism.'

[66] Alan Gilbert, 'Segregation: Aggression, and Executive Power: Leo Strauss and 'The Boys," 421-425.

[67] Cited in *Ibid.*, 424-425.

[68] Cited in Cal Thomas, 'For Secretary of State, John Bolton is best choice.'

[69] John Podhoretz@jpodhoretz, May 8, 2018.

[70] Some of the horrible treatment Edward Said received from his critics is detailed by Tom Paulin in 'Writing to the moment;' and in a documentary about Said, which included lengthy interviews with him, by *Media Education Foundation* called 'Edward Said on Orientalism.'

[71] Irving Kristol, *Neoconservatism: The Autobiography of an Idea*, 7.

[72] Christopher Hitchens writes

> Part of the charm of the regime-change argument (from the point of view of its supporters) is that it depends on premises and objectives that cannot, at least by the administration, be

publicly avowed. Since Paul Wolfowitz is from the intellectual school of Leo Strauss—and appears in fictional guise as such in Saul Bellow's novel *Ravelstein*—one may even suppose that he enjoys this arcane and occluded aspect of the debate.

See Christopher Hitchens, 'Machiavelli in Mesopotamia.'

[73] Jenny Strauss Clay, 'The Real Leo Strauss.'

[74] Catherine Zuckert and Michael Zuckert, *The Truth About Leo Strauss*, 3.

[75] Peter Minowitz makes similar claims in his interview with Scott Horton. See Scott Horton, 'Straussaphobia: Six Questions for Peter Minowitz.'

[76] In an exchange with Scott Horton, Minowitz concedes he is unaware of the existence of Strauss' May 19, 1933 Löwith letter in which the latter clearly expresses admiration for the Julius Caesar's authoritarian rule. This is noteworthy given Minowitz's self-professed expertise in Straussian thought. See *Ibid.*

[77] Leo Strauss, *Gesammelte Schriften, Bd. 3: Hobbes' politische Wissenschaft und zugehörige Schriften, Briefe,* 624-25, cited in Susan Shell, "To Share the Vanquished and Crush the Arrogant: Leo Strauss's Lecture on 'German Nihilism,'" 186.

Chapter Three: Duplicity & Democracy

[1] John Bolton, 'Full Address at Oxford Union.'

[2] Charles Krauthammer, 'At Last, Zion.'

[3] *The Jerusalem Post*, 'Charles Krauthammer Lauded by Netanyahu, 'We Were as Brothers';' Eve Harrow, 'Charles Krauthammer: A unique voice in our world.'

[4] Ali Abunimah, Nigel Parry and Laurie King, 'Republican Party leader calls for ethnic cleansing of Palestinians on prime time talk show.'

[5] Iranian students studying in foreign lands including the US were amongst those greatly affected by the US' economic sanctions. A devaluing in Iranian currency brought about by these initiatives meant many students struggle to or could no longer afford to pay their fees and associated costs. *Al Jazeera* is amongst those to have reported on this situation, see Samira Damavandi, 'Why Iranian students in US are crowdfunding to pay their tuition.'

[6] *Newsmax TV*, 'James Woolsey to Newsmax TV: Sanctions Key to Stopping Iran.'

[7] *Ibid.*

[8] Dowd, Maureen, 'I'm With Dick. Let's Make War!'

[9] *Ibid.*

[10] Bernard D. Nossiter, 'Israelis Condemned by Security Council for Attack on Iraq.'

[11] Robert Tucker, 'The Middle East: Carterism Without Carter.'

[12] Meir Soloveichik 'Jews and Power: Tradition, Literature, and Politics.'

[13] Bret Stephens, 'The Queerest Denial.'

[14] Mark Wallace has strong ties to the neo-conservative movement, which are best evidenced by his serving as deputy campaign manager for the 2004 re-electing of George W. Bush and Dick Cheney, and serving as CEO of the Tigris Financial Group, which is an investment group controlled by Thomas Kaplan. See Eli Clifton, 'Billionaire's sketchy Middle East gamble: Meet the man betting on war with Iran' and Mark Wallace and Irwin Cotler, 'In Case You Missed It, "To Protect Human Rights, Companies Must Pull Out Of Iran."'

[15] See for e.g. Gregory Vlastos, Paul Sunstein, and Robert Gordis, reply by M.F. Burnyeat, 'Further Lessons of Leo Strauss: An Exchange;' Shadia Drury, 'The Esoteric Philosophy of Leo Strauss;' Arthur M. Melzer, *Philosophy Between the Lines: The Lost History of Esoteric Writing.*

[16] Steve Tesich, 'A Government of Lies.'

[17] *Ibid.*

[18] Cited in Mark Tapson, 'The War to Destroy Christian America.'

[19] *Ibid.*

[20] John Bolton, 'Full Address: Oxford Union.'

[21] Ilan Peleg, *The Legacy of George W. Bush's Foreign Policy: Moving Beyond Neoconservatism*; Jonathan Monten, 'The Roots of the Bush Doctrine.'

[22] Roger Cohen, 'Obama's American Idea;' Greg Grandin, 'The Strange Career of American Exceptionalism.'

[23] For an appreciation of the long history of neo-conservative prejudice against non-Jewish-American minorities see, Norman Podhoretz, 'My Negro Problem-And Ours.' *Commentary Magazine* has played a leading role in promoting these ideas, see, Jason D. Hill, 'My 'Black Lives Matter' Problem;' James Kichik, 'The Rise of Black Anti-Semitism;' Milton Himmelfarb, 'Is American Jewry in Crisis?' Bret Stephens has called the Black Lives Matter movement a "big lie" and "nonstop conspiracy." For a rundown of Stephens' controversial public commentary see Hamilton Nolan, 'The Best of Bret Stephens: Your Newest *New York Times* Opinion Columnist.'

[24] John Bolton, 'Full Address at Oxford Union.'

[25] Greg Jaffe, 'Obama's new patriotism: How Obama has used his presidency to redefine 'American Exceptionalism.''

[26] Lindsey Bever, 'Report: Rudy Giuliani tells private dinner 'I do not believe that the president loves America.''

[27] *The Algemeiner*, 'Livid Giuliani Contrasts Obama With Netanyahu: 'That's a Man Who Fights for His People, Unlike Our President.''

[28] See Ron Csillag, 'Bret Stephens: U.S. Jews Are Not Single-Issue Voters.' Stephens tells Csillag:

> ...for all the whiff of scandal and legal jeopardies he's [Netanyahu] in, has been a steady and successful prime minister. Diplomatically, he expanded the range of Israel's relationships in a way that scarcely can be imagined when I was

editor-in-chief of the *Jerusalem Post*. In terms of security, Israel is probably more secure today that it has been in quite some time.

The Weekly Standard has led the charge amongst neo-conservative outfits to support Netanyahu. See for e.g. Neil Rogachevsky, 'After Netanyahu;' Vivian Bercovici, 'The Corruption Scandal that Could Upend Israeli Elections: Who is to blame?.'

[29] For an appreciation of the venomous, disproportionate and hypocritical response by neo-conservatives against Arab and Muslim leaders, particularly Palestinian leaders accused of corruption, see Jonathan Schanzer, 'Huge Verdict Is the Price the Palestinian Authority Pays for Not Controlling the P.L.O;' Michael Rubin, 'The Middle East's Real Bane: Corruption.'

[30] Vivian Bercovici, 'The Corruption Scandal that Could Upend Israeli Elections: Who is to blame?.'

[31] Press Release from the Rudy Giuliani Presidential Committee, Inc., 'Rudy Giuliani Announces Foreign Policy Team Members.'

[32] *The Times of Israel,* 'Giuliani: Sanctions creating the conditions for revolution in Iran;' *Iran Freedom*, 'OIAC Holds Up, "The Path To Freedom – The Alternative."'

[33] Brent D. Griffiths, 'Giuliani: Trump is 'committed to' regime change in Iran.''

[34] Senator Marco Rubio, 'S.1 Strengthening America's Security in the Middle East Act of 2019.'

[35] *Ibid.*; Justin Logan, 'Where the Neocons Went, Rubio Is Following.'

[36] Eli Clifton, 'Following Paul Singer's Money, Argentina, and Iran (Continued);' *Council on Foreign Relations*, 'A Conversation with Senator Marco Rubio;' *Right Web*, 'Marco Rubio.'

[37] See for e.g. Bret Stephens, 'Obama Is Pushing Israel Toward War;' Dov Zakheim, 'The Iran Nuclear Agreement: Tehran 'Achieved All It Wanted';' Irving Kristol, 'Obama's Israel Problem.'

[38] Rohan Davis, *Western Imaginings: The Intellectual Contest to Define Wahhabism.*

[39] Meir Soloveichik, 'Jews and Power: Tradition, Literature, and Politics.'

[40] John Mearsheimer and Stephen Walt, *The Israel Lobby and U.S. Foreign Policy.*

[41] Many authors have written about the anti-Palestinian rhetoric accompanying Israeli Defence Force atrocities perpetrated against the Palestinian people including during the Second *Intifada.* See for e.g. Joseph Massad, 'Are Palestinian children less worthy?' in which he claims:

> In the second intifada (2000-2004), Israeli soldiers killed more than 500 children with at least 10,000 injured, and 2,200 children arrested. The televised murder of the Palestinian child Muhammad al-Durra shook the world - but not Israeli Jews, whose government concocted the most outrageous and criminal of stories to exonerate Israel.

See also Rebeeca L. Stein, ''Fake News!:' the view from Israel's Occupation;' Greg Shupak, *The Wrong Story: Palestine, Israel and the Media.*

[42] Suzanne Goldenberg, 'Rioting as Sharon visits Islam holy site.'

[43] Exact numbers of those killed remains underdetermined because many bodies were buried in the ruins, deposited in massive graves, and transported away from the killing fields to other sites in trucks. Imprecise estimates range from 300 to 3000 victims. See Linda A. Malone, 'The Kahan Report, Ariel Sharon and the Sabra-Shatilla Massacres in Lebanon: Responsibility Under International Law for Massacres of Civilian Populations,' 374.

[44] *Israeli Ministry of Foreign Affairs*, '104 Report of the Commission of Inquiry into the events at the refugee camps in Beirut- 8 February 1983.'

[45] Amnesty International delegate David Holley reported: "The military operations we have investigated appear to be carried out not for military purposes but instead to harass, humiliate, intimidate, and harm the Palestinian population. Either the Israeli army is extremely ill-disciplined or it has been ordered to carry out acts which violate the laws of war." See Lama Jamjoum, 'The Effects of Israeli Violations During the Second Uprising "Intifida" on Palestinian Health Conditions," 54. For an understanding of the immediate economic impacts associated with *First Intifada* see *World Bank*, 'Twenty-Seven Months -- *Intifada*, Closures and Palestinian Economic Crisis: An Assessment;' *World Bank*, 'Fifteen Months -- *Intifada*, Closures and Palestinian Economic Crisis.'

[46] Matt Rees, 'Streets Red with Blood.'

[47] *Jerusalem Quarterly* Editorial, 'The Uses of Anti-Semitism,' 3.

[48] Luis Sanchez, 'Bolton: Recognizing Jerusalem as Capital of Israel 'Enhances the chances for peace.''

[49] Reuel Marc Gerecht, 'The New Rouhani, 15-16.

[50] Michael A. Ledeen, 'Easy Prey: Can We Even Pray?'

[51] Goldberg's actions as a Prison Guard during the First *Intifida* have not received the kind of widespread attention from the US mass media that it deserves. This is surprising given we are now living in a post-Abu-Ghraib world, where the US has appeared to demand more accountability from its own citizens when it comes to the treatment of Arab and Muslim prisoners. Whether or not Goldberg's actions as a prison guard working for a colonial Israeli regime resonate with the banal kind of evil described by Hannah Arendt is a discussion for another time. So too is Goldberg's ability to continue to maintain positions of influence within popular US media organisations, receive popular journalistic awards and enjoy privileged access to both the Israeli and US political establishments in spite of his war crimes. One wonders whether the marked differences in terms of social and intellectual capital between Goldberg, and Lynndie England and her colleagues, who were prosecuted for prisoner abuse, played a determining role in the disparity in punishments (or lack thereof in Goldberg's case). Goldberg himself has, rather unconvincingly, sought to deflect attention from his actions using satire. See Jeffrey Goldberg, 'Jeffrey Goldberg's Israeli Prison Secret Exposed!' For a detailed description of Goldberg describing his role in the abuse of a Palestinian

prisoner see his biography *Prisoners: A Story of Friendship and Terror*, in which he states:

> It was February 1991...at a place called Ketziot...that a friend of mine named Yoram tried, in my presence, to beat senseless an Arab by the name of Abu Firas...Yoram, whom I knew to be gentle but at that moment had blood in his face, was beating Abu Firas on the head with the handset of an army radio. The headset weighed five or six pounds, and it was sharp-edged. Abu Firas was hurt. Most men taking a beating like this would scream blue murder, but Abu Firas didn't. I was impressed...It was quite a sight – a yeshiva Jew, a God-fearer-, delivering a bloody beating...We were standing near the solitary confinement cells...No one else knew we were there..." Get this dog out of here," he said, pointing to Abu Firas...I told Abu Firas to move. Then I went in search of someone to take Abu Firas to the infirmary. I found another military policeman, and handed off the wobbling prisoner, who was now bleeding on me. "He fell," I lied.

[52] Jeffrey Goldberg, 'Who is Stephen Walt?'

[53] T.S. Eliot, *Four Quartets.*

[54] *Christians United for Israel*, ''Pastors' Briefing Events;' *Christians United For Israel,* 'Who We Are.'

[55] *The American Israel Public Affairs Committee*, 'A Light Unto Nations.'

[56] See for e.g. *Chabag.org* 'The Miracles of the Six Day War: June 9, David and Goliath;' Yaakov Katz and Amir Bohbot, *The Weapon Wizards: How Israel Became a High-Tech Military Superpower*; Rob Eshman, 'The Hidden Hero of the Six-Day War.'

[57] Dov Zakheim, 'Practicing Jews Serving in the National Security Community;' *The Tikvah Fund,* Norman Podhoretz interview with Eric Cohen: 'Norman Podhoretz – Reflections of a Jewish Neoconservative.'

[58] Elliott Abrams, 'Two Words.'

[59] Meir Soloveichik, 'Jews and Power: Tradition, Literature, and Politics.'

[60] Norman Podhoretz, *Why are Jews Liberals?*; Joshua Muravchik, *Making David into Goliath: How the World Turned Against Israel.*

[61] It is noteworthy that neo-conservatives supported the 2006 censorship campaign targeting the play *My Name is Rachel Corrie* in New York, and have since rallied against the play's performance around the world, on account the production, which was based on the life of Corrie as told through her diary entries and personal emails, is pro-Palestinian and anti-Israeli. Steven Plaut, whose extensive links with the neo-conservative movement include working for the *Middle East Forum*, writing for *FrontPageMag* and working alongside prominent neo-conservatives such as James Woolsey at the *Ariel Center for Policy Research,* lambasted the play for glorifying Corrie's "suicide as part of her campaign for the "right" of Palestinian terrorists to murder Jewish civilians in Israel." Plaut

described the production as a failed attempt at "deconstruct[ing] the young terrorist as a golden-haired lover of peace and poetry, striving for love and beauty in a world beset with pain." He claims the "70-minute propaganda play" is a "pro-jihad agitprop" this is "about as morally compelling as would be a similar play about Horst Wessel." As is so often the case amongst neo-conservatives, Plaut has deployed Holocaust rhetoric as part of his attempt to silence and discredit critics of Israel's occupation (Horst Wessel was a Berlin leader of the Nazi Party's *Sturmabteilung* who was made into a martyr by Joseph Goebbels following the former's murder in 1930). See Steven Plaut, 'Celebrating Rachel Corrie: Israeli Tax Dollars at Work.'

[62] Nissan Mendel, 'David and Goliath.'

[63] Aaron Shuster, 'Israel's Role and the Way Forward.'

[64] Joshua Muravchik, *Making David into Goliath: How the World Turned Against Israel*, xi-xii.

[65] *Ibid.*, xii, 102.

[66] *Ibid.*, xxvii.

[67] Noah Beck, 'Can Israel Survive Obama?

Chapter Four: Beginning the Sense-Making Process

[1] Leo Strauss, *Persecution and the Art of Writing*, 35

[2] Jim George, 'Leo Strauss, Neoconservatism and US Foreign Policy: Esoteric Nihilism and the Bush Doctrine;' Patricia Owens, 'Beyond Strauss, Lies and the War in Iraq: Hannah Arendt's Critique of Neoconservatism;' John G .Mason, 'Leo Strauss and the Noble Lie: The Neo-Cons at War;' Danny Postel, 'Noble lies and perpetual war: Leo Strauss, the neocons, and Iraq;' Shadia Drury, 'Gurus of Endless War.'

[3] Rohan Davis, *Western Imaginings: The Intellectual Contest to Define Wahhabism*, 162, 172

[4] J.R. Martin and P.R.R. White, *The Language of Evaluation: Appraisal in English*.

[5] Jan Nuyts, 'Cognitive Linguistics and Functional Linguistics,' 840

[6] For an in-depth understanding of these different approaches to language see Jan Nuyts, *Aspects of a cognitive-pragmatic theory of language*; Jan Nuyts, *Autonomous vs. non-autonomous syntax*.

[7] For a basic understanding of the usage-based linguistics approach see Holger Diessel, 'Usage Based Linguistics.'

[8] Suzanne Eggins, Introduction to Systemic Functional Linguistics: 2nd Edition, 3

[9] J.R. Martin and P.R.R. White, *The Language of Evaluation: Appraisal in English*.

[10] For examples of neo-conservatives, and those closely aligned with the movement, seeking to both absolve themselves and shift the blame for their long history of violence-promoting ideas and actions, especially in the case of the Iraq War, see Jonah Goldberg, 'The Term 'Neocon' Has Run Its Course;' Douglas

Murray, 'Neoconservatism: Why We Need It;' David Brooks, 'The Era of Distortion;' Dana Milbank critiques Richard Perle's speech where he, amongst other things, denies the chief role he played in the orchestrating the Iraq War, see 'Prince of Darkness Denies Own Existence.'

[11] J.R. Martin and David Rose, *Working with Discourse: Meaning Beyond the Clause*, 43-44

[12] Mikhail Bakhtin, 'Discourse in the Novel;' Valentin N. Vološinov, *Marxism and the Philosophy of Language.*

[13] Martin and White, *The Language of Evaluation*, 99

[14] *Ibid.,* 102

[15] *Ibid.,* 97-98

[16] Martin and White, *The Language of Evaluation,* 108-109

[17] Donald Trump @realDonaldTrump, 8.24pm, July 22, 2018

[18] James A. Neuchterlein, 'Neoconservatism & Irving Kristol;' Garry J. Dorrien, *The Neoconservative Mind: Politics, Culture, and the War of Ideology*; Irving Kristol, *Reflections of a Neoconservative: Looking Back, Looking Ahead.*

[19] Amongst the most prolific neo-conservatives to Tweet about Iran are John Podhoretz @jpodhoretz, Bret Stephens @BretStephensNYT and Frank Gaffney @frankgaffney.

[20] Martin and White, *The Language of Evaluation*, 112-113

[21] William Kristol, 'BHL: So It's War.'

[22] Douglas Kellner, 'Bushspeak and the Politics of Lying: Presidential Rhetoric in the 'War on Terror';' Piki Ish-Shalom, ''The Civilization of Clashes:' Misapplying the Democratic Peace in the Middle East,;' Rohan Davis, *Western Imaginings: The Intellectual Contest to Define Wahhabism.*

[23] I have previously undertaken this task in relation to how neo-conservatives have gone about interpreting and representing Wahhabism, see Rohan Davis, *Ibid.*

[24] David Hills, 'Metaphor.'

[25] George Lakoff, 'Metaphor, Morality, and Politics Or, Why Conservatives Have Left Liberals In the Dust.'

[26] David Hills, 'Metaphor.'

[27] George Lakoff, *The Metaphors We Live By.*

[28] George Lakoff, 'Metaphor, Morality, and Politics Or, Why Conservatives Have Left Liberals In the Dust,' 1

[29] *Ibid.,* 5

[30] Wayne C. Booth, 'Metaphor as Rhetoric: The Problem of Evaluation,' 56

[31] Susan Greenfield, *Mind Change: How Digital Technologies are Leaving Their Mark on our Brains.*

[32] Wayne C. Booth, 'Metaphor as Rhetoric: The Problem of Evaluation,' 56

[33] Karen Cerulo, *Deciphering Violence: The Cognitive Structure of Right and Wrong.*

[34] John McCain @SenJohnMcCain, 2.34am, February 5, 2007

[35] John Podhoretz @jpodhoretz, 4.01am, February 5, 2007 cited in Jill Langlois, "McCain compares Iran's Ahmadinejad to monkey in tweet ."

---

[36] Pigs are typically understood as *haram* in Islam; they are understood to be especially dirty, and considered harmful to the health of humans. Relevant and often cited verses in the Quran attesting to this include: *6:145* when Allah remarks in reference to the flesh of swine (pig), "for that surely is impure" and *5:60* "Shall I inform you of [what is] worse than that as penalty from Allah? [It is that of] those whom Allah has cursed and with whom He became angry and made of them apes and pigs and slaves of Taghut. Those are worse in position and further astray from the sound way."

[37] Guy Gugliotta and Douglas Farah, '12 Years of Tortured Truth on El Salvador.'

[38] Bret Stephens, 'The Essential Wall' ('The Way We Live Now (in Israel)')

[39] Alan M. Dershowitz, 'Why deterrence won't work against Iran.'

[40] There exists a plethora of articles produced by neo-conservatives and neo-conservative media outfits emphasising the violent nature of the Palestinians and suggesting this in inherent to their being, whilst at the same time ignoring all other aspects of their lives. Among the most cutting articles are; Frank Gaffney, 'Seeing the Threat for What it is;' Bret Stephens, 'Palestine: The Psychotic Stage;' Evelyn Gordon, ''Palestine' is a Civil War Waiting to Happen;' Steven Plaut, 'The Truth About the 'Apartheid' Wall.'

[41] Rohan Davis, *Western Imaginings*, 151

Chapter Five: A New Holocaust

[1] British Broadcasting Commission, 'Panorama: The War Party.'

[2] Jeffrey Goldberg, 'A Little Learning: What Douglas Feith knew, and when he knew it.'

[3] Bill Keller, 'The Sunshine Warrior;' Eric Schmitt, 'Paul Dundes Wolfowitz.'

[4] Tom Schachtman, 'It's Time to Abandon 'Munich';' David A. Bell, 'Not Everything Is Munich and Hitler;' Jeffrey Record, 'Using (and Misusing) History: Munich, Vietnam, and Iraq;' Jeffrey Record, 'Retiring Hitler and " Appeasement" from the National Security Debate.'

[5] *Pew Research Center* reports that in 2010 there were just over 5 and a half million Jews in the US, and 243 million Christians. Its projections for 2020 are 5,700,00) Jews and nearly 253 million Christians. See *Pew Research Center: Religion and Public Life*, 'Religious Composition by Country, 2010-2050.'

[6] *Pew Research Center: Religion and Public Life,* 'Pentecostals in the Evangelical Tradition.'

[7] *Ibid.*

[8] Michael Horowitz, 'New intolerance between crescent and cross.'

[9] Diane Bedermen, 'The Troubling Influence of the 'Jihadist Psychopath.''

[10] Bruce Thornton, 'Terrorism in the Therapeutic Age.'

[11] Bernard Lewis' views, particularly those relating to US foreign policy and Islam in general, are so similar to neo-conservatives he is offered mistaken as such. In reality he is better characterised as a liberal intellectual whose strong interventionist and ethnocentric convictions overlap with the neo-conservative

approach to the political. It is precisely these shared ideas that helped both groups of intellectuals to unite in their advocating for the US invasion of Iraq.

[12] Clifford D. May, 'Intellectual Leader [On Bernard Lewis].' This article originally appeared on the *Foundation for the Defence of Democracies* website, however has since been removed. It can now be located on the *Middle East Forum* website.

[13] Cited in Alan Gilbert, 'Segregation: Aggression, and Executive Power: Leo Strauss and 'The Boys,' 425

[14] Clifford D. May, 'Intellectual Leader (On Bernard Lewis).'

[15] Debra Rubin, 'Author decries radical Islam's 'culture of death.''

[16] Thane Rosenbaum, 'Hamas's Civilian Death Strategy.'

[17] Jennifer Rubin, 'Rand Paul's Confused Foreign Policy Speech.'

[18] *Post Staff Report*, 'Loose Lips.'

[19] *Ibid.*

[20] Reconstructions of the Pearl Harbor attacks that have proven particularly popular amongst American audiences include the Hollywood blockbuster movie *Pearl Harbor* and The US Office of War's *December 7th: The Movie* – footage from this propaganda film has since been portrayed as 'real' in documentaries by major US mainstream news media including *The New York Times* and *CNN*. See David Austin Walsh, 'The New York Times recycles John Ford Pearl Harbor footage' and *History News Network* 'CNN's Pearl Harbor Mistake.'

[21] Box Office Mojo, 'Pearl Harbor.'

[22] Box Officer Mojo, 'Pilot / Aircraft.'

[23] Box Officer Mojo, 'Romantic Drama.'

[24] Gordon William Prange, Donald M. Goldstein and Katherine V. Dillion, *At Dawn We Slept: The Untold Story of Pearl Harbour.*

[25] For an account of Hilary Clinton's comments about the 'Deplorables' see BBC, 'Clinton: Half of Trump Supporters 'basket of deplorables';' Clark Mindock, 'Hillary Clinton doubles down on use of word 'deplorable' to describe past two years under Donald Trump.'

[26] It is noteworthy that Jeff Jacoby is a member of *Young Israel of Brookline* in Brookline, Massachusetts, which was founded with the aims of increasing the popularity of Orthodox Judaism amongst the local Jewish-American population, and at the same time countering the Jews increasing assimilation into American secular society. These aims and goals align perfectly with the religious and political aims and goals expressed by leading neo-conservatives such as Norman Podhoretz and Elliott Abrams, that Jewish-Americans should be tending towards Orthodox expressions of Judaism and rejecting more liberal interpretations. According Podhoretz and Abrams, Jewish-Americans adopting more liberal interpretations of Judaism often results in them becoming both supporters of the Democratic Party and less supportive of the Israeli state. See Norman Podhoretz, *Why Are Jews Liberals?*; Elliott Abrams, *Faith or Fear: How Jews Can Survive in a Christian America.*

[27] For an insight into Daniel Pipes' more recent warmongering see, 'The Case for Supporting Assad,' in which he claims:

> Evil forces pose less danger to us when they make war on each
> other. This (1) keeps them focused locally and (2) prevents
> either one from emerging victorious (and thereby posing a yet-
> greater danger). Western powers should guide enemies to
> stalemate by helping whichever side is losing, so as to prolong
> the conflict.

For an understanding of his anti-Islamic rhetoric see, Daniel Pipes, 'Lessons of
the War in Gaza,' in which he claims "the civilized and moral forces of Israel"
are engaged in a "face-off with [Islamic Palestinian] barbarism." The *Center for
American Progress* lists Pipes and the Middle East Forum; a Philadelphia-based
neo-conservative outfit he founded, as the core participants within a large group
of US-based organisations and intellectuals who have promoted anti-Islamic
rhetoric and policies. See, *Center for American Progress,* 'Fear Inc.: The Roots
of the Islamophobia Network in America.'

[28] Bin Laden wrote "Some American writers have published articles under the title
'On what basis are we fighting?' These articles have generated a number of
responses, some of which adhered to the truth and were based on Islamic Law,
and others which have not. Here we wanted to outline the truth ...Why are we
fighting and opposing you? The answer is very simple: 1) Because you attacked
us and continue to attack us. a) You attacked us in Palestine... The blood pouring
out of Palestine must be equally revenged. You must know that the Palestinians
do not cry alone; their women are not widowed alone; their sons are not orphaned
alone. See, *The Guardian*, 'Full text: bin Laden's 'letter to America.'

[29] *The Charter of Allah: The Platform of the Islamic Resistance Movement
(Hamas)* states:

> Thus, our nucleus has formed which chartered its way in the
> tempestuous ocean of creeds and hopes, desires and wishes,
> dangers and difficulties, setbacks and challenges, both internal
> and external. When the thought matured, the seed grew and the
> plant took root in the land of reality, detached from temporary
> emotion and unwelcome haste, the Islamic Resistance
> Movement erupted in order to play its role in the path of its
> Lord. In so doing, it joined its hands with those of all Jihad
> fighters for the purpose of liberating Palestine.

See also, *The Palestine National Liberation Movement: Fatah, Internal Charter*,
which reads:

> This movement and this work are a national trust and a historic
> responsibility. You must shoulder the precious trust and
> recognize the historic responsibility. You must prepare yourself
> to inspire the spirit of organized revolutionary work in every
> Arab soul that is sincere to Palestine and that believes in its
> liberation.

See also, Lebanon Renaissance Foundation, *The New Hezbollah Manifesto*, which addresses the movement's changes since its open letter in 1985; and The *PLO Charter of 1964*, which states: "The people of Palestine determine its destiny when it completes the liberation of its homeland in accordance with its own wishes and free will and choice."; For a basic understanding of the key role the liberation of Palestine plays in motivating Palestinian Islamic Jihad see Scott Atran and Robert Axelrod, 'Interview with Ramadan Shallah, Secretary General, Palestinian Islamic Jihad (Damascus, Syria, December 15, 2009).'

[30] See Frank Gaffney Jnr, "Seeing the threat for what it is"; Caroline Glick, 'Ehud Olmert's "Convergence" Plan for the West Bank and U.S. Middle East Policy.'

[31] Judy Maltz,'Islamophobe and 'Great Friend of Israel' Frank Gaffney Reportedly Joining Trump Team.'

[32] Eli Clifton, 'Trump's Muslim Ban: Thanks To Supreme Court Decision, Bogus Polling, And AIPAC Funding.'

[33] Those choosing to use of the phrase 'Armenian Holocaust' rather than 'Armenian Genocide' include Robert Fisk, *The Great War for Civilisation: The Conquest of the Middle East*, 53-71; Richard G. Hovannisian, *The Armenian Holocaust: A Bibliography Relating to the Deportations, Massacres, and Dispersion of the Armenian People, 1915-1923*.

[34] Darcy, DiNucci, 'Fragmented future;' Tim O'Reilly, 'Web 2.0: Compact definition?'

[35] William L. Hosch, 'Web 2.0: Internet.'

[36] Frank Gaffney, 'Holocaust 2.0'

[37] Judea and Samaria are the biblical names for Israeli-occupied West Bank excluding East Jerusalem. The terms are commonly used by those operating under the assumption this land has been promised to Israel by God as stipulated in the Hebrew Bible. Relevant biblical verses include Genesis 12:7 where God revealed himself to *Avraham Avinu* (Abraham) in Schechem (modern day Nablus in Samaria) declaring "To your offspring I will give this land." And Genesis 13:17-18: "Go, walk through the length and breadth of the land, for I am giving it to you. So Abram went to live near the great trees of Mamre at Hebron, where he pitched his tents. There he built an altar to the LORD." The standard interpretation of the Hebrew Bible holds that God promised specific land to the offspring of Abraham's son, Isaac. Isaac was born to Abraham's first wife Sarah and it is through them that Jews trace their lineage. *Avraham Avinu* (Abraham) roughly translates in English as 'our father Abraham.' For examples of neoconservatives and pro-Israeli movement intellectuals using these biblical terms in relation to the perceived threat posed by a nuclear Iran see Caroline Glick, 'What the Left is Really After;' Caroline Glick, 'Israel's Arab Cheerleaders,' Norman Podhoretz, 'Bush, Sharon, My Daughter, and Me.'

[38] John Holmes, UN Under-Secretary-General for Humanitarian Affairs and Emergency Relief Coordinator, wrote of the Occupied Territories after visiting in 2010: "It is a big open air prison...Half the population is unemployed, if there is food in the shops people don't have money to buy it. It's a rather desperate, depressing situation where people are easily falling prey to despair. See,

China.org.cn, 'Blockade turns Gaza into 'big open air prison.'" In more recent times, David Halbfinger and Iyad Abuheweila of the *New York Times* reported that in Gaza "living and dying is the same thing...[it] is little more than an open-air prison." Their viewpoints are revealing given the *New York Times* has proven itself to be far more receptive to a pro-Israeli posture than shining a line on injustice in the Palestinian Territories – the recent hiring of well-known neo-conservative Bret Stephens helps to support this claim. See, Iyad Abuheweila and David M. Halbfinger, 'For Gaza Protester, Living Or Dying is the 'Same Thing.' *The New York Times'* pro-Israeli and anti-Palestinian has been revealed by many scholars undertaking extensive documentary analysis of its recent and past reporting in relation to the Arab-Israeli conflict. See, Janice Terry and Gordon Mendhenhall, '1973 US Press Coverage on the Middle East Author;' Chang Kuang-Kuo and Geri Alumit Zeldes, 'Three of Four Newspapers Studied Favor Israeli Instead of Palestinian Sources;' Issam S. Mousa, 'The Arab Image The New York Times;' Daniel Okrent, an editor at the *The New York Times*, has also admitted there exists "structural geographic bias" that favours Israel. The paper's correspondents live inside Israel and not the occupied Palestinian territories, meaning they are more likely to interpret the conflict from Israel's point of view. See, Daniel Okrent, 'The Hottest Button: How The Times Covers Israel and Palestine.'

[39] Frank Gaffney, 'ObamaBomb: Holocaust 2.0'

[40] Robert Lawrence Trask and Peter Stockwell, *Language and Linguistics: The Key Concepts*, 293

[41] M.A.K Halliday, *Linguistic Studies of Text and Discourse*, 48

[42] Kyle Mantyla, 'President Huckabee's Foreign Policy? 'If We Don't Fear God, Nobody Will Fear US.''

[43] *Ibid.*

[44] Mark Helprin is most famous for his fictional work *Winter's Tale*, which was adapted into a Hollywood feature film. He has also worked as an Op-Ed writer for leading mainstream US newspapers like *The Wall Street Journal, The New York Times, The Washington Post* and *Los Angeles Times.*

[45] Bret Stephens, 'Stephens: Worse than Munich.'

[46] *MSNBC*, 'Must-Read Op-Eds for Tuesday, Nov. 26;' *Unity Coalition For Israel*, 'Stephens: Worse Than Munich.'

[47] For a breakdown of the military funding the US provides Israel see, Alia Chughtai, 'Understanding US military aid to Israel.'

[48] Dov Zakheim, 'Fund Israel's Military, Not Its Settlements: Washington should link part of its defense aid to Jerusalem's settlement funding.'

[49] For a general understanding of Dov Zakheim's support for Israeli settlements see, Dalia Karpel, 'What's Wrong With This Picture;' Dov Zakheim, 'Obama Should Give up on East Jerusalem.'

[50] For an appreciation of the widespread anger amongst neo-conservatives about the BDS Campaign, see the following texts produced by neo-conservative outfits: *American Israel Public Affairs Committee*, 'Oppose Boycotts of Israel;' Benjamin

Weinthal and Asaf Romirowsky, 'What Americans Can Learn from Europeans about Fighting BDS.'

[51] *American Enterprise Institute*, 'AEI's Organization and Purpose.'

[52] Quoted in Michael Flynn, 'The War Hawks.'

[53] Jonah Goldberg, 'Huckabee's Hitler comparison that wasn't.'

[54] *Council on American-Islamic Relations*, 'Hijacked by Hate: American Philanthropy and the Islamophobia Network,' 45, 86; *Center for American Progress*, 'Fear Inc.: The Roots of the Islamophobia Network in America,' 21

[55] *The Times of Israel*, 'Dutch populist Wilders faces huge backlash on Moroccan critique;' *RT News*, 'Ban the Koran? Geert Wilders speaks out on his radical views.'

[56] Max Blumenthal, 'The Sugar Mama of Anti-Muslim Hate.'

[57] Jeff Jacoby, 'Pipes's effective path to peace.'

[58] Robert Mackey, 'Fox News Apologizes for False Claims of Muslim-Only Areas in England and France;' *Southern Poverty Law Center*, ''No-Go Zones:' The Myth That Just Won't Quit.'

[59] Alan M. Dershowitz, 'Why deterrence won't work against Iran.'

[60] Claudia Rossett, 'For Hotel Hosting Ahmadinejad, Just Another 'International Event.''

[61] *Ibid.*

[62] Noam Chomsky and Edward S. Herman, *Manufacturing Consent: The Political Economy of the Mass Media.*

[63] A favourite online tool used by neo-conservative outfits is to publish the views of others / promote the idea, that Chomsky is a 'self-hating Jew.' This allows neo-conservatives to establish some distance between them and these ideas so that they can deny claims of racism. Daniel Pipes' *Middle East Forum* as well as the *Gatestone Institute* are among the neo-conservative outfits to have utilised this technique. See for e.g. *Middle East Forum*, 'A Friend's Encounter With Chomsky' where the author claims "I had heard from friends on the faculty at MIT that Chomsky was an egomaniac and a self-hating Jew"; and, Alan Dershowtiz, 'Chomsky Calls Russian Interference a Joke - Blames Guess Who?' where an online participant in the discussion writes "Noam Chomsky is the prime paradigm of the pathologic self-hating Jew." These kinds of online forums are moderated, meaning views deemed to be extremist, offensive or similar, will be often removed by moderators. It is telling the aforementioned submissions have not been removed.

[64] Clifford D. May, 'A brief history of Jew-hatred.'

[65] Norman Podhoretz, 'Hannah Arendt on Eichmann: A Study in the Perversity of Brilliance;' Sol Stern, 'The Lies of Hannah Arendt;' Daniel Patrick Moynihan, 'Ex-Friendly Fire.'

[66] Alan Dershowtiz, 'Bernie Sanders: Knave or Fool?;' Seth Mandel, 'Why Bernie Sanders Doesn't Talk About Being Jewish.'

[67] Amir Tibon, 'Watch - 2020 Hopeful Bernie Sanders Says Netanyahu Leads 'Racist Government';' *Haaretz*, 'Bernie Sanders Says He Hopes Netanyahu Loses;' *FeeltheBern.org*, 'Bernie Sanders on Iran.'

[68] A survey of 1000 Jewish-American voters conducted in May 2019 by *Greenberg Research* for *the Jewish Electorate Institute*, which undertakes voter polling for Democratic candidates, showed Sanders favourable/unfavourable rating to be 51/43. This was far superior to Trump's 26/70, but behind fellow Democratic Presidential nominee Joe Biden 66/29. See, Ron Kampeas, "Most American Jews are concerned about anti-Semitism and disapprove of Trump, survey finds."

[69] Philip Lopate, 'Resistance to the Holocaust,' 90

[70] Jonah Goldberg, 'Huckabee's Hitler comparison that wasn't.'

[71] Texts in which Jonah Goldberg deploys Holocaust rhetoric when writing about the 'radical Islamist' and political Liberal enemies include, 'Obama's tough talk is poisoning America's relationship with Israel;' *Liberal Fascism: The Totalitarian Temptation from Mussolini to Hilary Clinton.*

[72] Peter Novick, *The Holocaust in American Life*, 9; Charles Murray, 'Jewish Genius;' Rabbi Harold Kushner famously made comments about Jewish brilliance relative to non-Jews during his debate with Christopher Hitchens at the *Connecticut Forum*. Kushner remarked "statistically the only long-term effect circumcision seems to have on people is it increase their chances of winning a Nobel prize." See, *The Connecticut Forum*, 'God: Big Questions...Bigger Questions.'

[73] Peter Novick, *The Holocaust in American Life*, 9

[74] Elie Wiesel, '1986 Nobel Prize acceptance speech;' Elie Wiesel, 'Art and the Holocaust: Trivializing Memory.'

[75] Valentin Voloshinov, *Marxism and the Philosophy of Language*, 95

[76] Daniel Patrick Moynihan, *The Negro Family: The Case for National Action*; Norman Podhoretz's comments about Black Americans are cited in Andrew Hartman, 'The Neoconservative Counterrevolution.'

[77] Monica Crowley, 'Speech Delivered at Stop Iran Rally in Times Square, New York.'

[78] See for e.g. Monica Crowley, *What the (Bleep) Just Happened?*; Monica Crowley, Bill O'Rielly, et al. "The Holy War Begins;" Monica Crowley, 'Monica Crowley: Syrian airstrikes show Trump has learned from history.'

[79] *Right Web,* 'Family Security Matters.'

[80] *Ibid.*

[81] *Center for Security Policy*, '2013 Mightier Pen Award: Honoring Diana West.'

[82] John Wagner, 'Trump national security spokeswoman Monica Crowley to forgo post amid plagiarism charges.'

[83] Jacob Heilbrunn, *They Knew They Were Right: The Rise of the Neocons*, 11

[84] Charles Krauthammer, 'Charles Krauthammer: If we really mean 'never again,' must stop Iran nukes.'

[85] *Simon Wiesenthal Center*, 'Speech by PM Netanyahu to a Joint Meeting of the U.S. Congress.'

[86] Alvin Felzenberg, 'Benjamin Netanyahu for President in 2012?'

[87] George Orwell, *1984*, 103

[88] Jack Khoury and Barak Ravid, 'Netanyahu's 'Wild Beast' Quote Was Apartheid-speak, Says Chief Palestinian Negotiator;' Liel Leibovitz, 'Fibi Netanyahu.'
[89] Abdulaziz Ahmet Yasar, 'Israeli wants to be 'in Africa' but to keep Africans out of Israel;' Azad Essa, 'Israel: no country for black people.'
[90] Ilan Lior, 'Netanyahu on African 'Infiltrators:' We Will Return South Tel Aviv to Israelis.'

Conclusion

[1] Hannah Arendt, *On Violence*, 17.

Index

www.ingramcontent.com/pod-product-compliance
Lightning Source LLC
Chambersburg PA
CBHW061007280326
41935CB00009B/867